"a touching love story . . . er
the emotional quality and color of a good historical novel . . ."

C. Melvin Aikens, professor emeritus,
University of Oregon

BEAUTIFUL AS THE RAINBOW

Nashimoto Masako, a Japanese Princess
against All Odds for Love, Life,
and Happiness

SONG NAI RHEE

Inspiring Voices®
A Service of Guideposts

Inspiring Voices books may be ordered through booksellers or by contacting:

Inspiring Voices
1663 Liberty Drive
Bloomington, IN 47403
www.inspiringvoices.com
1-(866) 697-5313

ISBN: 978-1-4624-0706-4 (sc)
ISBN: 978-1-4624-0708-8 (hc)
ISBN: 978-1-462-40707-1 (e)

Library of Congress Control Number: 2013914676

Printed in the United States of America.

Inspiring Voices rev. date: 9/18/2013

"People call me the tragic crown princess . . . But I have experienced love and happiness as a woman. I have also had dreams and hopes as beautiful as the rainbow . . ."

(Yi Bangja, 1985, p. 12)

In 1962, Princess Nashimoto Masako (梨本方子) became Yi Bangja (李方子) and a Korean citizen. Bang-ja (方子) is Korean pronunciation of Masako (方子).

This story unfolds against the background of the mortal Korea-Japan conflicts during the 20th century and is based on Yi Bangja's publications, including:

Jinaon Seweol (Reflections on my Life), Yeoweon Press, Seoul, 1967 (in Korean)

Baram buneundaero, Mulkyeol chineundaero (Following the Wind, Going with the Flow), Hanjin Press, Seoul, 1980. (In Korean)

Nagareno Mamani (Going with the Flow), Keiyusha, Tokyo, (1983). (In Japanese)

Seweoliyeo Wangjoyeo (My Life and the Joseon Royal Dynasty), Jeongeum Press, Seoul, 1985 (in Korean)

The author is deeply grateful to Principal Kim Woo, the chief administrator of Jahye School and the Yi Bangja Memorial for granting him permission to use and adapt contents and photos of Yi Bangja's publications for this story.

Supplementary information is provided by works included in References, and the author expresses his appreciation to their authors and publishers.

All photos, unless referenced, are adapted from Yi Bangja's publications or created by the author.

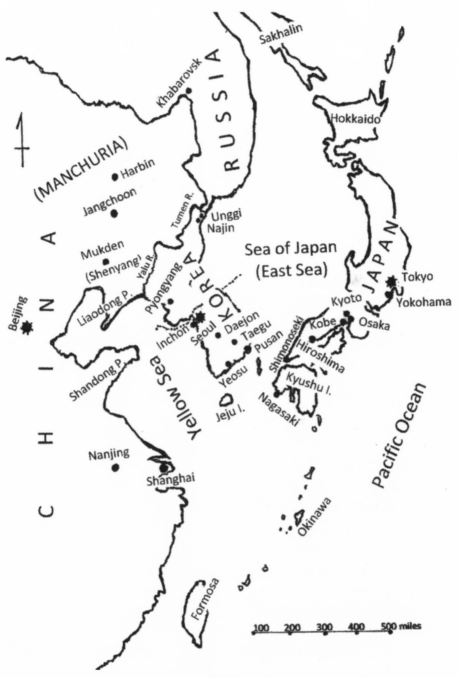

Map of the Far East

TABLE OF CONTENTS

PROLOGUE

Fate's Cruel Joke

"The queen is dead! Her Majesty, the Queen, has been murdered!"

The frantic shouts of a shaken palace guard broke the silence of the Seoul morning as the sun was just breaking out in the eastern horizon with its rays touching the majestic sky lines of Gyeongbok Palace and the gently flowing waters of the Han River.

It was in the early morning of October 8, 1895.

A group of terrifying Japanese soldiers and restless ex-samurai had broken into the forbidden inner private quarters of Gyeongbok Palace, the political center of Korea's Joseon Kingdom, slashing and slaying every palace guard in their path.

The Throne Hall in Gyeongbok Palace

In savage rage, they were looking for Queen Min, the consort wife of Gojong, the king of Korea.

When they found her, after frenzied room to room searches, they brutally and mercilessly cut down the queen in the face of her terrified and helpless palace ladies-in-waiting.

The queen was slim and slight but still a beautiful woman at 44.

After thrusting a sword into the queen's abdomen once, twice, and thrice, some twenty of the bloody samurai soldiers violated the dying queen in turn, continuing their acts of desecration even after she had stopped breathing. The murderers then cut out the breasts of the queen and those of the palace women.

As their final act of savagery, they mutilated the queen's body with their swords from head to toe. They then dragged the slim, torn body outside, wrapped it in a blanket, doused it with kerosene, and burned it to ashes, leaving no trace of the queen.

When Japan embarked on the modern era under the leadership of Emperor Meiji in 1868 it eagerly aspired to become an imperialist power like the Western nations.

In addition, to solve the problems of its growing urban population and limited arable lands it set its eyes on the Asian continent and chose Korea as its first target of conquest.

In 1876, with armed threats the Meiji government forced Korea to sign an unequal treaty with Japan, which opened a way for ambitious Japanese to freely move into Korea and begin their economic and political exploitations.

Following its victory against Imperial China in the Sino-Japanese War in April, 1895, the Japanese in Korea became more aggressive, strangulating Korean interests in business, commerce, finance, and even in the political arena.

Gojong and Queen Min concluded that the Japanese were determined to destroy their nation and sought to protect Korean independence. Of the two, Queen Min was more forceful and determined in her opposition to the Japanese high-handed tactics and ambitions in Korea.

The Japanese were enraged, calling the queen "a shrewd fox" to be eliminated.

In August, 1895, Ito Hirobumi, Japan's first prime minister under Emperor Meiji, chose Viscount Miura Goro, a retired general in Japan's Imperial Army and a trusted fellow samurai from his hometown of Hagi in Yamaguchi Prefecture (old Choshu Domain), as resident minister extraordinary and plenipotentiary in Korea.

Miura had power and permission to do whatever he wanted to do, and his mission was to resolve the "Korean problem."

Within a few weeks of his arrival in Seoul, Miura, firmly convinced that Japan's conquest ambitions in Korea would be thwarted by Queen Min, adopted an assassination plan code-named "Operation Fox Hunt."

With meticulous planning, he organized a death squad consisting of regular Japanese soldiers, restless ex-samurai seeking adventure, and Japanese civilians with expansionistic ambition.

At 3 o'clock in the morning of October 8, Miura's assassination team was given the order to find and murder the queen.

It was Japan's first open act of diabolic trampling of modern Korea, making itself a mortal enemy of Koreans for years and decades to come.

Following the death of Queen Min, Gojong took Lady Eom, his favorite court lady-in-waiting, as his second wife, impressed by her intelligence, wisdom, and political sagacity.

Within a few days of the bloody murder, the Japanese aggressors, feeling triumphant, put pro-Japanese Koreans in key government positions, quickly turning Joseon Kingdom into a Japanese puppet.

Lady Eom advised Gojong to take refuge in the Russian Embassy for his personal safety as well as for launching counter offensive measures against the Japanese. Russian friendship with Gojong would soon lead to the Russo-Japanese War, but that is another story.

Two years later in 1897, Gojong had a son by Lady Eom and named him Yi Eun. He would become Korea's last crown prince.

Three years later, in 1900, far away across the ocean in Tokyo, an imperial princess was born in a palatial mansion built, of all people, by Miura Goro, the Japanese official responsible for the murder of Queen Min, the wife of Gojong, Yi Eun's father.

The princess was named Masako.

Sixteen years later, in 1918, Imperial Japan's rulers decided that Princess Masako would marry Crown Prince Yi Eun "to enhance peace and harmony between the Japanese and the Koreans and Korea-Japan union."

A noble Japanese princess born in a house built by Miura Goro was bidden to marry a Korean, whose father was long in mourning over the death of his beloved consort wife, Queen Min, murdered by Miura Goro!

Was it humor, or was it a cruel joke which Fate plays on hapless humans from time to time?

An ancient Hebrew wise man lamented on the fickleness and cruelty of Fate:

> The race is not to the swift,
> Or the battle to the strong,
> Nor does food come to the wise,
> Or wealth to the brilliant,
> Or favor to the learned;
> But the time and chance happen to them all.
> Moreover, no man knows when his hour will come,
> As fish are caught in a cruel net
> Or birds are taken in a snare
> So men are trapped by evil times,
> That falls unexpectedly upon them.
> (Ecclesiastes 9:11-12)

Surely, in the summer of 1923, similar thoughts were going through the mind of Princess Masako, cloistered in the quiet recess of Rinnōji Temple, deep in the forest of Nikko, musing about the cruelties, uncertainties, and contradictions in her own life.

She had come to the temple to escape the steaming heat of Tokyo's summer, but in reality she was running away from the world of grief and pain in search of peace and tranquility of mind.

Born in the Nashimoto branch of Japan's imperial family, she was among the most privileged.

Reared in a palace and educated at Gakushuin, the Peers School and the elite academy for sons and daughters of Japan's imperial household and other royal and aristocratic families, she was elegant, refined, and proper in all things royal and Japanese. She was also stunningly beautiful.

It was therefore only natural that she was being groomed to be betrothed to a prince, no less than Crown Prince Hirohito, the future Emperor of Japan.

Political and military rulers of the newly emerging Empire of the Sun, however, decided to offer the beautiful princess as a sacrifice on the altar of Japan's imperialism. She, they conspired, must marry Yi Eun, the crown prince of Korea's Joseon Kingdom, whose national independence they were strangulating with their conquest ambition.

As Korea was forced to become a part of Japan, so was Masako forced to become a part of Korea to symbolize the union of the two nations in mortal conflict.

Like a fish in a net or a bird in a snare, Princess Masako turned and twisted to live, to be free, and to be happy, and being painfully aware that events in her life were beyond her control she decided to accept her destiny.

The imposed destiny, however, would not control her, for she decided to become a heroine, not a victim of her misfortunes, driven by her passion for love, life, and happiness.

Masako's story is about the human soul empowering a victim of misfortunes and an unwished destiny to become a hero, transforming adversity into patches of paradise.

Yi Eun's Royal Family Relationships (abbreviated)

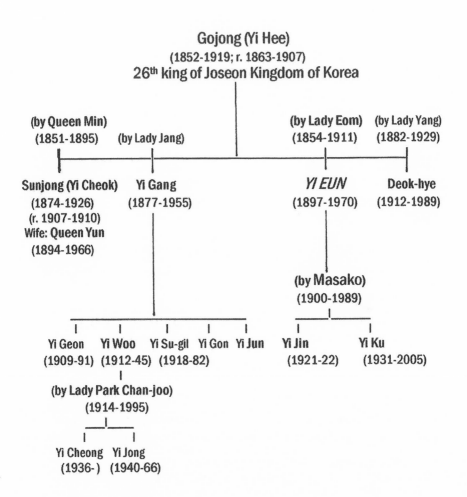

Yi Eun's Royal Family Relationships

Nashimoto Masako's Imperial Family Relationships (abbreviated)

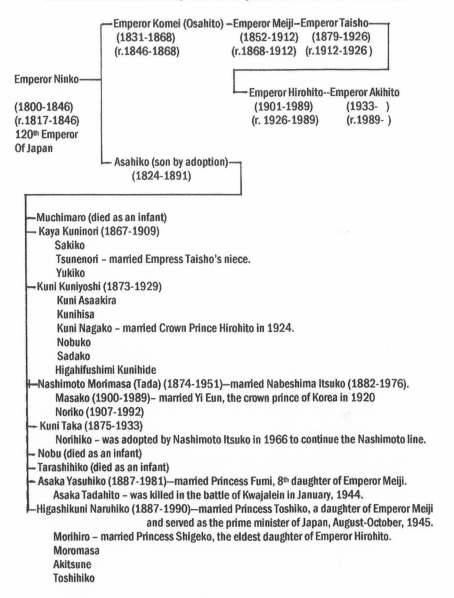

┌─Emperor Komei (Osahito) –Emperor Meiji–Emperor Taisho─┐
    (1831-1868)   (1852-1912) (1879-1926)
    (r.1846-1868)   (r.1868-1912) (r.1912-1926)

Emperor Ninko──

(1800-1846)
(r.1817-1846)
120th Emperor
Of Japan

└──Emperor Hirohito--Emperor Akihito
    (1901-1989)   (1933-)
    (r. 1926-1989)   (r.1989-)

└── Asahiko (son by adoption)─┐
    (1824-1891)

─Muchimaro (died as an infant)
─ Kaya Kuninori (1867-1909)
    Sakiko
    Tsunenori – married Empress Taisho's niece.
    Yukiko
─Kuni Kuniyoshi (1873-1929)
    Kuni Asaakira
    Kunihisa
    Kuni Nagako – married Crown Prince Hirohito in 1924.
    Nobuko
    Sadako
    Higahifushimi Kunihide
─Nashimoto Morimasa (Tada) (1874-1951)—married Nabeshima Itsuko (1882-1976).
    Masako (1900-1989)– married Yi Eun, the crown prince of Korea in 1920
    Noriko (1907-1992)
─ Kuni Taka (1875-1933)
    Norihiko – was adopted by Nashimoto Itsuko in 1966 to continue the Nashimoto line.
─ Nobu (died as an infant)
─Tarashihiko (died as an infant)
─ Asaka Yasuhiko (1887-1981)—married Princess Fumi, 8th daughter of Emperor Meiji.
    Asaka Tadahito – was killed in the battle of Kwajalein in January, 1944.
─Higashikuni Naruhiko (1887-1990)—married Princess Toshiko, a daughter of Emperor Meiji
                   and served as the prime minister of Japan, August-October, 1945.
    Morihiro – married Princess Shigeko, the eldest daughter of Emperor Hirohito.
    Moromasa
    Akitsune
    Toshihiko

Nashimoto Masako's Imperial Family Relationships

CHAPTER 1

PRINCESS NASHIMOTO MASAKO— BIRTH AND EARLY LIFE

"Masako, Masako, where are you?"

"Masako, my dear child, I am looking for you. Here I come . . ."

In a playful spirit, Itsuko, her mother, was tiptoeing toward her family flower garden where little Masako was happily lost among myriads of sweet-smelling flowers in red, blue, yellow, pink, lavender, and white.

Itsuko had been chatting with a visitor, while all the time watching Masako from the corner of her eye.

Every spring, the flower garden was Masako's most favorite place. As her small feet gently moved from flower to flower she imagined herself as a butterfly and thought she was in heaven. She specially liked orchids and pink plum blossoms.

"Oh, Mama, aren't these flowers gorgeous? I just love them. And they smell so good."

Little Princess Masako, in her colorful kimono and just as beautiful as the flowers around her, smiled as Itsuko held her hand tightly.

"Mama, I saw Daddy riding on a big horse today! And there were so many soldiers and people singing and waving flags. Did you see Daddy?"

Little Masako was remembering a huge military parade which she went to watch with an aunt earlier in the day. It was in celebration of Japan's victories in its recent war with Russia. Itsuko, as the wife of

1

Prince Nashimoto, was on the viewing stand with a group of Imperial dignitaries and military officers.

"Yes, my dear, I saw Daddy too. He looked awesome on the big horse and with his long sword."

"But, Mama, at the parade, all the soldiers were shouting, 'Emperor, Emperor, Long Live the Emperor!' What is an Emperor?"

Bright, pretty, pure and innocent at four and half, little princess Masako was also a curious child.

"Oh, the Emperor is the most important man in all of Japan."

"He is also your Big Uncle."

"Really?" Exclaimed Masako with her big brown eyes.

The Big Uncle was Emperor Meiji, who had led feudal Japan into the modern age as a newly emerging empire through its spectacular victories in wars with China and Russia, in 1895 and 1905 respectively.

Princess Masako was born on November 4, 1901, at #3, Kojimachi, Chiyodaku, in Tokyo, as the first daughter of Prince Nashimoto Morimasa, the fourth son of Prince Kuni Asahiko., descended from Emperor Ninko (1800-1846).

Emperor Ninko, the 120th emperor of Japan, had two sons: Osahito, a biological son by his wife, Fujiwarano Naoko, and Asahiko, by adoption. Osahito became Emperor Komei (1846-1868) and became the father of Emperor Meiji (1868-1912). Asahiko became the father of Prince Tada and 15 other princes and princesses by different wives.

Prince Tada was born on March 9, 1874. On December 2, 1885, he became head of the Nashimoto collateral Imperial family upon the resignation of his cousin Prince Kikumaro. The following year he assumed the name Morimasa.

Like all males in Imperial families, Prince Nashimoto attended the Military Academy and became a professional army officer. Proud of his impressive Kaiser mustaches, popular for Japanese military officers in those days, Morimasa was a fear-inspiring warrior—strict, stern and generally of few words.

Masako's mother, Itsuko, was the second daughter of Marquis Nabeshima Naohiro (Chokudai), the former lord (daimyo) of Saga Domain in Kyushu. Under the Meiji government, the Nabeshima clan gained membership in Japan's new nobility, and Marquis Nabeshima served as Japan's ambassador to Italy in the late 1800s.

While Nabeshima was in Rome, Itsuko was born; therefore, he named his new daughter "Itsuko," meaning "a girl born in the capital of Italy."

Slender and graceful, Itsuko was known as "the most beautiful woman" within the Imperial household and all royal families in Tokyo. She was well educated and fluent in Italian and French.

Skilled in conversation, she was pleasing to everyone she met. She was also diligent and caring. During house-cleaning times, she would work along with her servants, and with her skills in sewing and embroidery she would make gloves, socks, and other things her children needed.

Nashimoto Masako' family
From left: Itsuko, Prince Morimasa, Noriko, and Masako

Masako's childhood home, the Nashimoto Palace, was located near the offices of the Imperial Household Ministry and the residences of the Lord Keeper of the Privy Seal and the Imperial Household Minister.

The palace, consisting of various Japanese and Western style buildings, stood in a grand park-like setting. It was maintained by a large staff including more than 30 male and female servants, under the supervision of the Imperial Household Ministry.

When Masako was nine years old, her family moved to a new grand palace built in Japanese style on a beautiful eight acre plot in Aoyama.

In addition to residential buildings, it had an impressive gate, a pavilion, and a fresh water lake with a water fountain. Within its courtyard were towering trees, bamboo groves, and many flowering plum blossom trees. Strangers took the new palace as a beautiful temple.

Morimasa, Masako's father, was a highly disciplined military officer, maintaining a same daily routine of waking up, breakfast, and going to work every day with ritualized punctuality.

He was a man of few words, but when she spoke he was always exact and proper in his speech. His stern demeanor made Masako a bit guarded and uneasy at all times.

As a child Masako feared her father especially when his hot temper flared. When angry about something, he roared like a lion. Cowed, everyone, including her mother, Itsuko, knelt on their knees, trembling with fear.

As no one stirred or made a noise, Masako would try to rescue the situation with the only tactic which she knew worked. Mustering all her courage, she would approach angry Morimasa, begging him with both hands on her knees to forgive everyone, especially Itsuko, her mother. She did not know what she was begging forgiveness for, but she would keep begging until her father calmed down.

At an early age, Masako already was revealing a character trait: she was unwilling to let a bad circumstance ruin her day. She would meet it face to face rising above it with courage and tenacity.

If Itsuko naturally endowed Masako with beauty, charm, and grace, from her warrior father she received gifts of bravery, courage, determination, and tenacity. In time, these warrior traits would transform her into a fighter extraordinaire with charm and grace.

Morimasa took a special pride in his Kaiser mustaches and took pains in caring for and culturing them. Every night and during meals he would tie them to his ears to keep them straight and unruffled. Masako found the warrior father's daily ritual quite amusing as well as entertaining.

In religion, Masako knew only Shintoism, the official religion of Japan's Imperial clan. Shintoism taught that all Imperial families were descendents of their sun god, Amaterasu Omikami.

As such, they were considered divine, and from early on, Masako's life was well guarded and protected. She was not allowed to go shopping or ride street cars on the way to school. She was forbidden from mingling with the children of commoners.

Except for mealtimes and family outings, Masako and her sister did not interact with their parents closely; consequently, they rarely crossed them.

"We spent so little time together at home that we never did anything to upset our parents, and we were never physically punished," recalled Masako.

Twice a year, Imperial families had gatherings at the detached beach palaces of Shiba and Hama. There they were entertained with music, dancing, and magician's performances.

Masako's family often spent summers at the Maeda family's cottage at Nikko. There, they would visit with the Crown Prince who became Emperor Taisho in 1912. They would also enjoy the company of Prince Hirohito who became Emperor Showa in 1926, sharing fruits and cookies in a garden.

One winter, Masako celebrated Christmas at the palace of Prince Kuni, her uncle. She was enchanted by a Christmas tree beautifully decorated with colorful lights and balls. Later in the evening all children received gifts including cookies and toys.

When Masako was about four years old, Japan was caught up with war spirit as it was fighting a war with Russia. Children sang military marching songs and played war games. Masako remembered playing a brave army field nurse, carrying a wounded soldier on a cot to "an army field hospital" and wrapping "a wounded hand" with a bandage.

When Masako was six years old, her sister Noriko was born. They each had a servant looking after their needs. Because of the age difference, they rarely fought.

A year later, in April, 1908, Masako enrolled in the Girls' Department at Gakushuin.

Gakushuin, or Peers School, was the most prestigious educational institution in Japan, established originally in 1847 in Kyoto by Emperor Komei for the children of Imperial families.

In 1877, with the active support of Emperor Meiji, Gakushuin was moved to Tokyo, near the Imperial Palace, and opened to other children of nobility.

In 1884, it also became a government school to educate children of prominent commoners such as members of the Mitsui financial group. Gakushuin was under the jurisdiction of the Imperial Household Ministry.

Gakushuin was headed by prominent scholars and scientists, as well as famous admirals and generals, including General Nogi Maresuke, the celebrated commander of Japan's Third Army, which defeated the Russian Army at Lyushun, Manchuria, during the Russo-Japanese War. He was also Masako's principal.

Among students of the Boys' Department at Gakushuin was Hirohito, Masako's distant cousin and of the same age. Masako's school mates in the Girls' Department included Nagako, her first cousin. In time Hirohito would become the Emperor of Japan, and Nagako would be Hirohito's wife and the Empress of Japan.

General Nogi was appointed as the principal of Gakushuin in 1906, specifically for the purpose of training and educating Crown Prince Hirohito.

Masako remembered her Gakushuin days as one of the happiest times of her life.

Gakushuin (Peers School)
Masako's French class

Each school day, as with other students, she was escorted to and from school by a guardian. The guardians would wait in their designated waiting rooms until classes were over, and while waiting, they would idle their time away with sewing or embroidering. During recesses, Masako would run to the waiting room to comb her hair or straighten her school dress.

Like a typical girl, she liked to wear pretty silk dresses and don colorful ribbons, but under the rules and regulations set by her school principal, the stern and strict General Nogi, she had to settle for plain and simple outfits.

On national holidays, however, such as New Year's Day, the Emperor's birthday, and National Founding Day, the rules were lifted and all the school girls, including Princess Masako, jumped into a day-long fashion extravaganza.

Masako liked playing in the school playground and participating in the school's annual sports events and talent shows. She specially enjoyed reading poems in French.

Occasionally she went to the Imperial Palace with her mother, who was a close friend of Empress Teimei, the wife of Emperor Taisho (1912-1926). While her mother visited with the Empress, Masako would play in the Imperial courtyard, picking flowers in the Imperial flower garden.

On each school day there were five classes, each lasting 50 minutes. During the first 6 years of elementary education, Masako's favorite classes were fine arts (painting), history, and language and literature.

Included in the Gakushuin education was instruction on matters of propriety and ethical values for just and righteous living based on Confucian and other eastern wisdom. Students were taught to value trust, honesty, responsibility, duty, and respect for the elders.

During her Gakushuin days, two things happened, that had lasting impact on Masako's consciousness: a fire that destroyed her beloved school building and the death of Emperor Meiji. As she watched the building engulfed and disappearing in an inferno she realized for the first time in her life how painful it was to lose something she valued.

When Masako was eleven, in 1912, Emperor Meiji died, and General and Mrs. Nogi committed suicide as an act of loyalty to the Emperor. Two years later, amidst the falling of April cherry blossoms, Empress Shoken, the wife of Emperor Meiji, also died.

Through the deaths of these people so close to her, Masako became aware of the fact of death, and at the same time she felt sadness and the preciousness of life as well as "a sense of human mortality like the falling cherry blossoms."

As she advanced to middle school years, school life became more involved but more fun for Masako. In addition to regular classes, her weekly school lessons included piano, koto (a Japanese stringed instrument), flower arrangement, tea ceremony, calligraphy, waka (Japanese song/poetry), and French.

Each day was full and busy, but Masako was immensely enjoying all that she was learning, for she knew that the school was preparing her to become a good and enlightened wife.

As she was growing into puberty, Masako also began to think about her future. She would dream of marriage, having a home, and living a happy life as a princess married into another Imperial family, like her mother before her.

CHAPTER 2

A LIGHTNING BOLT

On August 3, 1917, as happened every summer, Masako, her mother, and her sister were enjoying their summer vacation at a quiet and serene beach cottage in Oiso, located southwest of Tokyo. Masako's father was on military duty at Utsunomiya, and could not join the vacationing family.

It was a beautiful morning with the sun brightly shining on the blue waters of the Pacific Ocean.

After several days of rain, the trees and grass looked fresh and clean, and the flowers in the cottage garden were ablaze with enchanting colors. Sweet fragrance was in the air.

At sweet 16, Masako, petite and naturally endowed with fair skin, big brown eyes, distinct eye brows, and gracefully pleasing looks, was charming and beautiful like the pink magnolia blossom in the spring.

Masako in 1917

Her upbringing in the imperial culture and years of disciplined education at the Peers School (Gakushuin) gave her an elegant, refined, and dignified demeanor. In all settings she was decorous, composed, and proper.

But that morning, she lost all her usual composure.

Walking into the cottage living room, Masako picked up the *Yomiuri Women's Supplement* lying on a table, and as she was nonchalantly browsing the front page her eyes stopped at two photos side by side.

In one photo was herself, dressed in a traditional kimono, and in the other Prince Yi Eun of Korea, dressed in a military uniform. Next to the photos was a headline in bold letters: Matrimonial Engagement of Crown Prince Yi Eun and Princess Nashimoto Masako of the Nashimoto Prince Family.

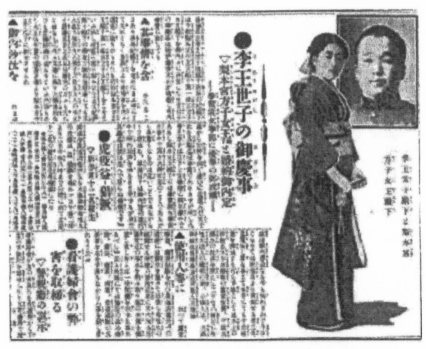

*August 3, 1917 news report on Masako's betrothal
to Korea's Crown Prince Yi Eun
Source: Naver.com, Yi Bangja*

"What is this?!" Masako screamed.

"Why to a Korean?"

"Why do I have to learn about my own marriage from a newspaper?"

"Why didn't they discuss the matter with me first?"

"It was like a bolt of lightning striking my forehead," Masako recalled the moment.

She was in absolute consternation. Her head was swinging in dizziness, and the printed letters on the newspaper were playing tricks on her bleary eyes. Her legs and hands were shaking uncontrollably.

She felt like collapsing, but holding herself with all her energy she brought her eyes to the headline once again. There was no mistake. It was about her and her engagement to Crown Prince Yi Eun of Korea.

"I don't know whether I was angry or sad, but I cried and cried," Masako said as she reminisced of the morning that jolted her with the first shock of her life. And with it, suddenly gone were the bright sunshine and the serenity of the August morning that had greeted her.

Itsuko, her mother, who had come into the living room, quietly watched Masako lost in confusion and consternation. With tears streaming down her grimacing face she looked as if she were begging for forgiveness.

"I wish I could have told you about this earlier," she muttered with a painful look.

"I know you are utterly shocked by the news, but we could not help it. Actually, the Minister of the Imperial Household has been to our house several times to inform us that the engagement was the will of the Emperor Taisho, and plead that we accept the Emperor's will . . ." Itsuko explained with dismay as she was wiping away her tears.

"We refused each time," Itsuko continued, "but the Emperor himself has decided on this matrimony for the purpose of enhancing the relationship between Japan and Korea . . . and as an example for all citizens of Japan. We had no choice but to accept the Emperor's will. It will be hard and difficult for you I know, but . . ."

The decision was actually made by Japan's two supreme military leaders of the time: General Yamagata Aritomo, the head of Imperial Japan's military cliques, and Field Marshal Terauchi Masatake, the first Governor General of Korea who was slated to be the next prime minister of Japan.

Together the two men controlled the politics of Japan and made all decisions affecting the Empire. They agreed that the marriage would hasten the union of Japan and Korea.

While Masako's parents were nervously waiting for an appropriate moment to tell Masako about the news of the secret Imperial decision, the media jumped the gun by reporting it as a top social event of the day.

In traditional Japan, down through the first half of the 20th century, marriages were often arranged by parents. Individual freedom and choice in romance and marriage were limited.

This was especially so within Imperial families. No one could object to or refuse "the will of the Emperor." Even more so if the decision was already made public in the media.

Masako reluctantly realized that her fate had been sealed by forces beyond her control, and sensing the agonies which her parents had been bearing in oppressive silence she tried to comfort Itsuko.

"Mama, I understand. However difficult my life may become, I will do my best to live according to your and father's wishes . . ."

"Thank you, Masako, for your kind words. I know your father will be greatly comforted . . ."

Itsuko, who, for days had been tormented inside, took a deep breath and warmly embraced Masako.

In reality, however, for Masako that was the beginning of her interminably discomforting anxiety and sleepless nights as questions kept bombarding her confused and rattled head.

"How can I marry a foreigner?"

"What is this grand role I am to play in the Japan-Korea union?

"How can I live with strangers in a foreign country with a different language and customs?"

Sensing that Masako was troubled by such concerns, Itsuko assured her that she would be helped with able teachers to learn all about Korea, its language and customs before the marriage.

Furthermore, Itsuko took special pains to explain that she had accepted the Imperial decision on the condition that Masako and Crown Prince Yi Eun would live in Tokyo after marriage, not in Korea.

Her parents' assurances notwithstanding, Masako first had to convince herself about the future and the destiny willed and determined for her by others. The harder she tried, the more nightmarish her struggles became. Each day, she wished it were all just a dream.

At night she would walk into the darkness wishing that she would disappear forever as part of the darkness. Sometimes, she wished desperately she would be dead without anyone knowing.

"They tell me that," she screamed in silence, "this is for the purpose of enhancing Japan-Korea unity . . . ! But why should it be me? Why do I have to be the one? I know nothing about Korea. For me, it is just a country far away . . ."

Masako had thought about marriage and home, but her vision of it was more like the case she was familiar with—her own home and her own parents. Like Princess Itsuko, her mother, Masako dreamed of marrying into an Imperial family in Tokyo and raising children in a princely palace.

In fact, starting a year earlier, Masako was being groomed by the Imperial Household Ministry to become the wife of Crown Prince Hirohito, a distant cousin. Naturally, her father, Prince Nashimoto Morimasa, was most excited and was biting his nails as the grooming process was proceeding.

Then one day, Prince Nashimoto was called into the Imperial Palace for a meeting with Emperor Taisho. Relishing the happy thought that his daughter had been selected to be the new Crown Princess and future Empress of Japan, Prince Nashimoto walked briskly to the Palace.

"Today, the Emperor is going to give me the good news about Masako and Crown Prince Hirohito," he said to himself happily. He was feeling as if the flowers along the path were smiling for him, and the birds in the air singing for him.

To his utter consternation, however, the Emperor informed him that Masako had been selected to marry Yi Eun, the Crown Prince of Korea.

As Prince Nashimoto stood before the Emperor, stunned and dumbfounded, Field Marshal Terauchi, now the prime minister, standing near, tried to break the tense silence of the moment:

"Emperor has made this decision for the sake of Japan's future. We need to unite Japan's Imperial Court with that of Korea in order to strengthen the union of the two."

Terauchi was subtly pressing for a positive response from Prince Nashimoto.

"But, why does it have to be my daughter? How can she bear such an enormous burden and endure all the hardships which she will face?" Prince Nashimoto protested to himself in an unbearably painful silence. Unable to give the Emperor a response, Prince Nashimoto returned home deeply distressed and downcast.

For several days, Prince Nashimoto and Itsuko agonized over the fate of their daughter, with Itsuko crying into sleepless nights. In the end, with repeated calls from the Imperial Household Ministry for a speedy response, they had no choice but to consent. Masako would be married to Yi Eun of Korea.

Even though no one in the Nashimoto Palace knew at the time, Princess Masako had become a victim of politics among rival military factions seeking to establish a favorable relationship with the Emperor.

In considering the selection of Crown Prince Hirohito's wife and future empress of Japan, the Imperial Household Ministry had three candidates: Princess Tokiko of the Ichijo-oka Family, Princess Nagako of the Kuni Family, and Princess Masako of the Nashimoto Family. Nagako and Masako were first cousins.

Yamagata Aritomo, who had the upper hand as the leader of all the military factions, supported Princess Tokiko. He rejected Masako and Nagako for medical reasons. His physicians (conspiring?) reported that Masako was sterile and Nagako color-blind.

In rejecting Nagako, Yamagata faced fierce opposition from her supporters. Some of them sought to assassinate Yamagata, while others mobilized renowned physicians, including those at Tokyo Imperial University Medical School, for medical tests.

When the final medical report cleared Nagako of color blindness, Yamagata gave up his political positions as well as his noble status. And five months later, on January 18, 1919, Nagako was formally chosen to be Japan's Crown Princess and the wife of Hirohito.

As Masako reflected on these events after more than 6 decades, she said:

"His Highness Crown Prince Yi Eun and I thus became victims of a fierce power struggle among scheming military factions of Japan."

"As for Princess Nagako," she continued, "she was my first cousin, and I was so very proud of her becoming the Crown Princess. She was not only elegant and graceful but bright and had a beautiful heart. She was also a great singer."

CHAPTER 3

KOREA AND YI EUN IN JAPAN'S CLAWS

King Gojong and Lady Eom, Yi Eun's parents

Yi Eun was the seventh son of Yi Hee (1852-1919), the 26th king of Korea's Joseon Kingdom (also known as the Yi Royal Dynasty) founded in 1392 by General Yi Seong-gye of the Jeonju Yi Clan. Yi Hee's official title was Gojong. He was on the throne of Joseon Kingdom for 43 years from 1864 to 1907.

Yi Eun was born in Gyeong-Un Palace (now called Deoksu Palace, located near the present Seoul Plaza Hotel and old Seoul City Hall) on October 20, 1897, three years before Princess Masako.

His mother was Lady Eom, a court lady and a woman with keen intellect and political sagacity, whom Gojong chose as his consort after Queen Min was murdered by the Japanese two years earlier.

Gojong was 40 years old when Yi Eun was born. Consequently, the young prince became an object of Gojong's special affection and attention.

Yi Eun as Crown Prince of Joseon Kingdom in 1907

Yi Eun was short in height and on the chubby side, but he was physically strong with broad shoulders. He was of stout character and was often praised in the royal court for his keen intellect, literary acumen and upright character.

In August, 1900, Yi Eun was designated as Prince Yeong, and seven years later, in 1907, as the Crown Prince of Joseon Kingdom. As such, Yi Eun was slated to become king of Joseon Kingdom in due time, but Japan's aggressive moves in Korea turned its affairs upside down, and prevented him from ever sitting on the throne of his kingdom.

Imperial Japan made certain that Yi Eun, Korea's Crown Prince, would remain in its claws until he died.

In the 1870s, during its rapid modernization under Emperor Meiji, Japan began to exert its economic and territorial aggressions abroad, and especially on Korea.

Japan's heavy-handed tactics in Korea quickly led to confrontations with Ching Dynasty China, which had long maintained suzerainty over Korea, as it did also with other neighboring nations.

Japan decided to remove this obstacle in the path of its economic and political ambitions vis-à-vis Korea, and on August 1, 1895 it declared war on China.

Trained and advised by the British Royal Navy, the foremost naval power in the world of that day, Japan's Imperial Navy, combined with its Imperial Army, achieved a decisive victory over China. The Japan-China Peace Treaty, signed at Shimonoseki on April 17, 1895, effectively ended China's influence in Korea. Japan now had a relatively free hand to aggressively push its economic exploitations of Korea.

When the Korean monarchy, under the influence of its powerful Queen Min, the wife of Gojong, was gravely alarmed and sought to stem Japan's increasingly hostile encroachments, Miura Goro, the Japanese Minister Plenipotentiary in Seoul, decided to eliminate the Queen.

On October 8, 1895, Miura ordered his hand-picked assassins from Japan to murder her in cold blood in her own palace residence.

In the face of Japan's aggressive moves, Gojong turned to Russia for protection and support, and on February 11, 1896 he fled to the Russian Embassy in Seoul.

In extending its helping hand to Gojong, however, Russia had its own ulterior motives. After establishing its dominant position in Manchuria it was actively seeking to secure its economic and commercial hold in Korea as well.

At the urging of nationalists zealously promoting Korean independence, Gojong left the Russian Embassy a year later, on February 20, 1897, and on October 12, he declared the establishment of Daehan Jeguk (Empire of Korea) and became the Emperor of Korea.

Japan considered the Russian encroachment in Korea unacceptable, and on January 10, 1904, it declared war on the Russia of Tsar Nicholas II, to drive the Russians, the last remaining foreign presence, out of Korea.

Japan defeated Russia, and on September 5, 1905, Japan and Russia signed the Treaty of Peace at Portsmouth, under which Russia recognized the Korean peninsula as part of Japan's sphere of influence.

As the sole foreign power in the peninsula now, Japan actively pursued its aggressive designs on Korea.

Toward that end, in November 1905, Emperor Meiji appointed Count Ito Hirobumi, his closest confidant and Japan's leading elder statesman of the time, as his special emissary to Korea. Ito's primary mission was to secure a treaty establishing Korea as Japan's protectorate and thereby lock it firmly in its claws.

Korea was an ancient nation, but through its long history of many thousand years it had become a victim of its unique geography more times than its people wished to count. Surrounded by nations and peoples much larger than themselves, Koreans had been invaded from all directions time and again: by the Chinese on the west, by the Mongolians in the northwest, by the Manchus in the north, by the Jurchens in the northeast, and by the Japanese in the south.

Each foreign invasion left Koreans utterly devastated and destitute, but each time, like a phoenix they rose up again from the ashes and rebuilt their homes, their villages, their cities, and their nation, continuing brilliant cultural advancements begun during Korea's bronze age of the pre-Christian era.

And in the course of a thousand years between 400 B.C. and 600 A.D. Koreans taught the Japanese, their southern neighbor, how to grow rice, build dams and irrigation dykes, weave and make clothes, breed and ride horses, raise silkworm, fashion iron and steel tools, and make stoneware potteries, among others.[1]

During the 6th and 7th century A.D., Korean teachers, technicians, architects, tile makers, craftsmen, and artists went to Japan to help build their first capitals, first at Asuka and later at Nara. Holding exalted positions, Korean Confucian scholars taught the Japanese how to read and write as well as how to manage and administer, while Korea's Buddhist priests were planting Buddhism and building first Buddhist temples in Japan. In the process Korean architects taught the Japanese how to make tiles and build sturdy tile-roofed buildings supported by foundation stones.[2]

In time many Koreans settled in Nara, becoming elite members of Japanese society. Some of them, like the Soga clan, rose to become supreme leaders of the land while others became members of Japan's royal family through marriage. One of such Koreans in Japan's royal family was Takano no Niigasa, a descendent of Baekje King Muryeong of Korea. She married Emperor Konin (770-781) and gave birth to a son who became Emperor Kammu (781-806 A.D.), one of the greatest monarchs of ancient Japan.[3]

Koreans, who outnumbered native Japanese population in the ancient capital area by 8 to 2, named it Nara according to a Korean word, *nara*, meaning land, country, or nation. They called their mother land *kun-nara* (main or original land) and their newly settled land *sae-nara* (new land). In time, *sae* part dropped out, and the new land came to be called simply Nara. But the Koreans and local Japanese continued to call Korea *kun-nara* or *kudara*, the latter being a phonetically evolved version.

In the days of Goryo kingdom (918-1392) Korean ceramic technicians charmed the world with their bluish colored celadon ware of exquisite beauty. In 1234 Korean printers invented the world's first movable metal type, preceding Gutenberg of Germany by two centuries.

During Joseon kingdom (1392-1910) Korean artisans perfected ceramic technology producing magnificent porcelain ware which some Japanese samurai lords admired and valued to the point of deifying them. In the late 1600s Korean ceramic artisans helped develop Japan's entire porcelain industry including the famous Karatsu Ware, Hagi Ware, Arita Ware, Satsuma Ware, and Agano Teaware.

In the course of its five hundred-year history, the Joseon Kingdom also gave birth to world-class leaders, including Great King Sejong and Admiral Yi Soon-shin. The former led a group of scholars, in early 15th century, in the invention of the *hangeul* alphabet, one of the greatest marvels among human inventions, enabling Koreans become literate easily without having to learn difficult Chinese characters. Admiral Yi Soon-shin proved himself to be a brilliant naval strategist against Japanese invaders in 1592, eliciting awe and admiration even from his enemies.

By the middle of the 19th century, however, the old kingdom had signs of wear and tear. Corruption among government officials was rampant, peasant rebellions were frequent, and Confucian scholar-officials charged with the responsibility of running the government and maintaining peace, justice, and order in the land were caught up in interminably self-destructive factional politics.

When foreign merchant ships, first from England and France and later from Russia and US, approached its shores seeking to trade, its leaders reacted violently, knowing the harm which the Europeans had done to China in the Opium War of 1839-1842. Even though some practically minded intellectuals were clamoring for reform, opening to the West, and modernization of the nation's economic and military systems, the political establishment of Joseon Kingdom, dominated by the conservative Confucian elites of the *Yangban* class, clenched their fist and decided to turn to their Confucian past more firmly than ever.

In 1866 Daeweongun, King Gojong's father and the de facto ruler of Korea as Gojong's regent since 1864 (Gojong was only 12 years old when he was placed on the throne), decided to reject all things Western and close up the country to Westerners. As part of his national exclusion policy, Daeweongun put to death more than 8000 Korean Catholics and nine French missionaries.

Japan, likewise had closed up its shores to Westerners early in the 1600s except one isolated and tightly controlled port at Nagasaki, but in 1854 under armed threat from the United States, Japanese feudal lords signed a treaty with the US for trade. Soon Japan signed a similar treaty with other Western nations. By the 1860's many Japanese recognized that the Shogunate, the government of feudal lords, was incapable of leading their country and by force replaced it with an imperial system by making Meiji new ruler of Japan in January, 1868.

Having recognized the power and superiority of Western technology and Western products, Emperor Meiji issued a decree opening Japan completely to the West, and soon Japan embarked on massive and rapid industrialization. Thus while Korea was closing up its shores to the West in 1866 Japan was opening up all of its ports to the West, to Western science, Western technology, and Western ideas.

In 1873 Daeweongun retired, and Gojong, now 21 years old and more progressively minded, assumed his direct royal reign. But by then Korea, endowed with more antiquated bookish Confucian scholar-officials than properly trained military officers, was too weak to withstand Japan which was already well on its way in modernizing its military.

When Ito Hirobumi arrived in Korea in November, 1905, Japan had demonstrated its military superiority by defeating China and Russia in two wars.

With his overwhelming military force, Ito Hirobumi immediately went to work, demanding Gojong, and his cabinet ministers to sign a treaty under which Korea would relinquish to the Japanese resident-general in Seoul its jurisdictions on all international relations. The so-called "Protectorate Treaty of 1905" was drafted by Ito Hirobumi himself. In effect, Ito was demanding Gojong and his government that they place Korea under his control.

When the King and his ministers refused to sign, Japanese soldiers stormed the foreign ministry to forcibly take its official seal, which Japanese officials themselves affixed to the document. It was November 17, 1905, and Emperor Meiji promptly appointed Ito Hirobumi as the first Resident-General of Korea.

Clearly, it was an act of naked aggression by Japan against Korean sovereignty in its weak moment, and Gojong, angry with Ito Hirobumi and Japanese aggression, decided to carry out his lonely war against Japan by appealing to the international community.

On February 1, 1906, Gojong published an open letter in the *Korea Daily News* proclaiming that as the Emperor of Korea he did not approve the treaty and that Korea desperately needed the protection of world powers.

The following year, on April 22, 1907, Gojong secretly sent a delegation to the Second Hague Peace Conference in the Netherlands to expose the injustices done to Korea by Japan. The plan failed, however, due to adverse interference by Japan and England, its ally and a major colonial power.

Ito Hirobumi decided to use the incident for further aggression on the Korean sovereignty. He forced Gojong to abdicate as the Emperor of Korea and put Yi Cheok, one of Gojong's sons and a person of limited mental and physical ability, on the throne. Ito's intention was to use Yi Cheok as an instrument of his political aggrandizement.

On July 20, 1907, Ito forcibly effected the change in a strange royal succession ceremony conducted without the personal participation of Gojong and his son. Under duress, Yi Cheok thus became Sunjong, the 27th king of Joseon Kingdom.

Having removed Gojong, the last major obstacle to Japan's aggression in Korea, Ito Hirobumi, on August 1, forced King Sunjong and his cabinet to sign a new agreement, which gave the Japanese resident-general power and authority over all matters of Korean internal administration. Immediately thereafter, Ito Hirobumi disbanded all elements of the Korean army.

Tightly held in the claws of Japan, Korea's history as an independent nation was thus rapidly coming to an end.

On August 7, Gojong crowned ten-year old Yi Eun as the Crown Prince of Joseon Kingdom. In due time, he would succeed Sunjong and become the king of Korea. Born in a wrong time, however, Yi Eun would never sit on the throne, for Ito Hirobumi decided to take Korea's Crown Prince away from Korea to Japan in a permanent exile.

He assured Yi Eun's father, Gojong, that he was taking Yi Eun to Japan for study at Japan's best schools, but his real intent was to take him away from Korea and turn him into loyal Japanese. To enhance his objectives, Ito, already the *defacto* ruler of Korea, had himself appointed by Emperor Meiji as Yi Eun's Teacher Extraordinaire. He wanted to put Yi Eun under his personal control.

In preparation for the boy prince's exile mentally and psychologically, Ito had removed Yi Eun from his parents in Gyeong-Un Palace to the Nakseonjae, a separate royal residence in another part of Seoul. There, he would spend the last 22 days of his boyhood life in his homeland before being shipped to Japan.

As a boy Yi Eun had spent much time at the Nakseonjae, studying or playing in its beautiful garden among its trees and rocks. Those rocks and trees would be etched in his memory forever, keeping his longing for his homeland alive throughout his life in exile.

As expected, the entire Yi Royal Court in Seoul erupted in fury as the news spread.

"I will never let my son leave me. He is just a little child," screamed Lady Eom, Yi Eun's mother. "No, No, No!" Likewise, Yi Eun's father protested vehemently. "As Korea's Crown Prince he must be educated in Korea and not in Japan," he declared.

The Nakseonjae

"What a pity! His Majesty, the Crown Prince, is only 10 years old!" Court ladies who had been looking after him since his infancy wailed aloud with sadness and anger.

All the furies, all the objections, and all the wailings were to no avail. Emperor Meiji himself issued a decree ordering Yi Eun to come to Tokyo.

To placate Gojong and Lady Eom, Ito Hirobumi promised them that Yi Eun would return to Seoul once a year during summer vacations. That promise offered them some comfort, and on that condition, Gojong and Lady Eom gave their final permission.

Then Gojong conveyed his only and final advice to his son, just before his departure, while they were alone. Taking a piece of paper, he wrote with a brush PATIENCE and said to him, "Above all, be patient, and be patient again. Until the right time comes, endure all hardships and obstacles which come in your way." That advice would guide Yi Eun throughout his life in exile.

Thus on December 5, 1907, Yi Eun, now 11, boarded the Manshu Maru, a Japanese navy ship, to begin his life of exile in Japan. Ito personally accompanied him.

Behind him he was leaving all of his childhood friends, close relatives, his nurse mothers, his familiar play grounds, his beloved father, and most of all, his dear mother.

Ito Hirobumi, the Resident-General of Korea and Yi Eun's Teacher Extraordinaire, was the architect of Imperial Japan, called by many "the George Washington of modern Japan." Born of a low-ranking samurai of the Choshu Domain (current Yamguchi Prefecture) in 1841, he was captivated by the Western civilizations early in his life. At 22, he went secretly to London to study British naval sciences at University College. While in England, he became convinced that Japan had to be westernized, especially in the military, to remain free from Western colonialism.

Following the fall of the old Tokugawa Shogunate and the restoration of Emperor Meiji to the position of supreme power in Japan, Ito gradually rose in the political ladder, and in 1885 became Imperial Japan's first prime minister (1885-1888).

He helped draft the Constitution of the Empire of Japan promulgated in February, 1889.

Known as the Meiji Constitution, it centered on authoritarian rule, severely restricting civil rights. It was modeled after Prussia's authoritarian constitution.

That same year, Ito became head of the Privy Council, which advised the Emperor on all key issues of the Empire, thus becoming the real power behind the scenes. Beginning in 1892, he served as prime minister three more times, 1892-1896, 1898-1899, and 1900-1901.

It was during his second term as prime minister that Japan intensified its aggressive actions in Korea, declaring war on China (Sino-Japanese War of 1894-95) to remove China's influence there and also murdering Queen Min, the wife of Gojong, who stood in his path.

Ito was a shrewd and clever political strategist and tactician. Unlike Field Marshal Yamagata Aritomo, his colleague from Choshu Domain and a political rival, who advocated outright annexation of Korea with armed forces, Ito was a gradualist. Believing that Japan was not ready militarily to challenge Western powers abroad, particularly England and the United States, he decided to take over Korea step by step, by attrition, through political and diplomatic maneuvering.

One of Ito's major strategies, in this regard, was weakening the power of Joseon Kingdom's Yi Royal Court and Yi royal household. And as the first step he decided to send Yi Eun, the young Crown Prince, out of Korea and place him completely under Japanese control in Japan.

Arriving in Tokyo, Crown Prince Yi Eun received a royal welcome from Emperor Meiji and all the members of the Imperial Court. The news of his arrival quickly spread throughout Japan.

His new home was a beautiful and spacious palace in Toriisaka section of Tokyo, provided and cared for by Japan's Imperial Household Ministry with a large retinue of officers, cooks, gardeners, drivers, and servants. All of Yi Eun's personal and household expenses would be paid with money sent from the Yi Royal Household Administration in Seoul.

Beginning January, 1908, Yi Eun received private instruction in Japanese language, Japanese history, world geography, and other subjects from some of the best scholars and teachers of Japan, for a period of three years.

Yi Eun was accorded the same status of Crown Prince as that of Crown Prince Hirohito of Japan with all the respect and honor thereof. And the Imperial Household Ministry made certain that all his physical needs were met and that he lacked nothing in material comfort.

He was, however, forbidden from returning to Korea or visiting his family in Seoul.

Emperor Meiji himself would occasionally invite him over to the Imperial Palace for dinner as well as tea and friendly chats. From the Emperor down to cooks and servants, Japan's Imperial establishment went out their way to make Yi Eun feel welcome and comfortable.

All the warm welcoming gestures notwithstanding, for the eleven-year old boy, snatched from his parents, family members, friends, and his familiar home, his life was one of unbearable loneliness, longing, and bewilderment.

Most of his waking hours, the little boy looked forlorn and deserted. In his demeanor, there was no sign of energy or any joy. Each night he cried himself to sleep while longing for his mother. Likewise, back in Seoul, Lady Eom, his mother, was twisting and turning in her endless wailings for her only son, now gone from her.

Ito Hirobumi with Yi Eun in Japan
c. January, 1908
Source: Naver.com, King Young-chin/Yi Eun

One day, in his longing for the happy days he had spent in the Nakseonjae, he wrote a friend in Seoul and asked him to send him a few pebbles from the Nakseonjae garden where he used to play as a child. When the pebbles arrived, he held them in his hands with tears rolling down his cheek. Those pebbles became his companion for many years, comforting his lonely soul.

About two years later, on October 26, 1909, Yi Eun learned that his Teacher Extraordinaire, Ito Hirobumi, was assassinated by Ahn Joong-geun, a Korean patriot and a nationalist, at Harbin,

Manchuria, where Ito had gone to hold a political meeting with Vladimir Kokovtsov, a Russian leader in Manchuria.

Ahn decided to kill Ito for "his crimes against Korea and the Korean people" and particularly for the Treaty of Protectorate which he had forced on Korea. Three of six shots from Ahn's pistol hit Ito in the chest, and he died shortly after.

Ahn killed Ito hoping that the assassination would bring the plight of Korea to the attention of international powers for justice. He also believed that the elimination of the brain behind Japan's military adventurism would enhance the peace of East Asia.

For the first time, Yi Eun, now 13 years old, became aware of himself and his place in the context of Japan-Korea conflicts, and he had a heavy sense of burden vis-à-vis his mother land, the land whose king he was slated to become.

At the same time, he realized that he was shackled and powerless as others decided on his fate and his destiny. He painfully became aware that he was a bird in a cage.

In the aftermath of Ito's assassination, Field Marshall Yamagata Aritomo, the fierce firebrand in Japan's politics, became the most powerful leader in Japan. And as the head of the Privy Council (1909-1922), he dictated all major decisions on Japan' military and foreign affairs.

In May, 1910, he had General Terauchi Masatake, another military firebrand, appointed as the new Resident-General of Korea. His mission was to effect speedy annexation of Korea.

Terauchi wanted to keep his plans secret, so immediately upon his arrival in Korea he closed down all Korean newspapers. Then with Yi Wan-yong, the Korean prime minister, he drafted the annexation treaty, and on August 29, 1910 he had the prime minister sign it.

In anticipation of strong reaction from the Korean populace, Terauchi disbanded all Korean patriotic organizations and quickly arrested leaders among Korean nationalists. A few days later, on august 29, 1910, Terauchi forced Sunjong to announce publically that he was no longer the king of Korea and that Korea was now a part of Japan.

Thus as of August 29, 1910, Joseon Kingdom was no more, and Korea became a Japanese colony against the will of its people.

Following the annexation, Japan established the Government General in Seoul, and the Resident-General became the Governor General of Korea, who would now rule Korea in behalf of Japanese government in Tokyo.

And to insure absolute control of Korea with military and police forces, Japanese government adopted a policy that only generals and admirals would serve as the Governor General.

The Yi Royal Court, which had maintained Joseon Kingdom for 500 years since 1392, was abolished. In its place the Government General created the Yi Royal Family Administration and placed it under the Government General and Japan's Imperial Household Ministry.

Upon hearing the news, Yi Eun, the Crown Prince of Korea, wailed as he watched as a hostage the passing of his kingdom and his nation from a faraway place across the ocean.

He wept because he was helpless. He wept for his kingdom that was no more. He wept for his father, for his mother, for his friends, and for his brother, Sunjong, who had just lost his throne.

On January 9, 1911, Yi Eun was enrolled in the Boys Department of Gakushuin as a middle school student. He excelled in his studies and became an honor student.

On July 20, he received an urgent telegram from Seoul that his mother had become gravely ill with typhus fever. Forbidden to leave Japan, however, he could only turn his face westward toward Korea and shed tears of longing and sorrow.

Lady Eom had also been longing for her son day and night. Every time she had a chance to see Terauchi she begged him to allow her to see her son at least just once, reminding him of the promise which Ito Hirobumi had made, but Terauchi refused with one excuse after another.

He feared that once Yi Eun returned to Korea he would stay, complicating Japan's position in Korea.

As Lady Eom was dying of high fever, she became hysterical and cried without end calling her son's name and asking, "Has the Crown Prince come? Where is the Crown Prince? Where is my son?" In the end, she died without ever seeing her son again.

When the word arrived in Tokyo that Lady Eom had died, Yi Eun collapsed. All of his pent-up emotions imploded. Only then, powers in Tokyo gave him the permission to visit Seoul.

Yi Eun hastened, hoping at least to view his mother's body, but when he arrived at Deoksu Palace he was forbidden to approach the room where his mother's body was laid for fear that he might also be infected by typhus.

For three weeks he stayed in a solitary room mourning and pining for his lost mother.

Then, after watching her buried in a royal cemetery on a hill, east of Seoul, he returned to Tokyo.

He had been forced to leave his mother at 11 when she was young and vibrant, and now he was forced to leave her again, this time in her grave, holding his aching heart being shattered to ten thousand pieces.

Terauchi, the Governor General of Korea, made it certain that Yi Eun would leave Korea, and the sooner the better.

Ever since Ito Hirobumi destroyed Korea's independence six years before, Korea had been seething with anti-Japanese movements, riots, and guerrilla wars against Japanese installations.

Independence movements were emerging among Korean intellectuals, with local media calling for a new awakening and new actions among the Korean populace. And many Koreans were hanging their hope on Yi Eun, the Crown Prince of Korea, for the revival of Joseon Kingdom.

Terauchi was determined to snuff out such hope among Koreans by putting him on a Tokyo-bound ship.

Back home in Tokyo, Yi Eun entered the Boy's Military School to receive military training, like all the princes of Japanese imperial families. He had spent eight months at Gakushuin. In May, 1912, he received the happy news from Seoul that he had a new princess sister. Her name was Deok-hye.

Being his only daughter, Princess Deok-hye became Gojong's special darling, an object of extraordinary affection. Likewise, to Yi Eun, though born of a different mother she was his only sister, and he deeply longed to see the baby princess.

In May, 1915, upon graduation from the Boys' Military School Yi Eun entered Japan's Military Academy, graduating two years later, in May 1917. Three months later, in August, he learned about the Japanese government decision regarding his marriage engagement.

When first informed by his secretary about the media report of his engagement to Princess Nashimoto Masako, he was silent. He knew that, as with all major decisions in his life he had no choice, even regarding his marriage.

But he had two concerns. First, he wondered how his father would react. Secondly, he could not help thinking about Maiden Min Gap-wan, to whom he had already been engaged.

Gojong, knowing about Japan's long-held political practice of establishing marriage alliances with peoples it subjugated, wanted to make it certain that his son, the Crown Prince, would be married to a Korean from the Korean nobility; consequently, just before Yi Eun was taken to Japan in 1907, the Yi Royal Court hurriedly chose Maiden Min Gap-wan, of the same age, as the Crown Princess.

She was the daughter of Min Yeong-don, Korea's former ambassador to Great Britain and a high ranking officer in Joseon Kingdom. Selected out of 150 candidates brought to Deoksu Palace, the boyhood home of Yi Eun, Maiden Gap-wan was formally engaged to Yi Eun in the midst of solemn palace ceremony.

For Yi Eun, however, only eleven years old, all the palace commotions carried little meaning. He was a young boy more interested in playing with sticks and toys in the palace play ground.

Marriage was the last thing on his mind. As he matured, however, he understood the significance of his engagement to Maiden Min Gap-wan not only as a solemn act of the Yi Royal Court and Joseon Kingdom but his father's utmost wish.

The announcement about his engagement to Princess Masako, therefore, brought Yi Eun much anguish. First, he was concerned about the shock which his father would suffer at the news. Secondly, he agonized over the tragic fate of Maiden Min Gap-wan, who, according to Joseon Kingdom's rules on marriage, could never marry another man.

Having sealed Yi Eun's engagement to Maiden Min, Gojong was adamant in his opposition to the Japanese plan.

As the matter stood, Japan's plan to marry Princess Masako to Crown Prince Yi Eun could not go forward.

Governor General Hasekawa (successor of Terauchi) therefore commanded Gojong and the Yi Royal family to annul Yi Eun's engagement to Maiden Min. Under the Governor General's gun, they had no choice but to comply. Neither could they raise objections to Yi Eun's marriage to a Japanese woman.

On December 25, Yi Eun was commissioned as a second lieutenant and promptly assigned to the Imperial Guards (Konoetai) in Tokyo.

On January 13 of the following year, Yi Eun, now an officer in Japan's Imperial Army, went to Korea to report to Gojong. That was his first formal official trip to Korea since his departure as a child.

By then, his engagement to Masako had been sealed, and accordingly the main topic of conversation between Yi Eun and Gojong was the upcoming wedding ceremony.

CHAPTER 4

A Destiny Unwished

As the eventful summer of 1917 was drawing to a close, the Nashimto family returned to Tokyo, and Masako began her fall semester at Gakushuin. On the first day of school, she was greeted by classmates with congratulations, but some appeared to disdain her upcoming marriage to a foreigner.

As a person whose fate was already decided, she was feeling distanced from her classmates and a sense of loneliness overwhelmed her. Nevertheless, with a firm resolve to travel on the path destined for her, Masako decided to focus only on studies and to prepare herself for the long journey ahead.

Along with regular subjects taught at the school, she received tutorial instruction at home on classical Chinese, moral lessons, calligraphy, and the history and customs of Korea.

Along the way she learned that for more than two thousand years Koreans had been coming to the Japanese islands, introducing advanced culture and technology such as rice farming, metal tools, horses, writing, art, architecture, and Buddhism among other things.

She also learned that the Baekje people of ancient Korea were indispensable in the development of early Japan during the Asuka and Nara periods (c. 530-800 A.D.) and that a Korean woman of nobility, Takano no Niigasa, who descended from the Baekje royal linage, gave birth to Emperor Kammu (737-806 A.D.), one of Japan's greatest emperors. This awareness not only gave her a sense of affinity to Korea but also caused her to muse whether she might have the honor of reciprocating the Korean contribution to Japanese civilization and especially to Japan's imperial family.

But for now, more than anything, Masako wanted to know about Prince Yi Eun. What is he like? What kind of personality does he have? What does he think about this marriage? Does he hate me for being forced to marry me? These and many other questions kept bombarding her mind. She was both curious and afraid.

She remembered hearing as a child someone making a passing remark that a Korean prince had been brought to Japan as a hostage and that he was not even allowed to see his dying mother back in Korea. She also remembered hearing that when Joseon Kingdom was abolished by Japan, his status was demoted from Imperial Crown Prince to Crown Prince.

As she saw the Korean prince occasionally from distance at various Imperial Palace functions, she felt sorry for him. Otherwise, to Masako Yi Eun was just another stranger.

But now that she was soon to marry the stranger, his plight became very personal. She suddenly realized that he too was a bird in a cage and a victim like herself, and she felt being pulled toward him. And the more she studied about Korea and its recent tribulations and sufferings brought on by Japan, the more pain she felt. They were no longer Korea's or Yi Eun's tribulations but her own.

Masako's family decided that the wedding was to take place in January, 1919.

As the first act of wedding preparation, Princess Masako and her mother went to the Imperial Palace to pay a ritual visit to Emperor Taisho and Empress Teimei. Warmly welcoming the two, the Emperor and Empress offered whatever help they needed in the upcoming event. Empress Teimei gave a personal admonition:

"You have done well in accepting this special marital union. While it is a highly auspicious event my heart goes out to you because of the heavy burden placed on your shoulders. But this is also for the sake of our nation . . ." As Masako was leaving the Palace, the Empress wished her well.

Years later, Masako reflected on this moment: "My heart was filled with both sadness and gratitude. And at the same time, I could not help feeling anew the overwhelming weight of my responsibility."

In spring the following year (1918), Masako began her high school studies at Gakushuin. During the summer, she went to Kyoto where her father was serving as commander of an army division. This would be the last summer which she and her family would spend together. They decided to stay at Sansenen Temple, where her grandfather Asahiko had once served as chief of the temple.

While in Kyoto, Masako hiked the beautiful Hiei Mountain behind the city and visited various historical sites and places of attraction. It was a delightful and memorable summer.

Masako had not met Yi Eun yet, but as the autumn arrived, Masako and her mother formally started wedding preparations. In the midst of hustle and bustle she turned 17 years old on November 14.

As she realized that this would be her last birthday at her birthplace, a sense of fear gripped her about her new destiny. Even the congratulatory words spoken by 30 or more staff of the Nashimoto Palace made her somewhat apprehensive.

Everything was becoming "last this" or "last that". November 30, 1918 was her last day of school at Gakushuin. Her classmates held a farewell party for her.

On December 5, 1918, Emperor Taisho issued an Imperial edict granting his permission for the wedding of Princess Masako and Crown Prince Yi Eun.

*Masako dressed for the sacred farewell ceremony
at the Imperial Palace Shinto Shrine*

Three days later, on the 8th, Masako's engagement to Yi Eun was formalized at a special ceremony. Only then did Masako and Yi Eun meet face to face for the first time. Six days later, on December 18, Princess Masako and her parents went to Crown Prince Yi Eun's residence at Toriisaka for their first meeting, at which they chose January 25th, 1919, for the wedding date.

On January 9, the Imperial Palace conferred upon Princess Masako the Meritorious Order of Hokensho, an Imperial honor and decoration given to Japanese women for distinguished service. The Meritorious Order, Princess Masako assumed, was to both recognize and further encourage her in her willingness to accept a burden imposed upon her by her nation—marrying a Korean prince to enhance Japan's political ambitions.

Next day, Masako went to the sacred Shinto shrine on the Imperial Palace grounds to perform her last act as a Japanese princess by bidding farewell to the imperial ancestors. With this she completed all rituals required for the wedding.

Their first meeting was formal and brief, but instantly, the two felt being drawn to each other.

Yi Eun's gentle and warm demeanor put Masako at ease. Though a person of a few words, each word he spoke was measured and considerate. In every way he was royal and princely, she thought.

His broad and sturdy shoulders gave her a sense of assurance. But at the same time, amidst all the formal and polite conversations, she saw a lonely prince in a foreign land, long separated from his home and loved ones, and a prince without his kingdom and in much unspoken pain. She felt her heart going out to him—in some way to comfort him.

As for Yi Eun, this beautiful and vibrant young maiden was like an oasis in the desert. Ever since he was brought to Japan against his will as a young boy, he had been living in a confined environment in loneliness. He was like a bird in a cage, and always surrounded by stale and stifling middle-aged or older men only.

He had longed, in vain, for the warmth and affection of his parents and his boyhood friends back in Korea. And strictly forbidden to socialize with females, he had never experienced the joy or the affection of a woman even as a young man now in his early twenties. To the young prince starved of affection, Masako was a vision of possibility.

Following their first formal meeting, Yi Eun visited Masako every Sunday at her house while attached to the Imperial Guards in Tokyo. Masako eagerly welcomed his weekly visits for she was anxious to know as much as possible about her husband-to-be.

Along the way, Masako learned all about the tragedies of his homeland as well as about his heartaches and tribulations as a young hostage in a foreign land, and she painfully realized what a lonely life he had been living.

Yi Eun as an officer in the Imperial Japanese Army
Source: Naver.com, King Young-chin

She also discovered that despite all the heartaches, frustrations, and despairs he had suffered he was a genuinely warm, kind, and gentle person. More than that, Princess Masako realized that she and Yi Eun were two human beings sharing the same tragic fate, decided by powers beyond their control and brought together against their will. They, she felt painfully, were like butterflies entangled in the spider's web.

Each meeting brought her ever closer to him. Princess Masako was falling in love, and she developed a resolve from which she would never waver, heaven or hell.

"I am binding myself in marriage to his warm heart, and not anything else," she assured herself.

"The politics of Korea-Japan union is none of my concern. My utmost wish is to love and comfort him in his loneliness as his warm, caring wife and friend. That shall be my duty and my destiny," Princess Masako promised herself.

Masako met Yi Eun at the will of her nation's political and military rulers for a strictly political reason; nevertheless, she was firmly resolved that she would build a truly happy life with Yi Eun, in genuine love and trust.

CHAPTER 5

KOREA EXPLODES IN RAGE

O n January 21, 1919, Masako sent her trousseaus to Yi Eun's residence in Toriisaka.

Four days later, there would be the wedding, and she and Yi Eun would start a new home and a new family together. For a moment she was drifted away in a blissful dream of a happy home and smiling children playing in the yard.

As Masako and her family sat down for dinner in the quiet peace of the evening, Mr. Ko Hee-kyeong, Yi Eun's secretary, hurried into the house, panting.

"We have received a bad news from Seoul," he said in a halting voice. Even though it was freezing cold outside he was perspiring profusely.

"Crown Prince Yi Eun's father has collapsed with a stroke, and his condition is grave. The Crown Prince is leaving for Korea immediately." Mr. Ko then ran out of the house.

It was another bolt of lightning to hit Masako. She sat stunned, speechless.

"Only four days before our wedding! If he goes to Korea now, when will he return? What's going to happen to our marriage?" she murmured to herself full of anxiety, uncertainty, and even fear.

The family made no stir. In a deadening silence, they were all thinking alike: This can only be a bad omen for the marriage at hand. Masako, however, could not sit still. She quickly changed her clothes and ran to the station where Yi Eun would be boarding a train.

"I don't know what is going to happen to us. But right now, he is on his way to see his gravely ill father. I must bid him a safe trip and do my best to console him in this sad hour. That is what I must do," she repeated to herself as she ran toward the station.

The Tokyo train station was a crowded place, but Masako was able to spot Yi Eun. He was already on the train, standing next to a window, looking somewhat lost. She was eager to comfort Yi Eun with proper words of consolation, but seeing him face to face she could not utter a word. There was only a silence between the two.

The man standing before her had gone through so much already, she thought. As a boy he was forbidden from seeing his mother even when she was dying. Now, he is on his way to see his dying father. How heavy and unbearable will his sadness be if the king dies before he arrives?

As these thoughts were going through her mind, her heart was going out to a man already plagued with much heartache and yet another tribulation. Immobilized by sinking emotions, the two just continued to look at each other's face in silence. Only there were tears welling in Yi Eun's eyes.

Finally, Yi Eun opened his mouth.

"I am sorry."

Masako was about to burst into tears, but holding herself, she said:

"I will be waiting for you until you return."

That night, Masako could not sleep, thinking about Yi Eun and how sorrowful he looked at the station. She was full of regret, for she could not do anything in the way of consoling him.

Upon his arrival in Seoul, Yi Eun learned that his father, Gojong, the 26th ruler of Korea's Joseon Kingdom, had already died.

As Yi Eun entered Deoksu Palace where the king's body lay, Sunjong, his half-brother (deposed since 1910), rushed out to the courtyard to meet him. He had been attending at wake. Surrounded by hundreds of grief-stricken mourners, they embraced each other and wailed loudly, as they were overcome by their own grief not only over the death of their father but also the loss of their kingdom.

Their hearts were broken to a million pieces as they felt all the heartaches, the tribulations, and the humiliations which their father had suffered at the hands of the Japanese.

Amidst national mourning a rumor was spreading fast that Gojong was actually poisoned by the Japanese.

Ever since Japan took control of Korea in 1905 under the illegal Protectorate Treaty, Gojong had sought every means to expose Japan's illegal and unjust actions to the world community.

In 1907, he dispatched a secret mission to the Hague Peace Conference to appeal for international assistance against Japan. The mission failed, as it was sabotaged by Japan and its ally England. To punish him, Ito Hirobumi, the Resident General of Korea, promptly deposed Gojong from the throne.

And once again, when he learned that another international peace conference would be held in Paris on January 18, 1919, in the aftermath of the World War I, Gojong secretly planned to send a delegation to the conference to plead for Korea's independence.

In this plan, he was specially inspired and encouraged by President Woodrow Wilson's declaration of the Fourteen Points, which among other things emphasized the principle of self-government for occupied nationalities.

Gojong's secret plan was discovered by Japanese agents, and someone in the Government General decided that the deposed king had become a thorn in its neck and must be eliminated for good.

In the evening of January 20th, Gojong drank a cup of tea, as he did regularly before retiring to bed. A short time later, he started to complain about severe stomach pain and soon died. A rumor quickly spread that Japanese agents, using threats and bribes, had persuaded a palace physician to poison Gojong.

As the rumor spread among the mourning Korean populace, simmering anti-Japanese sentiments were about to explode in

44

volcanic proportion. Koreans were ready to fight Japan's oppression, which had become increasingly harsh and unbearable.

In 1916, General Terauchi Masatake had been succeeded by another ruthless military man, Field Marshall Hasegawa Yoshimichi, as the second Governor General of Korea.

While Terauchi was making vital decisions in Tokyo as Japan's prime minister, including Princess Masako's marriage to Yi Eun, Hasegawa was seeking aggressively to dominate in political, economic, commercial, and other vital sectors of Korea.

As Koreans became increasingly marginalized in their own land, without power or freedom, they decided to embark on independence movements not only within Korea but abroad, especially among Korean students and intellectuals living in China, Japan, Russia, and the U.S.

Their movements continued to spread even as they came under the ruthless suppression of the Japanese police inside Korea and Japan. Especially encouraged by Woodrow Wilson's call for self-government in occupied nations, Korean independence activists were waiting for the right time to rise up in masse and appeal to the world community for Korea's liberation from Japan.

In preparation for the D-day that would explode with their resistance, 33 leaders of various religious and educational organizations (16 Christians, 15 members of the Heavenly Way Sect, and 2 Buddhists) held secret meetings to draft a declaration of independence and plan the mass event. The draft emphasized peace, justice, self-government, and non-violence. Tens of thousands of copies were printed secretly for distribution to every corner of the land.

The death of Gojong and the national mourning for him catalyzed a mass uprising.

Already large crowds were gathering in Seoul from all parts of the country to attend his funeral, and their emotions were highly charged by the rumors that the Japanese had assassinated their former king. No time was more appropriate than now.

Gojong's funeral was to take place on March 3rd, so the leaders of the mass uprising chose March 1st as the D-day in respect for the deceased king. As a matter of principle, the uprising would be strictly a non-violent movement.

At 2 p.m. on March 1, 1919, the entire Korean peninsula, from the Yalu River to the South Coast, rocked and exploded. Koreans, young and old, men and women, simultaneously took to the streets, waving the forbidden Korean national flag and shouting, "Long Live Korea! Long Live Korean Independence!"

In Seoul, the drafters of the independence declaration, including Sohn Byeong-hee, Oh Se-chang, Choi Rin, and Kweon Dong-jin, gathered at Taehwa Pavilion to publicly announce Korean independence. Simultaneously, they informed the Government General of their declaration. They also dispatched copies of the declaration to the International Peace Conference being held in Paris.

At the very same time, about 5000 high school and college students gathered at the Pagoda Park in the center of the city and publicly read the declaration. Afterwards, they marched through downtown Seoul, shouting "Mansei! Long Live Korea! Long Live Korean Independence!"

Caught completely by surprise and shocked by the boldness of Korean defiance against its rule, the Government General responded quickly and ruthlessly with a reign of terror by unleashing its armed military *kempeitai* and police forces.

During the first two months of the uprising, more than 20,000 Koreans were killed or wounded, and more than 50,000 participants in the mass rallies were arrested. Japanese soldiers and police had no hesitation in carrying out wanton destructions of Korean villages and full-scale massacres of the peaceful demonstrators, in some cases decapitating the peaceful marchers with swords and fodder choppers.

On April 6, before daybreak while people were still sleeping, Japanese soldiers entered the village of Suchon-ri in the Suweon area south of Seoul, and burned down 38 houses out of 42, including a Methodist church. "The people rushed out and found the whole village burning. Some tried to put out the fire, but were soon stopped by the soldiers who shot at them, stabbed them with their bayonets or beat them. They were compelled to stand by and watch their village burn to ashes."[4]

This was Japanese retaliation against the villagers' hailing "Mansei!"—"Long live Korea and long live Korean independence!" just a few days before in a village gathering.

For the same reason, five days later the Japanese soldiers repeated their savage acts at nearby Hwasu-ri. ". . . sometime before daybreak, the villagers were suddenly aroused out of their sleep by the sound of gunfire and the smell of burning. Running into the open they found soldiers and police torching the houses and shooting and beating the people. Leaving everything, villagers fled for their lives, old and young, the mothers with their babies, and the fathers with the other children—all of them fled to the hills. But before they could make good their escape, many were murdered, shot by the soldiers, wounded and beaten."[5]

Four days later, on April 15, a Japanese army lieutenant named Arita Doshio led a group of soldiers and police to Jeam-ri village nearby. After gathering up more than two dozen villagers, including young children, he locked them inside the sanctuary of Jeam-ri Methodist Church and ordered his men to shoot them from outside through the windows. When a man pushed his child out through a window pleading with the Japanese to spare his life, they riddled the crying child's tiny frame with bullets. They had no mercy. They then torched the church, reducing the dead and dying people to ashes.[6]

When the soldiers came upon two women outside the church, weeping and pleading for their husbands' lives, they promptly beheaded one and shot the other, then covered their bodies with straw and burned them. The beheaded woman was only 19 years old, recently married to a young man who was burned to death inside the church. Then the Japanese soldiers burned the entire village of Jeam-ri, killing 39 additional residents in the process.[7]

The Memorial monument of the Jeam-ri Church Massacre
Twenty-three stone pillars represent 23 Jeam-ri adults, youth, and children
burned to death in the Jeam-ri Church sanctuary on April 15, 1919.
The large pillar with a circular hole symbolizes eternal hope and freedom.

Arriving at these scenes of carnage two days later, Dr. Frank William Schofield, a Canadian Methodist missionary working in Korea as a veterinarian and bacteriologist, became the first Western eyewitness to the evil that Japan was committing against Koreans. With his pen and camera, he exposed Japanese atrocities in Korea to the world.[8] Soon, he himself became a target of Japanese anger and an assassination attempt.

Under such a reign of terror, the Korean independence movement went underground in Korea, but it would continue unabated elsewhere, especially in China, Siberia, and the United States. The Korean spirit could not be vanquished with guns and bayonets.

Koreans had long shared their collective memory, generation after generation, of the wanton ravaging of their land, in 1592 and 1597, by tens of thousands of sword swinging samurai soldiers sent by Toyotomi Hideyoshi, Japan's supreme military ruler, to conquer

Korea. Wherever they stayed or passed through the Japanese troops carried out carnage after carnage against innocent Koreans, burning, pillaging, and slaughtering.

To Koreans, therefore, Japanese had historically been a people who were brutal and savage by nature and could never be trusted. The destruction and carnage of 1919 only reconfirmed and solidified their collective memory, and they resolved to fight and resist the Japanese to the death.

F. A. McKenzie, a Canadian reporter and another early Western eyewitness to the events of spring, 1919, commented, "The Japanese struck an unexpected strain of hardness in the Korean character. They found . . . a spirit as determined as their own. They succeeded not in assimilating the people, but in reviving their sense of nationality."[9] Dr. Schofield echoed the same observation through his "Unquencherable Fire" lectures in Canada and the US in April, 1920.[10]

In Tokyo, Masako received the news of Gojong's death the day after Yi Eun left for Seoul. She had been eagerly looking forward to meeting her future father-in-law. She expressed her feelings of sadness in a poem:

> Daily I pay my homage to His Majesty's portrait.
> I miss the presence of honorable father whom I have not met.
> I feel much sadness. Oh, how deep and unbearable
> Koreans' grief must be.

As she pondered that just in four days Gojong would have become her father-in-law, her sadness became even more unbearable. Having learned, through Yi Eun, all about the heartaches and tribulations which Gojong suffered while losing his kingdom, she had developed deep feelings of sympathy.

Then even as she was still struggling with a sense of personal loss and sorrow, she learned that her father-in-law-to-be was murdered by poisoning and that behind it was the Japanese Government General.

Masako shuddered in fright. At night she would be jolted out of her bed, startled and trembling with fear. She was completely at a loss in the face of man's inhumanity toward other human beings. "Murder by poisoning, conspiracy, scheming, and lies: Are these the way of Japanese politics and power?" she asked.

And as a Japanese she felt a deep sense of guilt. Gripped with oppressive and heart-wrenching emotions, she broke down and wept. She became even more unsettled as she pondered on her marriage being made amidst painfully difficult events such as these. "How many more tragic happenings will there be along the way?" she wondered.

Masako's fear and anxiety became more intense as she remembered something she had learned many years before: that the house at Gojimachi, where she was born, had been built by Miura Goro, the Japanese minister to Korea who had murdered Gojong's wife, Queen Min, in 1895.

She wondered if the coincidence portended a bad omen. At her sudden awareness that she too might meet similar dangers, she was so frightened she could not even breathe. She felt paralyzed.

Then on March 1, Masako learned from newspapers that Korea was exploding in its rage against the Japanese and was demanding freedom and independence.

The news brought the Japanese public as well as the Japanese government in Tokyo under a heightened state of tension. At the Imperial Palace was an atmosphere of grave concern.

As for Masako, each day was a nightmare. She was confused. She lost all sense of where her life was heading. At night she had strange dreams. Her father was gravely worried.

Her mother, normally of few words when around her father, blurted out:

"Did I not say that that this marriage was not right? How can the lad endure all . . . ?

Itsuko was protesting about Masako's engagement to a Korean, and at the same time she was regretting the consent she and her husband had given. A few minutes of tense silence followed.

Then Prince Nashimoto turned to his daughter and spoke in a serious and solemn voice:

"Masako, this marriage has been arranged strictly for a political purpose between Korea and Japan. When the relationship between the two countries turns bad, it will have a negative effect on your marriage. Knowing that, do you still want to marry Yi Eun? Are you confident that you can bear the painful consequences of marrying into Korea's Yi Royal Family?"

Once again, Masako was challenged to make a vital decision.

"When a person is in a crisis," she remembered the moment, "new courage surges forth. So it was with me. I had already made the decision and formed the resolve to love His Highness and become his life-time friend. I felt within my heart an unyielding force surging up to face any obstacles and to fulfill my hopes and dreams."

And facing her father, she replied:

"Father, please do not worry. The relationship between Korea and Japan may become bad, but I firmly trust in His Highness."

"What do you mean?" he asked.

"I know that our marriage has been arranged to enhance political union between Korea and Japan, but I am marrying His Highness, and not Korea."

Masako's father was reassured by her confident reply and said:

"You are right. As soon as His Highness returns from Korea we will select another day for the wedding. The sooner the better."

Her confident reply notwithstanding, Masako felt uneasy and unbearably lonely.

On March 3, the day of Gojong's state funeral, she offered a silent prayer before his portrait. Then she locked herself in her room all alone for the day, wondering through myriad confusing and unsettling thoughts.

Then, as Korean casualties were mounting in the March 1st independence rallies, Masako's family began to receive angry telegrams and telephone calls, day and night, from Koreans enraged with Japan. They were demanding that the family abrogate Masako's engagement to Yi Eun. The family was threatened with serious consequences in the event that Masako's marriage went forth.

For many days, Masako and her family were in a state of fear. Every time their telephone rang they shuddered, looking at each other. (She learned later that similar threats were being made to Yi Eun while he was attending his father's funeral back in Korea.)

In accordance with the mortuary protocols of Joseon Kingdom, Yi Eun was in mourning at Deoksu Palace ever since he arrived in Seoul on January 22.

On March 3, the Government General held a state funeral for Gojong in a military training camp, in accordance with Japanese Shinto mortuary protocols. Only 70 Koreans attended the ceremony.

The Korean people boycotted the Japanese ceremony, but when Gojong's bier left the camp for the Geumgok Royal Cemetery, thousands of Korean mourners appeared from everywhere along the path of the bier wailing in lamentation for their tragic king and their kingdom gone.

A few days after the funeral, Yi Eun returned to Tokyo. As soon as they learned of his arrival, Masako and her mother rushed to Yi Eun's residence in Toriisaka. They wanted to welcome him and convey their sympathies.

"We wish to express our heart-felt sympathies. We share your sadness in this difficult time," Itsuko said as Yi Eun greeted them.

"Thank you. I am very sorry for the concerns and worries I have caused," Yi Eun responded gently in an apologetic tone. That was all they said to each other, and yet they fully understood each other's feelings. Empathy in silence was more powerful than a million spoken words. To Masako's relief, she found Yi Eun exactly the same person she knew before. Even after the tumultuous two months of his stay in Seoul, through a long period of mourning, Japanese treacheries, and the explosive March 1 independence rallies, he had not changed.

He was still the same warm, kind, gentle, and considerate man as before. At last, she was relieved and freed from all the oppressive and unsettling thoughts which had been plaguing her. She could breathe once again.

Masako was deeply grateful and felt love and affection for Yi Eun surging in her heart more powerfully than ever. And once again, she made an oath to herself to love him and care for him.

"Yes, I will give him my love and my affections. Yes, I will do all my best to build a happy home for him filled with love and warmth. Yes, Yes, and Yes!" Again and again, she assured herself.

The new wedding day was set for April 28, 1920, a year later.

CHAPTER 6

FROM ECSTASY TO AGONY

The sudden death of Gojong and ensuing events provided Masako and Yi Eun more time to get to know each other and deepen their relationship.

During the 12 months from April 1919 to April 1920, they saw each other whenever Yi Eun could get away from his military duties. Sometimes their meeting would be for no more than 30 minutes as Yi Eun hurriedly dropped by between his military drills.

To Masako, every meeting and every visit, however brief, was pure joy and delight.

Masako's writing from those days reveal a young woman deeply in love, ever longing for her beloved, as seen in a poem written on August 2, 1919:

> On this day four years ago, when I was 16 years old, for the first time, the image of the man who would become my life-time companion was engraved in my heart.
>
> I had seen him before, but never did it occur to me that we would become related. Then he was just another stranger to me.
>
> Ah! today I cannot wait to see him and to visit.
> I so dearly miss him, and I am thinking only of him.

I am so very happy.

He is so bright and wise; he is healthy.
Even though he is from another country there is not a
trace of strangeness between us.

As soon as we say good bye I miss him and I want to see
him again. While waiting for him eagerly, I forget the
passing of time as well as any troubling thoughts.

A half day goes by quickly as I am wrapped with feelings
of bliss . . .

One day, while in a military field exercise, Yi Eun paid an
unexpected visit to Masako at her family's Oiso beach cottage. The
visit was brief. After he left, she wrote:

My beloved unexpectedly came to the beach where the
    ocean waves clap.
Tomorrow, again, my prince will go over the Hakone Pass.
I pray that neither storms nor the summer's hot sun will
    bother him.

As the spring of 1920 arrived, the entire landscape across Japan
was being transformed into a million beautiful multi-colored flower
gardens. Everywhere, happy crowds were gathering for cherry
blossom festivals, singing and dancing. It was a time of joyous
festivity for the renewal of life.

At the Palace of Prince Nashimoto Morimasa, people were busy
preparing for Princess Masako's wedding. Simultaneously, at the
palatial mansion of Prince Yi Eun in Toriisaka, two new rooms were
added, one for the newly married couple and the other for maids.

For more than ten years, the Toriisaka mansion saw only males. Now for the first time, its stale and stifling atmosphere would be lightened up with the presence of women. On April 26, two days before the wedding, Nakayama Teiko, the head maid, went to Prince Yi Eun's residence with two maids to prepare the arrival of Masako. It was the last logistic detail before the wedding.

The following day, Yi Eun was promoted to the rank of first lieutenant in the Imperial Army and also was decorated with the Grand Order of the Chrysanthemum.

At last, it was April 28. The wedding day arrived.

"The morning broke." Masako remembered. "As I awoke at dawn it was getting bright outside my window. Wrapped in the early morning fog, leaves on the trees were flapping in the gentle breeze.

"After a ceremonial bath, I went to the family shrine located in the southwest corner of the house and prayed for a happy conclusion of the events of the day.

"It was a bright sunny day. Everything was in order, and everyone, including the gardeners, looked fresh and cheerful.

"The cherry blossoms looked especially beautiful, as their petals were gently flying around in the air. It was like a beautiful dream, and I wanted to remember this day forever . . ."

It was customary for Japanese princesses to wear a traditional Japanese court dress at their wedding, but Masako chose a Western style dress in white color.

The moment a golden crown, decorated with diamonds and ostrich feathers, was placed on her head she felt her whole body becoming tense. She also felt her heart being weighted down as she became aware of the heavy responsibilities of the Crown Princess of Korea. She already knew fully about her tasks lying ahead, but the sensation from the weight of the crown prompted her once again to remember and strengthen her resolve.

Before heading to the wedding ceremony at Prince Yi Eun's mansion, Masako wanted to bid farewell to her parents. For weeks she had been trying to find proper words to say, but now she could not utter a word. Only tears were streaming down her face.

"Please, do not forget that you have heavy responsibilities. Be mindful of the values and the imperial standing of our family. I pray for your happiness."

Masako and Yi Eun on their wedding day
April 28, 1920

As Itsuko gave this advice in a solemn voice, Masako's father nodded his head, without a word. Masako saw tears welling in Itsuko's eyes.

Then Princess Masako headed to the wedding in a two-horse carriage provided by the Imperial Household Ministry, escorted by military honor guards. Prince Yi Eun, dressed in an officer's uniform, greeted and welcomed Masako.

Among dignitaries present for the occasion were Masako's uncles and aunts among others: Prince Asaka Yasuhiko and his wife, Princess Fumi, and Prince Kuni Kuniyoshi and his wife, Princess Chikako. They represented the imperial families on Princess Masako's side. Princess Fumi was a daughter of Emperor Meiji, while Prince Kuni, the father of Princess Nagako, engaged to Crown Prince Hirohito. Along with them there was Marquis Nabeshima Naohiro and his wife representing Masako's maternal side.

Representing the Yi royal family and Sunjong of Korea were Lee Wan-yong, Yun Taik-yeong, Yi Dal-yong, Lee Yun-yong, Song Byeong-joon, Jo Dong-yoon, and Min Yeong-chan. They were all alike pro-Japanese Koreans actively supporting Japanese causes in Korea. Lee Wan-yong, as the prime minister in Sunjong's cabinet, had contributed to Japan's annexation of Korea by providing Emperor Sunjong's official seal, which had been forcibly taken from under Queen Yun's skirt, where it was hidden. Also, representing Yi Eun was Prince Ito Hirokuni and his wife.

Even at this happy moment there was an element of bitter irony. Ito Hirokuni was at the wedding as the Minister of Japan's Imperial Household Ministry, which had jurisdiction over the Yi Royal family as well as over Yi Eun's life.

He was also the son of Ito Hirobumi, the arch enemy of Korea, who took control of Korea in 1905, deposed Emperor Gojong, Yi Eun's father, from his throne, and brought 11-year old Yi Eun to Tokyo as a hostage against his and his parents' will. For all those misdeeds, Ito Hirobumi had been assassinated in 1909 by Ahn Joong-geun, a Korean nationalist.

One can only imagine what thoughts were going through the mind of Yi Eun as he was being congratulated by the son of Korea's arch enemy and of his father and his mother.

But he was like a butterfly entangled in a spider's web. There was nothing he could do or say. The only thing he knew for certainty was that he loved Masako and that Masako loved him, and that was all that mattered.

Under a tense atmosphere, the ceremony ended without a glitch. At last, Masako felt truly at peace as she realized that she was now officially Crown Princess Yi Masako.

"I do not know what future the position of the Crown Princess holds," she said to herself, "but I know for certainty that it is my position, that it is the position I must keep, and that it is the position in which I will die."

"No matter what happens, I will move forward, with truth and a sincere heart, boldly and courageously," she said to herself firmly and confidently. That night, with their hearts firmly united, the couple sat on a sofa in their newly decorated room and held hands for the first time. The room was filled with the fragrance from white magnolias.

The following day, the newly married couple went to the Imperial Palace to report their marriage to Emperor Taisho and Empress Teimei.

"You have made a great contribution for the friendship between Korea and Japan. I wish you both a blessed and happy life," Empress Teimei spoke encouragingly.

For three days there were continuous parties and celebrations with countless numbers of congratulating guests streaming in and out of Yi Eun's mansion.

When Masako became Yi Eun's wife, her name was changed from Nashimoto Masako to Yi Masako, and her title from Princess to Crown Princess.

In her new home, with Yi Eun, Masako was blissfully happy like a typical honeymooner. Years later, she reflected:

"One happy day after another . . . This may be a too common expression, but it is the only way I can describe our married life together."

To become a helpful wife to her Korean prince, she endeavored to learn all things Korean. Every morning, after Yi Eun left for his work, she would invite Mr. Ko Hee-kyeong, Yi Eun's Korean secretary, and other Korean staff to her living room, and from them she would learn not only the Korean language but also about Korean customs, Korean food, and Korean dress.

With their help she practiced dressing in Korean clothes of the royal court, and the proprieties and mannerisms of Korean princesses.

One day, Masako wanted to surprise her husband, so she donned colorful Korean *chima* and *jeogori* (skirt and coat) decorated with blue circle dots, and was anxiously awaiting for his return from work.

As Yi Eun entered the house and saw beautiful Masako in a lovely Korean dress, he was excited. With a hugely surprised look, he exclaimed: "Oh! The Korean dress looks so lovely on you!"

By nature, Yi Eun was a man of few words, but he seemed thoroughly pleased and happy in that simple spontaneous exclamation. In Yi Eun's approving response, Masako saw a young man back in his Korean childhood reminiscing about his happy days surrounded by his mother and court ladies dressed in similar *chima* and *jeogori*.

Masako was very happy. From then on, she would often wear Korean dresses, which soon became one of her trademarks.

In time, Masako's skills in the Korean language also improved enabling her to read, write, and even speak simple sentences. To Yi Eun's delight, she would often try her Korean on him. Though imperfect, Masako's Korean speech was immensely charming and livened up the young couple's life.

In December, 1920, Yi Eun entered the Military Staff College. Its rigorous training program required long and arduous hours of study not only at the Staff College but also at home.

At times, he would stay up all night to complete his homework. Masako would sit closely by him, making tea or doing whatever she found helpful to her husband.

When Yi Eun was working on a project, she would watch and make suggestions. Upon learning later that her suggestions helped

Yi Eun pass with a perfect grade they would embrace each other and rejoice.

Yi Eun was not only a brilliant but also a hard-working student. He always completed his assignments on time and received superior evaluations.

One day, Yi Eun's superior confided to Itsuko: "His Highness Crown Prince Yi is an extraordinary person. Even among the imperial families, he is highly praised and respected for his virtuous character, generous heart, and brilliant mind. He is admired and adored by all."

When Masako heard this from her mother, she was so happy and proud.

"For a married woman," she mused, "nothing brings greater joy and happiness than the news that her husband is praised and respected by others."

Their happiest moment came toward the end of December when Dr. Suzuki, their family physician, informed Masako with a smile that she was pregnant. She was in the second month of her pregnancy.

When she gave the news to Yi Eun, he was overjoyed. Grabbing her hands, he exclaimed, "Is it true?" He was as happy as Masako. Having long missed his family, he was truly pleased at the thought of finally having his own child and his own blood kin. It would be the greatest blessing, he thought.

"Most of all please take care of yourself, so that we will have a healthy and strong baby," Yi Eun begged in an earnest and pleading voice.

Masako began to take extra measures for her health, not only for the baby's wellbeing and for themselves but also for the sake of the Yi royal lineage, for the baby would be destined to continue the 500-year old royal family line. That, she knew, was one of her most important duties as the Crown Princess of Korea.

Always focusing on the birth of a healthy child, she filled her mind with happy and pleasant thoughts. In all things, whether in walking, thinking, or doing chores, she tried to insure the health and wellbeing of her baby.

On March 24, 1921, there was a special ceremony marking the 5th month of her pregnancy. Following the ceremony, she began preparations for the arrival of the baby, buying baby clothes, baby blankets, and other necessary items.

Day by day, she could feel the baby inside growing active. Each morning she would take a walk around her garden and offer prayers for the baby—its wellbeing and its future.

On July 10, there was another ceremony, this time marking the 9th month of the pregnancy. Many congratulatory messages, including numerous telegrams from well-wishers in Seoul, arrived at Yi Eun's residence.

At last, on August 18, at 2:23 a.m., the long-awaited baby was born.

"It's a prince," someone shouted in an excited voice.

The word, prince, heard in a misty state of semi-consciousness, gave Masako an enormous sense of relief. As she realized that she had fulfilled her royal duty, giving birth to a prince who would continue the Yi Royal linage, she exulted with an overwhelming sense of joy.

Yi Eun had already arrived and was standing by her bedside.

"How wonderful! The baby is strong and healthy. Thank you for the hard work." As Yi Eun whispered into her ear, Masako cried and shed tears of joy and happiness.

She even felt triumphant. After all, her political enemies had kept her from becoming the crown princess of Hirohito on the ground that she could never bear a child.

Numerous praises and congratulatory words arrived at Yi Eun's mansion.

"The baby will become the 29th king of the Yi Royal Family."

"With the birth of the prince, the Yi Royal Family will finally be at ease and secure."

As he heard these words, Yi Eun was pleased and happy.

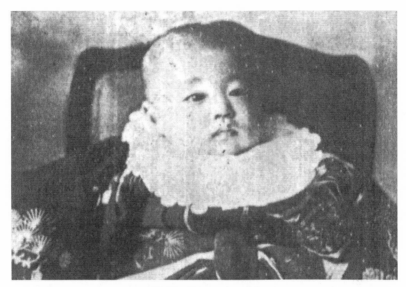

Yi Jin, 5 months old

The media carried headlines proclaiming that the birth of a new Yi prince was "the culmination of Korea-Japan union."

Such public declarations, however, meant little to Yi Eun and Masako.

"We were just happy as a father and a mother to have our own child. We expected nothing more," Masako recalled.

Seven days after the birth, Yi Eun and Masako named their first son Jin. Jin means "going forth; moving forward," and they hoped and prayed that their child would move forward with courage and happiness under all circumstances.

With Jin in their life, Masako and Yi Eun were in a state of ecstasy.

"Happy is the honeymoon, but even happier is watching your sweet baby doing cute things," Masako reminisced.

"When I held my baby tightly in my arms," Masako remembered, "I was so blissfully happy that I became completely oblivious to the affairs of the world. For my husband and me, just watching Jin was more than enough for a day's joy and happiness. A baby in our home added new life and freshness."

"Living in ecstasy," she wrote in a poem.
"What more can I hope for?
I am supremely blessed with a beautiful baby.
Our own child grows day by day,
Bringing new happiness to Daddy and Mama
With a bright smile!"

According to the protocols of the Yi Royal Family, Yi Eun and Masako were required to report their marriage to Sunjong in Seoul, formally and in person. (Sunjong had succeeded Gojong as Emperor of Korea in 1907. In 1910, he was deposed from the throne when Japan annexed Korea, and Sunjong was now the retired Emperor.)

The formal reporting was to be accomplished in the form of a traditional Korean royal wedding ceremony in the presence of Sunjong at Changdeok Palace in Seoul in accordance with ancient Korean rituals. For two years they had been putting off their Korea trip due to Masako's pregnancy and the birth of Jin. In April, 1922, they finally decided to make the long postponed trip.

The problem was what to do with Jin. He was only seven months old, and Masako felt quite uneasy about taking the baby on a long, arduous trip that would involve a long ocean voyage. The baby also needed the daily care of a lactating nurse.

Itsuko, Masako's mother, thought Jin was too young for the trip and strongly opposed his going. The Korea trip was too risky for the baby, she insisted. Accordingly, Masako was inclined to leave Jin in Tokyo during her Korea trip.

Others around her, however, informed Masako that Koreans, and especially the people in the Yi Royal family in Seoul, were eagerly waiting to see the new prince and insisted that she take Jin along.

Masako realized that even her baby's life was a sensitive public issue between Korea and Japan and that it was not a simple private matter. In the event that she did not bring Jin to Korea she would be deemed an irresponsible and inconsiderate woman, insulting the Korean protocols. She therefore had to respect Korean sensitivity.

Above all, Korea was Jin's ancestral land. Moreover, he was a prince destined to perpetuate the Yi Royal linage. Thus Jin's trip to Korea was not a private matter. Consequently, Yi Eun and Masako decided to take Jin along.

They left Tokyo by train on April 23, 1922, accompanied by a retinue of officials, nurses, and other attendants. Two days later they boarded the Shiraki Maru at Shimonoseki, bound for Pusan. The overnight sea voyage across the Korea Strait was rough, making everyone seasick through the night.

As the early morning sun rose, the ship approached the Pusan Harbor. Masako saw the land of her husband for the first time in her life with feelings of excitement mixed with deep anxiety.

As soon as the ship docked at Pusan Harbor, at 8:45 a.m., Prince Kang, Yi Eun's elder half-brother rushed to Masako's cabin, personally welcoming her and Yi Eun to Korea. This was followed by loud trumpet music from the Army, Navy, and Air Force, and the welcoming shouts of thousands of young students.

Masako was deeply moved. She saw and felt the heart-felt love and admiration which Korean people had for Yi Eun, their crown prince. She had not expected to receive such a roaring welcome.

Actually, before the trip Yi Eun had been undergoing mental turmoil. Although Masako and his son had given him relief from his Japanese life of loneliness and the stresses of his military duty, there was a lingering unrest deep in his soul.

The dethronement of Emperor Gojong and his subsequent death, as well as the explosive events of March 1, only three years ago, had intensified his internal anguish over his personal identity.

At times, deeply frustrated, he would scream to himself, "What am I? I am no longer a Korean. But neither can I become a Japanese. I have no choice but to live as a nobody and nothing!"

In social gatherings of Japan's Imperial families, conversations would abruptly stop when Yi Eun appeared. The same thing happened at military officers' social gatherings. Yi Eun was made to feel an alien, a person not to be brought into confidence.

Korean settings in Tokyo were no more assuring, and he always felt like a drop of oil floating on the water.

So the roaring welcome at Pusan Harbor was like a beautiful heaven opening with smiling angels beckoning their arrival. Masako was relieved, and she was happy for Yi Eun.

The train departed for Seoul at 9 a.m. Along the way, it made a stop at each station, where throngs of people had gathered to welcome Yi Eun and Masako to Korea, waving flags and shouting "Long Live the Crown Prince! Long Live the Crown Princess!"

When the train stopped, the station manager, the local community chief, and elderly men of nearby communities came aboard. Bowing low to the Crown Prince, they would greet him with flowers and fruits.

When the train approached the Choopong-ryeong Station high on the mountain, an old man, in his 80s and clothed in traditional court dress, came forward, bowing to the Crown Prince with tears on his face. He had once served in the Yi Royal Court in Seoul as the head of court retainers. He was now living in a remote mountain village.

When he heard that the Crown Prince and Jin, his son, would pass through the station, he was determined to greet them. Having carried his frail decrepit body over the rivers and mountains, he bowed and blessed Jin for a long and healthy life.

For the first time, Masako realized how deeply Koreans loved their country and how reverently they missed the Yi Royal Court which once ruled their land. She was deeply moved.

At 6:15 in the early evening, the train finally arrived at the Central Station in Seoul. Masako, Yi Eun, and Jin were personally greeted by Governor General Saito Makoto and the highest ranking members of the Japanese military and administrative bodies in Korea as well as by foreign ambassadors stationed in Seoul.

The Seokjojeon in Deoksu Palace

Escorted by armed soldiers of the Japanese cavalry, they rode in a beautifully decorated horse-drawn carriage to Deoksu Palace, where Yi Eun had been born twenty-five years before. Just outside the imposing Daehanmoon Gate of the palace was a large welcoming crowd of Koreans, young and old, in beautiful traditional Korean dresses in white, red, yellow, and blue colors.

Even after Masako and Yi Eun disappeared into the recesses of the palace, the crowd stayed on at the gate until dark, still savoring the short glimpse they had of the Crown Prince and the Crown Princess.

Inside Deoksu Palace, Masako and Yi Eun settled in the Seokjojeon Hall, a modern Western-style marble structure. Immediately, Yi Eun went to pay his respects to Sunjong in Changdeok Palace, about a mile away.

Changdeok Palace (frontal view)

April 27, 1922, Masako's first visit in Seoul, was a gorgeous day. The morning broke with bright sunlight and a crisp blue sky. The air was fresh.

Deoksu Palace in spring appeared as if floating among myriads of multi-colored flowers. Beyond the palace walls, Masako could see the beautiful Namsan Hill and its majestic pine trees. And in the distance, she gazed at the lofty granite peaks and deep valleys of the Bukhansan. It was a magnificent view.

At nine o'clock in the morning, three court ladies from Changdeok Palace arrived with Ms. Suminaga, who would serve as Masako's translator. They would prepare Masako for the formal Korean wedding ceremony, which was planned to take place the next day in the presence of Sunjong.

On that day Masako also met Lady Hwang, a court lady who served as Yi Eun's lactating nurse when he was a baby.

On April 28, the long awaited royal wedding ceremony and audience with Sunjong finally took place in the Daejojeon Hall of Changdeok Palace. This day also happened to be the anniversary of Masako's marriage to Yi Eun in Tokyo.

Ceremonial dresses and decorations prepared for the occasion were spectacular. When Yi Eun was young, his parents, Emperor Gojong and Lady Eom, had personally ordered them from Imperial China just for this day.

Each item was imbued with their love and care. Masako wished deep in her heart that Gojong had lived just two more years to see this wedding.

Yi Eun was dressed in *yongpo,* a royal robe of red color interwoven with a dragon design in golden threads. On his head was a royal crown of the Yi Royal Dynasty. Masako was attired in a court ceremonial dress of deep blue silk embroidered with 154 pairs of green-colored pheasants. It was the most beautiful court dress in Korea.

Her head was covered with a large ceremonial wig decorated with numerous accessories and an elongated golden hair pin. The wig was so heavy that a tall lady-in-waiting had to support it with her two hands from behind as Masako walked into the ceremonial hall and toward Sunjong and his wife, Queen Yun.

Masako's Korean wedding in Changdeok Palace
From Left: Princess Deok-hye, Masako, Queen Yun,
Sunjong, Yi Eun, and Jin in the arms of a court chamberlain

As for little Jin, he was dressed in a peach-colored robe with a black stripe design, his head covered by a ceremonial hood. He was brought to the hall in the arms of a court chamberlain.

The ceremony involved three hours of solemn rituals mixed with occasional pronouncements in medieval court language which only a few attendants understood. For Masako it was a long day, in a mystic land, of excruciatingly tense anxiety.

Totally absorbed in the solemnity of the ceremony she hardly remembered the details of the event. But when the ceremony ended, Masako and Yi Eun were now officially married in the eyes of the Yi Royal family, as the crown prince and crown princess of the Yi Royal Dynasty.

Thus the primary purpose of their Korea trip, reporting their marriage to Sunjong in Seoul, was accomplished. The wedding ceremony was followed by a celebratory banquet.

Masako greeted dignitaries of the Yi Royal family and visited with close relatives of Yi Eun. She did her best to communicate in her limited Korean, which the royal family found charming and delightful. They were warm and deeply appreciative of her having become Yi Eun's wife and companion.

Masako could feel the genuine love and affection of the Yi Royal family and felt she had at last become one of them as Crown Princess of the Yi Royal Dynasty. Once again she was blissfully happy.

On the following day, April 29th, Masako and Yi Eun went to Jongmyo, the Grand Ancestral Shrine of Joseon Kingdom, to report their marriage to Yi Eun's ancestors of 550 years. That final ceremonial act was followed by a series of receptions, parties, and outings. Each day was filled with one activity or another.

On May 4, they visited Jin Myeong School which Lady Eom, Yi Eun's mother, had established for the education of women before she died. Having long missed his beloved mother, he was filled with deep emotions.

As the time of their departure, set for May 8, neared, Masako and Yi Eun had mixed feelings. They knew they had to return to Tokyo, but still savoring the hearty, warm welcome which they received everywhere they went, they wanted to stay longer.

Yi Eun was even feeling a bit depressed and sad at the thought of leaving his boyhood home and all the happy memories of his father and mother. Amidst the mixed feelings, both were deeply grateful for the love and affection people showered on little Jin.

Before they came to Korea they had hoped and prayed that Jin would be loved by the people they would meet along the way, and they were gratified that he was. Little Jin was strong, healthy, and playful. Every palace woman loved to hold him and take him to her room, playing with the adorable child. With love and affection everywhere, Masako felt safe for little Jin.

The night before their departure, a farewell party was held at Injeongjeon Hall in Changdeok Palace. All members of the Yi Royal Family came and exchanged farewell greetings. Saying "Stay healthy and happy until we meet again," they were all warm and friendly to one another.

Sitting in the rear seat of their car on the way back to their lodging in Deoksu Palace Seokjojeon Hall, Yi Eun looked happy and pleased. "Masako, you have been superb through all the events of the past ten days," he said approvingly, putting his hand on Masako's.

"Everyone, including Sunjong and all royal family members, has been greatly impressed by you. They are all happy and thoroughly satisfied," he continued.

"Before I came I was worried, but everyone says you have every qualification to be a queen. I am truly pleased. Thank you," Yi Eun said with pride and appreciation.

"I am so happy that we came," Masako responded with a great sense of pleasure. "The way I feel at the moment, I want to stay longer in this place where you grew up."

Yi Eun smiled with genuine satisfaction. Then he said, "My only regret is that my father and my mother didn't get to see our Jin," Yi Eun was thinking about his parents who had died an untimely death.

Masako shared the same sentiment. In fact, because of Gojong's tragic death, many people were concerned for her safety when she arrived in Korea. Her Japanese bodyguards were always alert, checking every meal she took to make certain it had not been poisoned.

She now thought that these were all unnecessary worries. As she looked back on the roaring welcome, the love, and the affection which Koreans showered on her and her family during the past 10 days, she even felt a bit guilty about having had the unwarranted concerns.

But alas! The angel of death was just around the corner. In fact the calamity, with all its accompanying agonies, was already in the making.

As Masako's car was approaching the Daehanmoon Gate of Deoksu Palace, Mr. Sakurai, her Japanese attendant, came running, panting.

"Your highness, Prince Jin is not feeling well!" the officer shouted.

"What did you say?"

"The little prince is gravely ill!" the officer answered, trembling.

Masako suddenly felt dizzy. With her eyes going unfocused, everything was turning round and round. As she stumbled, rushing to Jin's room, Yi Eun grabbed her. In the room Masako saw a blue-faced baby throwing up gooey milk in blue-greenish color.

Only a few hours earlier, when she left for the farewell banquet, he was as lively, healthy, and playful as he had always been, but now he lay desperately struggling just to breathe.

Stunned and fear-struck, Masako felt suffocated, going unconscious. Trembling severely, she tried to get hold of herself with every ounce of her energy.

She was overwhelmed by fear that Jin might die. She was reliving the premonition she had before leaving Tokyo—that something bad might happen to Jin.

Soon doctors arrived, including Dr. Goyama, who had accompanied her during the trip, Dr. Shiga, the head of Government General Hospital, and a pediatrician from a local Japanese hospital.

After checking the sick child, they said, "It appears that the child has stomach indigestion."

Accordingly the doctors gave emergency remedies, but little Jin kept crying all night. The following morning, he was still throwing up chocolate-colored lumps of goo. His condition was worsening by the hour.

Sitting by little Jin's bedside, Masako asked, "How could this happen? How could such a thing happen to our child?" She prayed that all this was just a dream. She was willing to do anything, anything in the world if only someone could help Jim live.

Doctors assumed that little Jin had drunk spoiled milk. Masako, however, did not believe it, because Jin was throwing up not milk, but foreign food stuff. Spoiled milk, she thought, would not make the child so gravely sick, to the point of death. She wondered why this was happening during her last night in Korea.

She deeply regretted that she, as well as Jin's personal attendants, had lowered their guard on Jin during the past few days while he was basking in the affection and care of palace women.

In desperation, Masako called Dr. Miwa of Tokyo Imperial University Hospital, the most prominent pediatrician in Japan, to rush to Seoul.

Before Dr. Miwa arrived, however, Jin was dead, at 3:15 p.m. on May 11th. All the prayers, all the crying, and all the tears shed for Jin were to no avail.

As she watched little Jin taking his last breath, Masako slumped to the floor, wrenched and mangled to a million pieces. And holding the tiny, lifeless body she blurted out, "Why, why? He was only seven months old! He didn't hurt anyone; he was pure and innocent. Why did he have to die?"

Sensing that a Korean or Koreans angry with the Japanese had poisoned her son, she cried out, "Was it because his mother is a Japanese? If he had to die because he had Japanese blood, why not me? Why did they not kill me? Instead of the innocent child, they should have killed me!"

73

Hidden beneath all the roaring welcomes, warm smiles, love, and affection which Koreans showered on Masako, Yi Eun, and little Jin, there was also seething rage and hatred against the Japanese.

From the moment Japanese assassins murdered Queen Min years before, Japan became the Korean people's mortal enemy. The Korean animosity was intensified as Japan became ever more aggressive, strangulating Korea's national independence with one deceptive and high-handed tactic after another.

Japan's reign of terror forced thousands of Korean patriots and nationalists to flee abroad to China, Manchuria, Russia, and the United States, where they formed various organizations intent on carrying out political warfare as well as armed conflicts with the Japanese ruling in Korea.

The most prominent organization was the provisional government of Korea that had been established in Shanghai, China, in September, 1919. Its underground network of armed guerrillas, spies, and plotters was formidable.

In July 1921, Maiden Min Gap-wan, once betrothed to Yi Eun, fled to Shanghai and came under its influence. A high ranking officer in Korea's provisional government there assured Min Gap-wan that he and his comrades would avenge the wrongs done to her, though she personally declined the offer. The officer also believed that anyone harming Korea, be he the emperor of Japan or Korea's crown prince, must be assassinated.

In June, 1920, a month after Masako and Yi Eun were married, Kim Kyushik fiercely denounced the marriage in *La Coree Libre* (*Free Korea*), published in Paris, as a sham forced on a Korean crown prince against the will of the Yi Royal family.

Simultaneously, Korea's anti-Japanese guerrilla forces, under Hong Beom-do's leadership, killed 157 and wounded more than 300 Japanese soldiers at Bong-o Dong in southern Manchuria near Korea's northern frontier.

In October of the same year, the guerrilla forces, led by Kim Jwa-jin and Hong Beom-do, killed 1257 Japanese troops in a dozen battles at Cheongsan-ri, also in southern Manchuria.

Following the disastrous defeat at Cheongsan-ri, the Japanese army embarked on a reign of terror against Korean civilians and Korean communities throughout Manchuria, putting Koreans in Manchuria in a life and death struggle with the Japanese.

On May 4th, 1922, while Masako was still in Seoul, the *Dong-A Ilbo*, a popular Korean daily, carried an editorial decrying Japan's ruthless trampling on Koreans' political, economic, and financial life, destroying their very livelihood.

It condemned Japanese oppressions and high-handed treatment of Koreans. Highly charged emotionally, the editorial challenged Koreans to wake up and become vigilant. It was a rallying cry against the Japanese.

Then on May 6th, 1922, only two days before Jin became sick, *Doknip Shinmun* (*Independence News*), the official arm of the provisional government in Shanghai, denounced Yi Eun as "puerile" and "the betrayer of his own people." The crown prince of Korea, it accused, had become "an imbecile dulled by the charm of a beautiful and crafty Japanese witch."

Masako had been painfully aware of the Korean rage and hatred against the Japanese.

She even understood why Koreans would want to hurt a Japanese as an act of revenge for the deaths of Queen Min and Gojong. She also understood Korean anger regarding Japan's forced annulment of Maiden Min Gap-wan's engagement to Yi Eun.

She was only protesting why they killed innocent Jin instead of her.

Reflecting on that day decades later, Masako said: "In their effort to console me, people around me said, 'No, it can't be. No Korean would have wanted to hurt the little prince.'"

"But I didn't believe them. And I still don't believe them," she said unequivocally.

Masako was firm in her belief that Koreans, especially certain members of the Jeonju Yi Clan, did not want to allow a half-Japanese to contaminate the "pure Yi royal family line" and decided to eliminate him. "Otherwise, there was no reason for little Jin, only seven months old, to die," she uttered.

Then, with a long deep sigh of self-recrimination, she said, "In effect, I came to Korea to kill my little son."

That night, clinging tightly to her motionless child's body, Masako wailed endlessly. She didn't care about royal protocols or about anyone's reactions. She lost her usual composure. In a state of delirium she cried and cried loudly, as if her grief might be washed away by her tears.

Recalling that moment a few years before she died, she mused, "They say that with time grief is forgotten, but when I think of little Jin's death even today I cannot stop my tears."

"My heart is torn when I realize what an unfortunate child he was. I still feel guilty that he died because of me."

"I was only 22 years old when Jin died," Masako continued. "I was a mother, but I knew so little about the world. The shock at Jin's sudden death was too great for me to bear . . . I even thought about committing suicide, desperately wishing to be with Jin . . . His highness, my husband, was frantic in his effort to console and protect me. He feared I also would become a target of assassins."

On May 17, the Yi Royal Clan held a funeral for little Jin.

According to the mortuary protocols of Joseon Kingdom, no official funeral service was allowed for children, including princes and princesses, who died young before the death of their parents, for they were considered to have committed a filial sin against their parents by dying early.

Sunjong, grieving over Jin's death, made him an exceptional case, however, ordering the Yi Royal Family Administration to conduct a grand and solemn funeral ceremony for the little prince.

The funeral ceremony would be held in Deoksu Palace, Yi Eun's birth place, where he, Masako, and little Jin had been staying since their arrival in Seoul. The royal protocol, however, forbade Masako, a woman, from participating in the funeral ceremony. Likewise, she was forbidden to even view Jin's coffin once the rite of coffin-sealing had taken place.

The last thing Masako did for Jin was to place in his coffin a silk dress which Jin had worn, wool clothes she had knitted with her own hands, and a rabbit-shaped toy he used to play with.

A lady-in-waiting brought to Masako Jin's last photo taken before his death. It showed little Jin in the arms of a palace chamberlain at Masako's Korean wedding ceremony in Changdeok Palace only 19 days before. Holding the picture tightly to her heart, Masako wept uncontrollably . . .

Emperor and Empress Taisho in Tokyo dispatched Hara, an Imperial Palace attendant, to Jin's funeral as the official conveyor of their personal condolences. Crown Prince Hirohito and all Imperial families sent flowers.

At 10 a.m., a large bier carrying little Jin's body left the Daehanmoon Gate of Deoksu Palace, preceded by processional flags, in red, yellow, and green, bearing the little prince's name and title.

Masako in mourning during Jin's funeral

As the bier was moving out of the palace, Masako gazed on it from a distance and watched until it disappeared through the gate. Determined to see and remember little Jin's last journey, Masako held herself up with all her energy and grit, watching the procession's flags blow in the wind outside the palace wall. When she could see the flags no more, she returned to Jin's room, staying there alone all day.

At 4 p.m., a lady-in-waiting came and reported that the funeral and burial services were over. Soon many people visited her expressing their sympathy and condolences.

"Prince Jin has become the guardian deity of friendship between Korea and Japan," someone said. "Prince Jin's soul will be watching for the peace and prosperity of our two nations," others added. But to Masako, none of the statements had any meaning. They were nothing but vain, empty talk.

Jin was buried on a hillside in Cheongyang-ri, in the north-eastern outskirts of Seoul city, which Gojong had selected for a royal cemetery. Jin's tomb was named Soonginweon Tomb. On its left, a short distance away, was the Yeonghwiweon Tomb, where Lady Eom, Yi Eun's mother and little Jin's grandmother, was buried. Masako tried to comfort herself with the thought that little Jin was already in the arms of his beloved grandmother.

Little Jin's tomb in Cheongyang-ri, Seoul

When Jin was born, Masako had prayed that her little child would live a long healthy life, but that was not his destiny, she mused.

The day after Jin's funeral, Masako and Yi Eun prepared to leave Seoul for Tokyo.

First, they went to Changdeok Palace to bid farewell to Sunjong and Queen Yun.

With tears, Queen Yun sought to console Masako: "We know how painful it has been for both of you, but take heart and be strong and healthy. We will take good care of Jin's tomb, so do not worry."

Then, until 8:15 p.m., their train's departure time, Masako stayed alone in the room where little Jin took his last breath. Flashing before her closed eyes were snapshots of playful Jin laughing and giggling as he played with his favorite rabbit toy.

"When I came here," she said to herself with a sinking feeling, "he was with me, but I am going home without him."

As the train was passing Yongsan Station, near the Han River, Yi Eun, pointing his finger toward the east, said to Masako, "Cheongyang-ri is that way . . ." He was trying to tell Masako that somewhere in the easterly direction, under the dark sky, there was the Soonginweon Tomb, the hill where Jin was buried, whom she could never again see.

Gazing at the hills on the yonder side, shrouded in the dark of the night, Masako said repeatedly to herself and to little Jin, "My little child, good bye. Good bye. Stay well."

At seven the following morning, Masako and Yi Eun boarded the Keihukumaru and left Pusan Harbor.

The voyage back to Tokyo was too painful. Looking far on the horizon, she mused with a heavy heart, "It was such an exciting voyage on the Shiraki Maru three weeks ago. How could I have imagined that I would be leaving Korea with such sadness!?"

"When we were crossing this sea we were excited and happy, in spite of the rough waves and the sea-sickness, because Jin was in my arms. Today the sea is so calm and quiet, and yet in my heart I feel relentless agitations, like the swirling waves of the deep, dark sea." Engulfed by a sense of emptiness and the absurdity of life, Masako closed her eyes sobbing uncontrollably.

At Tokyo Central Station Masako and Yi Eun were met by a large crowd of Imperial families gathered to welcome their return. Among them were Masako's parents and her sister, Noriko. As soon as their eyes met they were in tears, unable to say a word.

Arriving at her home, Masako entered Jin's room. It looked exactly the same as when they had left. Only little Jin was missing.

Jin's death was a shock not only to Masako and Yi Eun but to the entire Nashimoto family. Noriko, only twelve years old and a student at Gakushuin, wrote for her class an essay on Jin's death, about the shock and pain which her family suffered.

"Finally, His highness Yi Eun, my brother-in-law, and my sister realized their travel to Seoul. On April 23, they left Tokyo with a plan to return on May 8. My nephew, Prince Jin, also went with them. Each day a telegraph message arrived, informing us that all was well with them.

"Then, on May 8, we received unpleasant news that they had to postpone their return trip because of Jin's sudden illness. It worried us increasingly as time passed. Mother was wondering if something was wrong with Masako's milk because of her overseas travel.

Whenever we gathered for meals, the main topic of our conversation was Jin. Prince Jin was the only grandson to our parents.

When Father said, "Prince Jin might die," Mother was visibly upset, scolding Dad for saying such an ominous thing. Tears were welling in her eyes, for even a mere imagining of Jin's death was unbearable for all of us.

That should never happen . . . I prayed. Our entire family was in a state of depression . . .

A telegram arrived with a message that little Jin's fever subsided a little, but that was only for a short moment. The following day, we received the worst—that Prince Jin was dead.

Father sat still with a blank look. Mother cried all day. I also cried in my room all alone. In the afternoon, I saw Father strolling in the garden, trying to suppress his grief.

I could not understand why such a healthy, lovely, and loved child had to die. He was so pure and so innocent, a child only seven months old. Such a short life . . .

During dinner time, Father said, 'Such an unfortunate child!' but could not continue. Mother cried and cried. I also cried. None of us had dinner that evening.

On our living room wall hangs the picture of smiling Prince Jin. But it is just a piece of paper. Jin is no longer in this world.

For days Masako sat with a blank stare. Confused and unable to concentrate on anything, she felt suffocated and depressed. Sometimes she could almost hear the cooing and babbling sounds of little Jin from his room. And sometimes when she opened the door to Jin's room, it seemed as if little Jin was greeting her with a bright and happy smile.

Day and night, while sitting or lying, everywhere in the house, all Masako saw was fleeting images of little Jin, and all she thought about was little Jin, nothing else.

She tried to describe in a poem the pain and agony in her heart:

"My grief will not end until I meet him again in the next world.
My baby's face is tearing my heart.
Happiness and agony are part of human life.

I will endure any agony Heaven gives me.
But the tears flow endlessly on my face . . .
Sleep well, my baby, my love. Sleep well.
Please look after the welfare of your fatherland and your
    people.
Please hear my pleas, for they come from your mother's
    grieving heart."

To Masako, those days were as bleak as death and more agonizing and more torturous than the death itself.

CHAPTER 7

RECOVERY AND RENEWAL

In her grief, Masako was not alone. The moment Yi Eun learned that his son had suddenly become gravely ill, he knew that his worst fears had come true. Better than anyone he was aware of the Korean animosity toward the Japanese and the Korean opposition to his marriage to Masako.

The sudden loss of his son in his own childhood home gave him pain and agony more than he could bear. But he could not verbalize his broken heart. Japan's imperial protocols forbade him, just as they did at the time of his parents' death. More than that, Yi Eun knew that his tears and wailings would only add to Masako's pain.

Sensing the depth of Yi Eun's agony and his silent grieving, Masako realized that she had to overcome her self-pity and rise above her troubled circumstance. "For His Highness' sake," she said sternly to herself, "I must recover. I must renew lest I become a burden to his troubled soul."

As Masako was striving for inner strength, one day Mrs. Maeda Saeko, her aunt and a devout Buddhist, brought her a copy of Buddhist Scripture along with a statue of Kannon, the Buddhist deity of love, mercy, and healing. She explained to Masako that copying characters from the Buddhist Scripture, using a brush with care and reverence, would bring peace and tranquility to her mind.

Kneeling before the statue of Kannon, Masako prayed for Jin, and each time she copied a Buddhist character, she filled it with Jin's soul, praying for Buddha's mercy. It helped her feel tranquility in her mind.

83

But sometimes Masako's grief and her feelings of resentment and regret would return, overwhelming her. Ceasing the religious rituals, she would spout in bewildered anger. "If we had been just an ordinary couple none of this would have happened. If our royal births had not brought us into this marriage, we would not have had our little baby killed . . ."

No matter how hard she tried, Masako could not forget little Jin. Day and night, her thoughts were all on Jin.

On bright sunny days she pitied her little baby lying deep underground, unable to see beautiful flowers or hear birds chirping. On rainy days she felt sorry, almost insanely, for the little child soaked wet but unable to move.

Masako missed little Jin, suffocatingly. On some days she wanted to run to his grave. At least she could embrace and caress his earthen grave and beautify it with her personal care.

At such times she just sat on her garden bench all day, her eyes gazing west toward Korea.

Masako, c. mid-1920s

As for Yi Eun, he kept himself busy in military training. It was his way of suppressing the agonizing thoughts of Jin's death and keeping himself sane.

Occasional setbacks notwithstanding, Masako's resolve to recover and renew sent her back to the ritual of copying the Buddhist Scripture time and time again. Becoming absorbed in the ritual and in Buddhist teachings on life and death, rebirth and Nirvana increasingly had a calming effect on her agitated soul.

As her normal life gradually returned, Masako had a new wish. She yearned to have another son for Yi Eun.

On August 18, 1922, Jin would have become one year old. On this first anniversary of Jin's birth, Masako's mind was filled with thoughts about little Jin, so healthy and lively only a year before. She could almost hear the sound of the new baby's cries filling her entire house.

Had Jin been still alive, there would have been the *dol-janchi*, a grand celebration for his birthday. Friends, relatives, and family members would have gathered, bringing gifts and wishes for a long life and happiness. She wept as she thought about little Jin, who was missing his *dol* celebration.

On that day Masako and Yi Eun built a small shrine in the corner of their garden to remember Jin and to pray for his peace and blessings. In the shrine they placed Jin's photo along with a strand of his hair and nail clippings. On an altar they also placed food and burned incense. Each time they placed food on the altar they looked at each other, wondering aloud, "Would our little Jin eat this meal?"

The shrine became a source of peace and comfort for Masako. Each morning upon waking she first would gaze at the shrine, thinking about little Jin. It soon became a part of daily ritual.

In the spring of 1923 Masako learned that she was pregnant again. No sooner was she exulting with the happy news than she lost the baby. The miscarriage, she thought, was caused by all the mental and physical stresses she had been undergoing.

"Life gives, and life takes away," she thought to herself. Once again, fate appeared to be playing jokes on helpless humans so dependent on mere shadows of happiness, now here and then gone in a moment.

That spring and then during the summer, Yi Eun was involved in strenuous military training exercises. While he was away for two weeks, Masako went to Rinnoji Temple in Nikko in order to escape the unbearable heat in Tokyo.

In reality, however, she was trying to get away from the world itself.

After repeated misfortunes she had come to a point where she loathed everything, large or small, whether meeting people, doing house chores, or looking proper and keeping social decorum. Nothing had any meaning, and she lost all desires. Buried deep in the forest, only listening to the chirrup of the cicadas and birds, she was seeking to find sanity.

And once again, she prayed for a new baby.

The sounds of a temple bell and the chanting of priests in the quiet of the morning and evening brought some renewal to her tired soul.

But Masako's hard-earned recovery was short-lived.

At 11:58 a.m., on September 1, 1923, only a few days after she returned from Nikko, Tokyo and Japan's entire Kanto region were hit by a massive earthquake, at the magnitude of 7.9-8.4. Amidst fire, tsunami, and tornadoes, more than 60 percent of the buildings in Tokyo and more than 80 percent of those in Yokohama were destroyed. The human toll was horrendous with 142,000 people dead and nearly 40,000 missing.

Amid the destruction and chaos the Japanese pubic, already severely distraught because of the great economic depression of the 1920s, became increasingly frustrated and angry with their government for being slow and unable to respond adequately in its rescue efforts.

To deflect the public anger against the government and to prevent explosive riots, the Cabinet of Prime Minister Yamamoto Gonnohyoe spread rumors through the official media that Koreans, along with socialists and anarchists, were setting Japanese homes on fire and committing rape and murder against Japanese women.

By September 4th, the fourth day of the earthquake, another rumor appeared: Koreans were poisoning wells and drinking water in an effort to kill Japanese citizens.

Using the rumors as a pretext, the Yamamoto Cabinet declared martial law. And as hoped by the government, the rumors quickly turned Japanese everywhere into frenzied mobs attacking and butchering Korean residents wherever found.

Organized into 3,689 vigilante groups, the mobs became like packs of angry hunting dogs, killing and mutilating thousands of Koreans, including young Korean students, with swords, picks, axes, bamboo sticks, and whatever weapons came to hand. Soon even Japanese police and soldiers joined the murderous mobs with their rifles and bayonets.[11]

The anger of the mobs was matched by their barbarity. They would tie Koreans to a utility pole, pull out their eyes and cut off their noses before killing them with a spear. Catching Korean women, the mobs would strip them naked, force them to dance before laughing and jeering crowds, and then thrust a sword or spear into their private part.

No Korean in Japan, including Yi Eun, was safe, so he and Masako took refuge in the compound of the Imperial Household Ministry, near the Imperial Palace. There, they spent a week in a temporary refuge tent.

As innocent Koreans were being butchered by the murderous vigilante mobs, Yi Eun was sad and angry. "Why is it," he protested in a shaking voice, "that whenever something bad happens Japanese blame Koreans? Koreans have been in a sad and unfortunate situation. Why do people want to kill them again, especially the many hapless common laborers? Japanese are engaged in utterly unjust acts!"

For Yi Eun and Masako it was a week of unbearable torment.

As Yi Eun was distraught and agonized with silent tears, Masako was equally troubled. As a Japanese, she felt guilty. But at the same time, she was helpless. She didn't know what she could possibly do to help assuage her husbands' sadness and anger.

Masako's dilemma was being caught between two loves and two loyalties. Japan was her birthplace and her motherland while Korea was her new home by marriage. Unable to take sides, she was utterly lonely. She could only accept her fate and endure her suffocating loneliness.

But when she learned that the brutal Korean massacre was instigated by the Japanese government with manufactured lies, she became enraged and despised the Japanese cruelty.

"For the first time," she confessed, "I felt with my own skin the cruel and barbaric character of the Japanese."

"How could the government have so many innocent Koreans killed just to escape public anger against its ineptitude? Is this the way of Japanese politics?" she lashed out.

Decades later, Masako revealed her innermost thoughts about Japan's sins against Korea. "Having witnessed personally such events between Korea and Japan," she said, "I know that Japan has committed too many misdeeds against Korea. It is a debt Japan can never pay back."

By September 16th, the Japanese government had achieved its main objectives. It deflected the public anger mounting against it in the aftermath of the great Kanto earthquake. Under the cover of martial law it also arrested and/or killed key leaders among Japanese socialists and anarchists who were arch enemies of the government.

With its goals met, the government finally ended the massacre with the announcement that the rumors were false! By then, more than 6,000 Koreans had been slaughtered in the Tokyo-Yokohama area.

In the days after the earthquake and massacre of Korean residents, Masako was in a state of despair and depression. She was utterly confused and lost. She feared for her future and that of Yi Eun. With recurring nightmares she was unable to sleep. In the middle of the night she would wake up, terrified.

Nothing made any sense. "What is the meaning of Japanese cruelty?" she asked. "Was it a big lie that our marriage would become the foundation of a peaceful relationship between Japan and Korea? What is the meaning of our marriage?"

Most of all, she bitterly lamented as she realized that little Jin, her beloved son, had died in vain. "Even the death of my son, Jin, has now become totally meaningless," she thought to herself.

As the dreadful September of 1923 was passing, so were the colorful flowers in her family garden.

The withering flowers reminded Masako of the ephemeral nature of life and made her wonder why and for what she was living. Like the flowers that wither and quietly disappear, she wanted to pass away quietly in her sleep.

For Masako, time was the only medicine.

And like a small patch of blue sky in the midst of dark clouds, there was a bit of joy to celebrate as the dreadful year of 1923 was drawing to a close. Yi Eun was promoted to captain in the Imperial Army, and at end of December he graduated from the Military Staff College, where he had been studying since 1920.

During the graduation ceremony Masako learned that Yi Eun had been an honor student. His professors heaped praises on him for his gentle spirit, exemplary conduct, and superior performance in military classes as well as in English and French. Especially in English conversation class he had no match. Yi Eun, the professors confided, was looked upon as a model for other officers to follow.

The celebrations and the high praises of her husband gave Masako some comfort and served to re-energize her spirit.

Following the graduation ceremony, Masako and Yi Eun left hurriedly for Korea. They wanted to visit little Jin's tomb in Seoul. The trip had been on Masako's mind ever since she returned to Tokyo nearly 20 months before, but she waited until Yi Eun's graduation from the Military Staff College.

During her last voyage to Korea, Masako was excited and full of anticipation, but this time she was numb to all feelings. Neither the rough waves on the sea nor the changing scenes along the way stirred her. Her mind was all on little Jin.

"Oh, how our little Jin must have missed us! And how eagerly he must have been waiting for us," she thought to herself, "It's been already 20 months!" Masako wanted to hurry, but the train from Pusan to Seoul seemed too slow. Her mind was moving faster than the train. In spirit, she was already at Jin's grave.

When the train finally arrived in Seoul on December 30, she wanted to head straight to Jin's tomb, but the Yi Royal family protocols forbade it.

First, she and Yi Eun had to pay respect to Sunjong and report Yi Eun's graduation from the Military Staff College. Also, on January 1, the New Year's Day, they had to pay homage at the Jongmyo Grand Shine of the Yi Royal Dynasty and exchange New Year greetings with other Yi Royal family members.

It was on January 3rd that Masako and Yi Eun were finally free to go to Jin's tomb. It was a winter day of bitter cold. The earth was frozen solid and the road was slippery.

On the way, Masako was deeply anxious, her mind running ahead of her body. She could not get there fast enough.

She became fidgety as the car carrying her and Yi Eun was barely moving on the icy road. She was fully aware of the reason, but still there was uneasy agitation in her eager and impatient soul.

When she finally arrived at the entrance of the royal cemetery in Cheongyang-ri, Masako saw two mounded tombs, one large and one small, perched on the hillside among tall pine trees.

The large tomb belonged to Yi Eun's mother, and the small one to little Jin. Under the winter's cold weather, grass and other ground vegetation had all died, exposing the reddish top soil of the tombs. There on the frozen hillside they looked awfully lonely.

"My darling, my dear baby, Papa and Mama have come," Masako whispered to herself as her eyes were brimming with tears.

She wanted to head straight to Jin's grave, but in accordance with ritual propriety she first went to the large tomb, trying to wipe away her tears. After paying homage to her mother-in-law, Masako walked to the little one.

As she stood before the little grave, images of little Jin leaped into her sight—smiling, playing, crying, sleeping, and crawling around his room . . .

"Oh, poor little Jin, he would be walking by now. He would be so adorable," she whispered again, unable to control tears flowing down her face.

An old Korean woman was standing by the grave, watching in silence. At one time she had been a court lady. When Yi Eun was a child she had served the prince as his nurse mother. Now she was living in a building attached to his son's grave, guarding and tending it.

Led by the old woman, Masako and Yi Eun entered her room, warmed by *ondol*, an under-floor heating system unique to Korean traditional houses. For a while they just cried in silence, holding each others' hands.

"Thank you from the bottom of our hearts," Masako said to the old woman tightly holding her hands. "You have been doing for our little Jin what even we, his father and mother, have not been able to do. Thank you, and thank you." Masako meant every word.

"Don't mention it, please," the old woman replied. "My loyal service to the little prince is the joy of my life and the reason for my living. I will do my utmost until I die." She was so sincere and so genuine.

Overcome by gratitude, Yi Eun caressed the old woman's shoulders and back. Tears were welling in her eyes.

Before leaving the cemetery, Masako and Yi Eun walked back to Jin's grave once more, gently treading the white sands in the cemetery path.

"Is Jin hearing the sounds of his Papa's and Mama's approaching footsteps? Does he see his Mama's tears of good-bye?" Masako wondered as she approached the little grave. After bidding her final farewell, she reluctantly turned around to descend the hillside, gazing repeatedly back at the grave.

The following day, on January 4, 1924, Masako and Yi Eun left Seoul and returned to Tokyo, where Yi Eun was to participate in the New Year military parade.

M asako's visit to Jin's grave was almost as painful as the day of Jin's funeral, but it was also the best thing to happen to her in 20 months. For the first time, she felt some peace in her soul and began to assume a more normal life.

In the course of twenty years, between 1924 and 1943, Masako would visit Jin's grave more than a dozen times.

Even though her body was in Tokyo her heart was always in Seoul with little Jin. Her friends have said that when Jin was buried in the Korean soil she also buried her heart there. In truth, she often said fondly that she had two motherlands: Japan where she was born and Korea where she would be buried.

As her life returned to normalcy, Masako once again began to enjoy the things that came as part of her life as an army officer's wife and an Imperial princess.

One of Masako's greatest joys was welcoming and entertaining her husband's friends, mostly fellow officers who thought Masako's home was the most fun place in Tokyo. When some of them showed up on a surprise week-end visit, Masako would hurriedly put together refreshments and *sake* on a living room table. There was nothing fancy, but the group would sing, talk, and visit until late. The men all seemed to hold her husband in high respect and trust, and made her very happy.

On New Year's Day each year, Masako and Yi Eun would go to the Imperial Palace reception, dressed in formal attire. As members of Imperial families, their duty was to stand behind the Emperor and the Empress while important dignitaries, including foreign ambassadors, appeared to bid their New Year greetings. The ceremony was awesome and colorful, delighting Masako immeasurably.

Such ceremonies, however, lasted from morning till night and left Masako and others exhausted. Standing all day motionless behind the Emperor was a daunting task, however colorful and pompous the ceremonies might have been.

Often, when she returned home from such ceremonies at night already exhausted, Masako would find a group of her husband's friends waiting in her living room. She would quickly change her clothes and prepare an impromptu party for them. It was always hard work, but it brought her joy and a deep sense of worth in her labor as she watched a group of tired and lonely soldiers having a happy time.

CHAPTER 8

EUROPEAN TOUR

When World War I broke out in 1914, the British government made an official request to the Japanese government for assistance against German forces operating in Chinese waters. In response, on August 23, 1914, Japan declared war on Germany and quickly seized German holdings in eastern China's Shandong Province.

Japanese forces continued their anti-German assaults, occupying German toe-holds in the Pacific Marshall Islands, Marianas, and Carolines. By the war's end in November, 1918, Japanese naval forces, including 12 destroyers, 17 transport ships, and 1 cruiser, were operating as far west as the Indian Ocean near Cape Town, and even in the Mediterranean Sea at Malta, transporting British troops and rescuing British sailors from sinking and damaged ships.

Its siding with the victorious European and American allies in the war brought huge rewards to Japan. In addition to acquiring German territories in China and the Pacific, and large economic gains through war period industrial productions, it emerged as a world power along with the "Big Four": Great Britain, the United States, France, and Italy.

Having emerged as a world power on the side of democratic nations, the Japanese people were eager to democratize their socio-political institutions throughout the 1920s. Various social movements emerged during the so-called "Taisho democracy period," calling for women's liberation, equal rights for all classes, universal suffrage, and cultural freedom.

In this atmosphere, the latest fashions from Paris, London, Rome, and New York became common sights on the streets of Tokyo and in upscale households.

In 1925, Universal Suffrage was enacted for all Japanese, although women would have to wait until 1945 to vote. Japanese politicians were also experimenting with party cabinets instead of relying solely on entrenched politicians and military generals to run the government.

Japan had indeed come of age. It saw itself as one of the great nations of the world. And in the fall of 1925, the Imperial Household Ministry suggested to Masako and Yi Eun that they take a European good-will tour. It would broaden their knowledge of the world, the Ministry explained, as well as give them an opportunity to study the conditions of various European countries in the aftermath of the war.

Emperor Taisho, the Ministry informed them, personally authorized the tour and would meet all necessary financial needs.

The Japanese government's real intent, however, was to show off to Yi Eun the power of Japan and the standing it was now enjoying. It reasoned that Yi Eun, impressed by the respectful recognition which Japan received from the great powers of Europe, would have a greater appreciation of Japan and more willingly accept Korea's becoming a permanent part of Japan. It hoped that Yi Eun, as Korea's Crown Prince, would never even so much as imagine restoring Korean independence from Japan.

Also, Japanese leaders, having received much negative publicity in the world media for its oppressive treatment of Koreans, wanted to tell the world that everything was now all right between Korea and Japan and that the union of the two peoples was progressing smoothly. "Look, here is the example," they wanted to tell all Europe.

Yi Eun and Masako, however, had a different purpose in mind, as they were after all political prisoners of the Japanese government. "Ever

95

since we were married" Masako explained, "we felt as if we had been confined in a bird cage with no real freedom. We wanted to be free to breathe, eat, talk, and think as we wanted. We also wanted to see and learn about the world first hand." And in their eagerness to get away from the stifling confines of Tokyo politics, they accepted the offer.

The tour would start on March 11, 1926. In preparation, Masako invited scholars to her residence for tutorial lessons on Europe— its history, economy, culture, society, and other relevant subjects. Masako was full of excitement, counting the days.

Suddenly bad news arrived from Seoul that Sunjong, Yi Eun's half-brother, was gravely ill. Instinctively, Masako thought to herself, "Once again, Fate is against us."

On March 1, Masako and Yi Eun made a hasty trip to Seoul, worrying that Sunjong might die any day. Upon their arrival at Changdeok Palace, however, they found his condition improved, and after explaining their planned European tour they returned to Tokyo to begin their tour on March 11 as planned, assuming that Sunjong's condition would continue to improve.

From Tokyo they maintained daily contacts with Seoul, to be kept updated on the progress of Sunjong's recovery. The news was not encouraging. He was still in serious condition, and they decided to postpone their tour until later.

On April 13 they made another hasty trip to Seoul upon receiving a message that Sunjong's condition was deteriorating rapidly. Masako carried with her a white silk cushion stuffed with bird feathers, which she made herself as a gift to Sunjong. She thought it would give him some comfort for his back and arms. Sunjong was deeply touched, thanking her again and again.

Masako was eager to do something, or anything, to help Sunjong— even attending him as a nurse at his side. The royal court protocols, however, stood in her way, and she could only watch helplessly as the last emperor of Korea lay dying.

Around one o'clock in the morning on April 25, Sunjong died, 19 years after he had succeeded his father, Emperor Gojong, in 1907.

Masako and Yi Eun had just left their bedroom to check on Sunjong when they received the sad news. Masako quietly wept, for she knew too well about all the grief, pain, disappointment, and sadness Sunjong had to bear throughout his life of 52 years.

Born on February 8, 1874 as the second son of Queen Min, Sunjong was soon chosen as the crown prince. By the time he was two years old, Japan had forced his kingdom to sign an unequal treaty allowing Japanese to freely move into Korea and wreak havoc.

When he was a child someone put poison in his tea. Though he survived the poisoning, he became permanently impaired both physically and mentally. He even became infertile and could not have children of his own.

At 21, he saw his mother, Queen Min, brutally murdered by Japanese assassins, the grief over which he would never overcome. Ten years later, in 1905, under the guidance of Ito Hirobumi, a scheming and aggressive Japanese politician posted in Korea, Japan began the destruction of his kingdom's independence by taking control of Korea's foreign affairs.

At age 33, in 1907, Sunjong saw Ito humiliate his father, Emperor Gojong, by forcibly dethroning him. The same year, he saw the same Ito Hirobumi sending Yi Eun, his 11 year old half-brother and crown prince, as a hostage to Japan.

Placed on his father's throne by Ito, Sunjong became Emperor, but in name only. Ito took over for Japan all the internal affairs of Korea, including military, judicial, and police jurisdictions, placing the entire Korean government under Japanese officials.

Finally at age 36, Sunjong saw his 519 year old Joseon Kingdom come to an end as Japan forcibly annexed Korea in 1910. Having ended his rule, even nominally, Japan demoted Sunjong from "emperor" to "king." (In defiance, however, Koreans would continue to call him Emperor Sunjong. Masako, identifying with Korean sensitivity, did likewise.) Then at 45, Sunjong saw his father, the former Emperor Gojong, dying poisoned.

As Masako reflected on these events, she realized that her own fate was inseparably tied up with Sunjong's grief-ridden life, because her being there at that sorrowful hour was also the result of Ito Hirobumi's and other Japanese politicians' manipulating her and Yi Eun's life. Masako too was a victim of the same scheming Japan, and she had a deep sense of humility, regret, and apology as well as anger, because Japan, her motherland, was the culprit behind the destruction of so many Korean lives and dreams.

Suddenly, breaking into Masako's reflections and the silence of midnight, a loud wailing sound came from the recesses of Sunjong's palace residence. It was the weeping of Queen Yun, his wife, mourning all alone in a darkened room.

Queen Yun was too young at age 33 to become a widow, and her wailing was that of one with a broken heart and unbearable pain and sorrow.

Masako realized that she also, as the wife of Yi Eun, who would soon succeed Sunjong, could end up with the same fate. Feeling the young widows' pain in her own heart, Masako joined her and wailed with her through the night.

According to the Yi Royal protocols, Sunjong's funeral was scheduled to take place on June 10, forty-seven days after his death.

On April 27, 1926, a royal coronation ceremony took place in Changdeok Palace, in which Crown Prince Yi Eun formally succeeded Sunjong as the 28th king of the Yi Royal Dynasty, though in name only.

Accordingly, Masako became the new queen of Korea. Following the coronation ceremony, former cabinet ministers of the Joseon Kingdom and senior officials of Japan's Government General in Korea solemnly presented themselves to the new king and queen in the Huijeong Hall in the palace.

The coronation was nothing more than an empty ritual, and it was a very sad day for Masako and Yi Eun. "It was," Masako recalled many decades later, "a coronation ceremony for a kingdom that was no longer in existence. Japan had ended it."

"Japan," she said, "was the new power in Korea. The former king was dead, and the new king was in name only. I knew how painful it was for His Highness, my husband, to stand in an old palace building among the court officials of old, with no power and no kingdom of their own."

Meanwhile as the news of Sunjong's death spread throughout the capital city of Seoul, there were stirrings of anti-Japanese sentiment. On April 28, Song Hak-seon, a 30 year old Korean nationalist, decided on the spur of the moment to assassinate Saito Makoto, the Governor General and de facto ruler of Korea. When Song saw Saito leaving the Changdeok Place with two other Japanese officials in a vehicle, he jumped into the moving car and stabbed Saito and another official with a specially prepared knife.

It turned out that Song was mistaken. Saito, the targeted Governor General, was not in the car. Of the two wounded Japanese, one died. Song Hak-seon was arrested, tried, and hanged promptly by the Japanese court on May 19. During the trial he told the Japanese judge that his only regret was that he failed to kill the Governor General.

On the day of Sunjong's funeral, 3000 mourners gathered from all around the country. All government offices, schools, and shops were closed, and there were endless parades of mourners, dressed in white robes and white hat.

Queen Yun, the young widow of Sunjong, collapsed as her husband's bier was leaving Changdeok Palace. For nearly seven weeks she had been in mourning with little food and water. Her weakened body, under the heavy weight of daily grieving, simply gave out at her last sight of her husband.

Masako remembered the day of her little Jin's funeral and how she too almost collapsed under the strain of her exhausted emotions and body. She rushed to the unconscious widow, nursing her, comforting her, and weeping with her.

As the funeral procession moved through the streets of Seoul toward the Yi Royal cemetery in Geumgok, east of Seoul, anti-Japanese demonstrations were becoming fierce at various locations in the city. Students were shouting "Long live Korea and Long live Korean independence!"

As in the March 1, 1919 independence movement following the death of Gojong, Sunjong's father, the whole country erupted in rage against the Japanese. Many were arrested, tortured, and tried by the Japanese authorities. It was the explosion of 1919 all over again.

Though in name only, Masako was now the new queen of Korea's Yi Royal Dynasty, with new duties and responsibilities.

Her lack of familiarity with all the Korean royal protocols notwithstanding, she did her absolute best. After more than two months of frantic activities, with little sleep and rest, Masako was completely spent and exhausted, physically and mentally.

On June 26, Masako and Yi Eun returned to Tokyo. Before she left Seoul, she wrote a poem about Queen Yun, the young widow.

> Did she know that it was a spring time when it arrived?
> She has confided herself in the deep interior of massive
>   palatial buildings.
> What a pity! Who would understand her broken and
>   lonely heart?
> While she stayed by the side of her Beloved, day turned
>   into night.
> Day and night she prayed for her Beloved's recovery.
> All the beautiful flowers fade away without her notice.

Soon after her return to Tokyo, Masako fell ill. Her exhausted body finally gave out. Under a high fever, she was in and out of consciousness. This condition continued for two weeks, and Masako thought she might die. As she pondered her possible death, she became overwhelmed with an awesome sense of guilt. "What would happen to the Yi Royal Dynasty's succession?" she asked herself.

She knew her death would constitute an unforgivable blow to her husband as well as the Yi royal linage. Gritting her teeth, Masako resolved to live at all cost, and her health gradually returned.

Before the year 1926 was over, Masako had to undergo another sad event. In the early morning of December 25, Emperor Taisho of Japan died after a long illness. This was especially hard on Masako, for since her childhood the Emperor had been close to her, always giving her kind personal attention.

That afternoon, Crown Prince Hirohito became the new Emperor. For Masako, it was a day of mixed emotions. On the one hand, she lost a dear personal friend in Emperor Taisho, and on the other hand, Hirohito, who might have become Masako's husband but for political rivalries among generals, became the new Emperor of Japan.

Instinctively, she also felt that Hirohito's coronation was the beginning of tumultuous years for Japan. Silently she offered a prayer for his well-being.

Three months later, on April 10, 1927, Masako and Yi Eun returned to Seoul to observe the first anniversary of Sunjong's death. After three weeks of activities, including a visit to Jin's tomb, they returned to Tokyo to prepare for their European tour, which had been postponed for more than a year.

With a new emperor on the throne, however, the Japanese government was having second thoughts about their travel abroad. And Yi Eun was no longer just a crown prince but a new king of the Yi Royal Dynasty, at least in name.

At the same time, since the Korean massacre during the Tokyo earthquake of 1923, Koreans' anti-Japanese sentiments and their independence movement had become fierce, making headlines in the world media.

An especially sticky issue for the Japanese government was the question of the formal status and title under which Yi Eun would be visiting various European nations: simply as "Prince Yi Eun" or as "King of Korea"?

The Japanese government feared that the latter title would give Europeans an impression that Korea still existed as an independent nation.

Yi Eun, normally of a moderate and accommodating personality, was adamant about proceeding with the planned trip abroad. He had been yearning to get away from Japan, to be alone in a country far away. As a hostage, in Japan he had been like a fish in a net. There was little he could do to liberate his people from the Japanese yoke, but he was deeply troubled and angry at Japan's harsh and oppressive treatment of Koreans in Japan as well as in Korea.

He was also feeling guilty about his comfortable life in Tokyo while his fellow Koreans were suffering. So he was determined to get away. He desperately wanted to have a space where he could breathe freely, away from Japan and away from Korea.

"I don't care about the status or the title," he declared. "I am willing to go simply as an individual or just as a human being."

Realizing that Yi Eun would not back down, his secretary, Viscount Ko Hee-kyeong, and another official representing the Yi Royal Household Administration, pleaded with Japan's Imperial Household Ministry, arguing that the tour had been authorized and funded by none other than deceased Emperor Taisho.

The Ministry finally granted its approval on the condition that Yi Eun and Masako would travel under "an informal and unofficial status" and would identify themselves simply as "Count and Countess Yi," not as "King and Queen of Korea."

Masako and Yi Eun were just as pleased, for they personally preferred traveling informally without having to deal with all the stifling formalities associated with official visits.

Their travel itinerary included France, Germany, England, Belgium, the Netherlands, Denmark, Sweden, Norway, Poland, Italy, and Switzerland. On the way they would stop in Shanghai, Hong Kong, Singapore, and Egypt.

At last, on May 24, 1927, Masako and Yi Eun boarded the Hakone Maru in Yokohama Harbor. It was a huge ocean liner weighing 10,000 tons, full of Japanese and international passengers, including businessmen, scholars, military officers, and tourists.

Yi Eun was 30 years old and Masako 26. Family members and many friends came to the harbor pier to say *bon voyage*. Even though they were on a personal, unofficial tour, they were accompanied by a retinue of seven, including a physician, a maid, and two army officers.

On the pretext of providing personal security, Miwa, a high ranking Japanese police officer from Seoul, also would accompany them as far as Shanghai. He was notorious for catching and torturing Korean nationalists.

The Imperial Household Ministry had also contacted all Japanese embassies in Europe regarding the royal couple's tour, requesting their utmost attention and assistance along the way.

When the ship arrived at Kobe Harbor on its way to Shanghai, Han Chang-soo, the head of the Yi Royal Household Administration, came aboard and informed Masako and Yi Eun that according to police intelligence reports, Korea's Provisional Government in Shanghai was aware of their overseas tour and was suspected of plotting something bad. He warned the couple to be extremely careful.

Yi Eun sat in silence, showing no reaction. Han Chang-soo was despised by Koreans for his excessively pro-Japanese stance. Yi Eun knew about this and personally disliked him.

Again, Han said, "Please be careful."

"I heard you," replied Yi Eun coldly. "I am willing to meet anyone wishing to see me. There is nothing to worry about!"

"Your Highness, absolutely not! You cannot meet them," Han protested.

"Did I insist that I will meet them? I am only saying . . ."

"The best thing for you is not to have any contact with anyone from the Korean Provisional Government. Even if you pass safely through Shanghai, there will be problems in Paris and at the Hague," Han sternly warned, mindful of Korean nationalists in those cities. Annoyed by Han's persistent nagging, Yi Eun finally brushed him aside, saying, "I told you not to worry about it. You have said enough. Our trip is of personal nature, so do not interfere anymore!"

The Provisional Government's plot was to kidnap Yi Eun and persuade him to join in the fight for Korean independence. By taking him away from Tokyo, it also wanted to carry out revenge for Japan's forcibly annulling Yi Eun's matrimonial engagement to Maiden Min Gap-wan, who was with the Provisional Government in Shanghai at that time.

At no point, however, was Yi Eun to be harmed physically.

When Masako had met Yi Eun for the first time, she knew nothing about Maiden Min, nor that Min and Yi Eun had been engaged for marriage but Japan had compelled her family to annul the engagement with threats in order to push Yi Eun into marrying Masako.

After Min's engagement to Yi Eun was annulled, her beloved grandmother died heart-broken in July 1918, and then her father on January 4, 1919, also heart-broken. Soon thereafter her family became destitute. Maiden Min had no choice but to flee Korea. She headed straight to Shanghai to join the Korean Provisional Government.

Masako learned about all this just before her wedding, but she could do nothing except feel deeply sorry for the young maiden. In the course of time she learned that Maiden Min Gap-wan was highly intelligent and well-educated and a person of virtue and fairness.

Masako even learned that Maiden Min, instead of blaming Masako for her personal misfortunes, felt sorry for her because Min knew that they were alike victims of politics beyond their control.

When the Hakone Maru arrived in Shanghai Harbor on the morning of May 30, Yi Eun and Masako were immediately met by Rear Admiral Araki of the Japanese Naval Fleet and Japanese Consul General Yata. The two warned Masako and Yi Eun against disembarking in Shanghai, and insisted they be transported to the Battleship Yakumo because of the Korean Provisional Government plot.

As they spent the night on the Japanese battleship, Masako said to Yi Eun, "Even here in Shanghai we are like birds in a cage. Aren't we? But I am happy that we are together."

It just happened that they were traveling with a bird cage containing a pair of canaries, given to Masako as a present when she was leaving the Kobe Harbor. Strangely the birds did not sing no matter what she did for them. As she kept wondering, one of her attendants said, "Canaries don't sing if they are together. They sing when they are separated from each other." He advised her to put the birds in separate cages.

Actually, when she received them as a gift they WERE in two separate cages, but Masako felt sorry for them and brought them together in one cage. She refused to heed the attendant's advice and kept the two canaries together in one cage. "It is all right even if they don't sing," she said to herself, "I want them to be happy together." "During the entire trip the birds never sang," she recalled, "but they remained happy together."

Masako was terrified at the thought of being separated from Yi Eun. "What would happen to me if my husband were kidnapped by someone?" "Alone I may sing and scream at the top of my voice," she said to herself, "but I would be absolutely miserable!"

Masako felt immensely blessed and fortunate that she and Yi Eun were together, and once again realized how deeply she loved him and depended on him.

Fortunately, the Shanghai plot never materialized, and the following morning the Hakonemaru sailed out of Shanghai Harbor for Hong Kong. Maiden Min Gap-wan, Masako learned later, vigorously objected to the plot to kidnap Yi Eun. She would go along only if both Yi Eun and Masako were brought together. She vehemently opposed any action that would separate the two.

The more Masako learned about Maiden Min, the more she admired her, and at the same time the heavier her sorrow became. She wanted to meet Min in person and tell her how sorry she was about all that had happened. All through Masako's life, she longed for such a day.

Maiden Gap-wan returned to Korea in 1947 and remained a virgin all her life. She died alone in poverty at age 67, three years before Yi Eun. Before her death she published a biography, "100 years of Unfulfilled Longing." Masako never had a chance to meet her.

The following day, as the Hakonemaru sailed out of Shanghai Harbor, Masako and Yi Eun stood on the deck gazing at the skyline of the bustling and crowded international city. Yi Eun looked distressed and even somewhat depressed, Masako thought.

Indeed, he was deeply absorbed in thoughts about his own pathetic and pitiful condition. Supposedly he was the king of Korea, and yet he was helpless to do anything for Korea or Koreans. While he was taking a world tour on a luxury ocean liner, his people were fighting and dying for Korea's independence.

Even in the city of Shanghai, spread out before his very eyes, Koreans living as alien refugees far from their homes and loved ones were fighting for his land's freedom. In desperation, they were even trying to kidnap him to enhance their cause, risking their lives, and he was hiding in a Japanese warship. "What a terrible irony all this is!"

Such thoughts, Masako assumed, were going through Yi Eun's mind, torturing him. Masako's heart ached. There was little she could do except to hold him tight and gently caress his face.

On June 6 they arrived in Hong Kong, a British colony. Known as the Pearl of Asia, it was an enchanting place, and for the first time Masako felt she was really in a foreign country.

Dazzling to her eyes were myriad people going to and from the work places and shoppers in colorful dresses. The steaming heat of the Hong Kong summer, however, was unbearable. The day happened to be the 62nd birthday of King George V of England, and huge celebrations were going on. Nine warships of the British navy, moored in the harbor, fired cannons into the air, shaking the city with loud reverberating sounds.

The following day the Hakone Maru sailed on, this time toward Singapore, another British colony. Along the way Masako and Yi Eun invited guests to their dinner table, sharing conversations on various subjects.

At times, they would be on the deck gazing at the vast ocean, marveling at the wonder of the mighty sea. Looking into the far distant horizon, with an infinite number of stars in the night sky and the endless waves of the deep blue sea, they became aware how small and insignificant they were.

"In the face of the Great Nature," Masako thought to herself, "we are so little and so powerless. We are nothing more than a tiny speck in the universe." At the same time she felt some relief from her heavy heart, so long mangled, bruised, and burdened down with sadness, anger, and resentment.

After four days of sailing the South China Sea, they arrived in Singapore on June 8. The tall palm trees along the harbor, waving in the warm gentle breeze of the south sea, were enough to enrapture the excited travelers from lands far in northern Asia.

Two days later they were in the middle of the Indian Ocean on their way to Egypt when their ship met a fierce storm, with 20 to 30 feet high waves rocking it from side to side. Terrified, Masako covered herself with a blanket and lay still in her bed. It reminded her of the stormy night when she first traveled to Korea with little Jin in her arms. As she closed her eyes, she suddenly saw flashes of her house in Tokyo and her dead baby son, Jin.

In the aftermath of the storm the Indian Ocean was a scene of brilliant sunlight and calmness, quickly liberating a depressed soul with laughter and feelings of gaiety. Masako felt as if the Ocean were saying to her, "It will be all right. You will have a beautiful future."

Masako and Yi Eun freely mingled with other passengers, including various foreigners, sometimes dining together and sometimes just visiting casually. For the first time in the seven years since their marriage, Masako saw Yi Eun visiting with cabin attendants, laughing and joking, unconstrained by all the stifling rules of his normal life. She was immensely happy and pleased.

The wonders of ancient Egypt—pyramids, sphinx, monuments, and mummies—were a testimony to the human past and tangible records of what humans can achieve, Masako thought.

Viewing these ancient historical remains, she wondered what the future would say about her and Yi Eun. Suddenly she was afraid and shuddered.

On July 4, they arrived in Marseille, France. It was America's Independence Day, and a joyous celebration was taking place in front of the U.S. Consulate Office, with colorful American flags fluttering in the wind. Yi Eun gazed at the ceremony intently. Then, turning to Masako, he said, "That's what national independence is all about. It brings freedom, joy, and happiness, something so precious and so wonderful to celebrate." In his voice there was a bit of melancholy.

"Your Highness, my darling, please don't despair. One day, Korea also will have its independence, and there will be great celebrations!" Masako said it quietly to herself, mindful of her Japanese attendant standing nearby.

After touring Paris, they went to Geneva, and then to London, where they met King George V and Queen Mary of Teck.

In Rome they had an audience with Pope Pius XI and Prime Minister Benito Mussolini.

They also visited the house where Itsuko, Masako' mother, was born. At one time it had been the Japanese ambassador's residence but was now a private home.

In every European capital they visited, from Paris to Stockholm, Masako and Yi Eun received a royal welcome and warm hospitality. They met the heads of states, and visited important historical and cultural sites including great museums, beautiful palaces, and majestic cathedrals.

Of the many places they visited, two in particular were of special significance to Masako and Yi Eun: Germany and Sweden.

On November 3 Masako and Yi Eun went to the presidential mansion of Germany to pay a visit to Paul von Hindenburg, the great general and statesman. He had passed 80, but was still robust and strong. While shaking hands, he held Masako's hand so tight she felt a crushing pain.

As an officer first in Prussia and later in Germany, Hindenburg fought in many wars including World War I. One of the wars in which he won great victories was the Franco-Russian War of 1870-1871. It happened that Yi Eun's specialty in military history was the Franco-Prussian War; consequently he had long been interested in the old general's life and thoughts.

Following Germany's defeat in World War I, Hindenburg became the president of Germany in 1925 and was trying to rebuild his country out of ashes. As he was explaining his reconstruction efforts, he said to Masako and Yi Eun, "At the present we are suffering and in great distress."

"The victorious allies," he continued, "are demanding from us an excessive amount of reparations money. France and Russia, in particular, have become unbearable. They are trying to bury us and destroy us so that we can never rise again. But we are rising again. We Germans have a strong spirit. We shall never despair."

Yi Eun heard these words as Hindenburg's message to him and to Korea that Korea would rise again. It was a word of immense encouragement. Many times afterwards he would say to Masako, "I see the soul and the power of Germany in Paul von Hindenburg."

Two weeks later, on November 16, they were in Stockholm. While visiting King Gustav V of Sweden, Masako and Yi Eun met Crown Prince Gustav Adolf, who had been to Korea about a year before. In

October, 1926, he had participated in the archaeological excavation of a royal tumulus of Korea's ancient Shilla kingdom.

To his great surprise, the Crown Prince helped find a dazzling golden crown with a phoenix design of the 5th century A.D. along with hundreds of other precious objects. In recognition of his personal involvement in the discovery, the tumulus was named *Seobongchon* in Korean (Tumulus of Sweden and Phoenix).

The spectacular discovery deepened the crown prince's interest in Korean history and civilization. Showing a beautiful Goryo period celadon from his personal collections, he said with excitement, "Such a magnificent piece of art does not exist in the West . . . Europeans generally think of China and India when they hear the word "Orient," but I believe that Korea has achieved an extraordinary civilization."

"The spiritual force behind such a brilliant civilization," he added, "is immortal. Nothing can destroy the spiritual force and creativity."

Crown Prince Gustaf Adolf knew about the plight of Korea and Yi Eun, and appeared to be conveying a message of encouragement to Yi Eun. He, Masako was certain, was trying to say to Yi Eun, "Your nation is in bad days now, but one day it will rise again and recreate a brilliant civilization." "Yi Eun was listening intently without saying a word, but he appeared to be deeply moved," Masako recalled the moment.

Masako and Yi Eun went to Europe to see and learn about the world first hand. They wanted to have freedom to see, to hear, and to talk as they wanted.

What they learned from Paul von Hindenburg of Germany and Gustaf Adolf of Sweden was more precious than all the gold and silver in the world. They were inspired and encouraged never to give up . . .

Masako and Yi Eun spent about four more months in Europe mostly in France and Italy. The great historical and cultural cities of Paris, Versailles, Rome, Naples, Pompeii, Genoa, Milan, Florence, and Venice left them with lasting memories of Europe's grandeur, past and present.

To Masako, every new sight and new scene was all so mystic and romantic. Marveling at the enchanting beauty and grandeur of this hitherto unseen world, she realized that she had been living like a little frog in a pond. Europe opened her eyes to the wider world and revealed new possibilities.

Europe even gave Masako an opportunity to go shopping for the first time in her life. As a princess, she was never allowed to shop or handle money. Such matters were all handled by her household servants.

One day while in Paris, she went to a bakery, picked out her favorite cake, and paid for it herself with money from her own purse, trying out her French which she had learned in her Gakushuin days. Sitting at a sidewalk table, she and a friend enjoyed a morning coffee. She was nervous through the whole transaction but counted it as one of the highlights of her European travel.

Masako in Paris

Finally, on March 3, 1928, Masako and Yi Eun boarded the Hakosakimaru, an ocean liner bound for Tokyo, arriving there on April 9. They were abroad for almost a year.

CHAPTER 9

PRINCESS DEOK-HYE, ANOTHER FATEFUL TWIST

At the pier were Masako's parents and many friends and relatives welcoming them home.

Masako's mind, however, was on a particular person, and her eyes were searching the crowd for Princess Deok-hye. "My dear Deok-hye, where are you?" she kept murmuring to herself.

It was during her Korean wedding ceremony in Seoul in 1922 that Masako saw little 9 years-old Princess Deok-hye for the first time, standing next to her at the ceremony.

Deok-hye was the only daughter of Emperor Gojong, born three years after Yi Eun had been taken to Japan. After Yi Eun's mother Lady Eom died, Gojong took Lady Yang, a former palace lady-in-waiting, as his consort, and she gave birth to Deok-hye on May 25, 1912.

Being the only daughter and the child of his old age, she basked in Gojong's affection. For Yi Eun, she was his only little sister, albeit by a different mother, and he loved her like a precious jewel. When five years old, Deok-hye was enrolled in a palace kindergarten that her father established specially for her.

Princess Deok-hye, c. 1925

Princess Deok-hye was shy, but also cute, playful, and bright. She loved music and dancing.

After her father, Gojong, suddenly died, she received special attention and love from Sunjong and Queen Yun, who had no children. She would often visit them and entertain them, singing new songs she learned at school.

From the moment she saw Masako, she fixed her curious eyes on the beautiful princess from a faraway land. Her shy but affectionate demeanor caught Masako's attention, and from that moment the lives of the two princesses would become forever inseparable.

Having learned about her father's death, poisoned by Japanese, Deok-hye dreaded Japan and the Japanese. She had fears and nightmares that she might also be poisoned.

Japan, however, decided to take her to Tokyo as a hostage as it had done with Yi Eun. She too would be thoroughly Japanized and would marry a Japanese, its leaders reasoned, in accordance with the policy which Ito Hirobumi had established.

Sunjong and Queen Yun vehemently objected. "Was not Yi Eun, the crown prince, sufficient in this hostage thing? Why would you also take a little 12-year old princess?" they protested. Powerless, however, there was nothing they could do.

On March 30, 1925, Princess Deok-hye, then 13 years old, arrived in Tokyo. Initially, she would stay with Masako and Yi Eun.

At the Tokyo train station, Masako was startled to find Deok-hye looking not only tired and haggard but distressed. There were none of the bright smiles on her face that Masako had seen before.

"How sad and scared she must be, having been forced to leave her home, her mother, and all her dear friends!" she thought to herself. Before Masako knew, tears were welling in her eyes.

"Princess Deok-hye, after a long journey across the rough ocean you must be tired out. Aren't you?" Masako said, trying to help with the princess' mood, but the little princess just cast her eyes down and made no response. Masako tried again, this time in Korean, but again there was no response. Nor was there any smile on her face.

Instinctively, Masako felt there was something drastically wrong, foreboding something bad to come. At the same time, Masako thought about Princess Deok-hye's mother, Lady Yang.

"Oh how sad and disheartened she must be! After losing Gojong, Deok-hye was her only joy. She was her life, now even she is gone!"

As a mother who had suffered the pain of losing a child, Masako fully understood Lady Yang's pain and felt it in her own heart.

That night, Princess Deok-hye slept with Masako, lying next to her. She seemed to feel more assured and more ease with Masako, and Masako was deeply gratified that Deok-hye accepted her as her sister-in-law with trust and affection. Gazing at her peaceful face in sleep, Masako said to herself, "What a pity! She has been forced to come here, to a land of strange customs and a strange language, with no friends."

"Oh poor little baby," she breathed a deep sigh, "she has been snatched out of her mother's hands! How homesick she must be.

How scared and distressed she must be!" Gently caressing the little princess' forehead, she uttered quietly, "My dear, please don't worry. I am here and I will always be with you. I will love you, comfort you, and look after you as your new sister and your new mother."

That same night, Yi Eun was seething with anger. He was deeply resentful of what Japan was doing to his little sister.

"Treacherous and devious people," he fumed, "How much more do they want? Am I not enough for their greedy ambitions? Why do they have to yank a little girl from her home, her mother, and all her friends? What are they trying to do to her?!" Deeply concerned for Deok-hye's well-being, Yi Eun begged Masako to look after her with special attention. Having already decided to do so, Masako readily welcomed Yi Eun's wish.

Even that wish, however, was frustrated when the Japanese government decided to send Deok-hye to Gakushuin, the Peers school designed to educate the children of Imperial families.

She came under the direct supervision of the Imperial Household Ministry, intent on Japanzing her. This led Yi Eun to an explosion, shouting in a loud voice,

"There is nothing I can do in this world as I wish!"

"Every time I want to meet a guest, see a movie, or go to a meeting I have to ask myself if it is all right with the government or if I am committing a political sin."

"When I enter a room where the subject of conversation happens to be on Korea, people immediately hush up turning away from me, and I pretend as if I am all hunky-dory. I feel like a man with a double personality!" "Now, little Deok-hye is suffering the same fate!" Yi Eun was raging.

Masako understood Yi Eun's anger and fully sympathized, but she did not know what to do. Besides, she knew that Yi Eun was not asking her to come up with solutions but only expressing his frustrations. Nevertheless, Yi Eun's torments became her own as well. And they reinforced Masako's resolve even more to care for the hapless princess struggling to survive in a foreign land, alone and living with fear and trepidation.

That was why the moment Masako disembarked the Hakosakimaru in the Kobe Harbor, she was frantically searching for Princess Deok-hye. She wanted to know how the little princess had been while she was abroad.

To Masako's relief, Deok-hye, now 16 years old, was healthy and cheerful. She was also enjoying her school activities at Gakushuin.

Fate, however, was not on Deok-hye's side. The following year, on May 30, 1929, her mother died of breast cancer, at the young age of 48. After losing Deok-hye, she had lived in loneliness and sorrow for four years in a town far away from Seoul.

Deok-hye dearly missed her mother and hoped to see her someday. There was now no someday. Overcome by shock and sadness, she locked her room to be alone, crying all day.

"What had happened to His Highness is happening to Deok-hye," Masako said to herself. When Yi Eun's mother died, he was in Tokyo, having never seen his mother since leaving her four years before. Upon receiving the news of her death, he also had collapsed in shock and sorrow.

At the time her mother died, Deok-hye was 17 years old, an age of emotional vulnerability, and Masako feared that all the emotional turmoil might be more than she could bear.

As Deok-hye was leaving for Korea to attend her mother's funeral, Masako held her hands and encouraged her to be strong, but she knew that nothing she said to the young woman could ease her sorrowful heart.

While Deok-hye was gone, Masako did not sleep well, waking up with nightmares in which she saw herself at the funeral, wailing along with other mourners. She herself was getting physically and emotionally all worn out.

Two weeks later, Deok-hye returned. Looking haggard, she said little, and as days went, she became more and more introverted.

By spring of the following year, Deok-hye was showing signs of a nervous breakdown. Sometimes her condition was so severe that her classmates at Gakushuin escorted her to Masako's house. Sometimes, even an innocent comment made by her friends would upset her to the point of hysteria.

In the summer of 1930, Masako kept Deok-hye at her house for rest and recuperation. She also took Deok-hye to a beautiful lake resort for a vacation. She tried her best to encourage the girl and strengthen her spirit. Nothing, however, seemed to help.

In the fall, when the new semester began, Deok-hye refused to go to school. All day long she would just lie in her bed without eating. In the middle of the night she would walk around all alone in the garden like a zombie.

One night she was to be found nowhere, not even in the garden. Masako and Yi Eun, along with others from the house, went out in search for her. Eventually they found her walking aimlessly in a lonely street. Each time this happened, Masako and Yi Eun were beside themselves with worry and anxiety.

Princess Deok-hye was by nature shy, but sometimes she was very cheerful and lively, happily talking about her future hopes and dreams. Eventually she wanted to return to Korea and become a teacher.

But now, she was gradually becoming a mental patient. Sometimes, she could not even recognize Masako and Yi Eun. When Masako, sometimes in tears, pleaded with her to be healthy and strong, she would make no response.

After many tests at a hospital, doctors concluded that Deok-hye was suffering "precocious dementia." Masako and Yi Eun tried every available treatment, but there was no improvement in Deok-hye's mental condition.

That fall, even as Deok-hye's mental condition was further deteriorating, the Japanese government decided to marry her to Count

So Takeyuki, a descendent of the feudal period lord of Tsushima Island. It was a Masako-Yi Eun marriage in reverse. This time a Korean princess was being forced to marry a Japanese nobleman.

Upon receiving the news, Masako and Yi Eun flew into a range. "What cruelty it is! How can they talk about marriage when Deok-hye is mentally sick and her condition has been deteriorating?!" They screamed. "First and foremost," they insisted, "every effort must be made to improve Deok-hye's health,"

Masako and Yi Eun strongly opposed the marriage decision for other reasons. They believed that Deok-hye would be happier if she returned to Korea, fulfilled her wish to become a teacher, and eventually married a Korean.

By the spring of 1931, to their delight, Deok-hye's health had improved almost miraculously. She was sharp mentally, recognized people, and had a hearty appetite. She freely engaged in conversations and was at ease with people around her.

At the tender and impressionable age of 19, Deok-hye was once again thinking about her future, her hopes and dreams.

Learning about Deok-hye's improvement, however, the government took up the marriage matter again. Masako and Yi Eun were adamantly against it. They wanted Deok-hye to continue in her education before any marriage decision.

Deok-hye had no interest in marriage, and she went into depression again. She stayed in her room for three days fasting and crying. Masako and Yi Eun entreated the government to leave Deok-hye alone, but all of their pleadings fell on deaf ears.

On May 8, 1931, Deok-hye was married to So Takeyuki, strictly "for the purpose of enhancing Korea-Japan union," as was with Masako and Yi Eun.

As Deok-hye appeared in a white wedding dress, looking haggard and uneasy, Masako quietly wept in sadness and anger, wondering about Deok-hye's uncertain future.

For some time, in the midst of all these tumultuous events, Masako was getting increasingly anxious and even worried about her persistent barrenness. For her, it was not just a personal matter. It had to do with the future of the Yi Royal Dynasty. The more she thought about it, the more anxious she became.

As the wife of Yi Eun, the 28th king of the Yi Royal Dynasty, she had a royal duty to provide a son to succeed Yi Eun. But since her miscarriage in the spring of 1923, nothing had happened, and it was among the foremost thoughts in her mind all through the European tour.

On October 18, 1929, more than six years after her last miscarriage, she went to Dr. Iwase, a gynecologist at the University of Tokyo. On the way she was watching autumn leaves falling on the ground. It made her sad as she wondered if she was becoming like one of the falling leaves.

Even her younger sister, Noriko, had a baby recently. "What's wrong with me?" she asked herself over and over again.

At the advice of Dr. Iwase, Masako underwent a simple surgery in her uterus to correct kyphosis, and desperately she waited for something good to happen.

At the end of the year, Masako and Yi Eun returned their mansion in Toriisaka to the Imperial Household Ministry. In its place, the Ministry built for them a large, beautiful English style mansion in Akasaka.

Early in spring of 1930, they moved into the new Akasaka mansion. Soon thereafter Masako learned that she was pregnant. Exceedingly happy, Masako felt like flying. So did Yi Eun. There was a new vitality in the house. At the same time, Masako had a premonition that she might have another miscarriage. She was right, and in April she lost the baby, a five month old male.

Everything came and ended like a puff of air, deepening her sense of despair. "What a wretched fate I have!" she cried out, "Is the God of fortunes forever against me? Why am I not allowed even just one happiness which other people enjoy?" Masako lost all courage to face Yi Eun.

Dr. Iwase confided to her that the miscarriage was caused by polyhydramnios, a complication in the uterus, and that if the baby did not die her own life would have been in grave danger. He also revealed that 8 out of 10,000 pregnancies had this problem. The doctor's words only made Masako feel sadder and more despairing. "Poor baby, he died for my sake," she moaned.

She then wondered why she was one of the unfortunate 8 out 10,000. A sense of despair was pressing down on her heart.

Throughout the year of 1930, Masako, among myriad other things, had been busy, sometimes at the risk of her own health, looking after sick Princess Deok-hye. All the stresses she was under undoubtedly contributed to her second miscarriage.

In July of 1931, still feeling tired and weak, Masako went to Doctor Iwase for a check-up. To her greatest surprise, the doctor revealed that she was in her 5th month pregnancy and that the baby was doing well. The news was a God-send. Excited and happy, Masako was determined to insure a healthy birth of her new child. "Oh God, please, please, help me this time," she earnestly prayed.

In the morning of December 29, 1931, at 8:22, Masako gave birth to a healthy boy just as the bright morning sun's rays were entering through the glass window of her room. Masako and Yi Eun named their new son Yi Ku.

CHAPTER 10

WAR TIME

T he birth of Masako's second son, Yi Ku, coincided with the start of Japan's war times, which began with the so-called Manchurian or Mukden Incident on September 18, 1931 and ended with Japan's unconditional surrender to the Allied Forces on August 14, 1945.

By 1931, Japan had emerged as a major world power along with England, United States, France, and Italy, as victors in World War I.

It had also achieved, to some extent, its imperialistic ambitions by bringing under its control Korea, Formosa, and the Pacific Marshall Islands, Marianas, and Carolines, as well as southern Manchuria.

Manchuria, with its vast plains and forested mountains, was particularly important to Japan's expanding economy and rapidly growing heavy industries, as a major source of raw materials.

In order to secure its economic interests there, Japan in 1915 forced China to sign a treaty granting Japan a 99-year lease of the Guandong or Kwantung District off the tip of the Liaodong Peninsula. Subsequently, Japan stationed in the territory one of its most powerful armies, which in time came to be known as "the Terrifying Kwantung Army."

Zhang Zuolin, the nominal Chinese warlord of Manchuria since 1911, gave Japan wide-ranging concessions in the region in return for its military support. However, on the morning of June 4, 1928, the Kwantung Army murdered Zhang Zuolin by bombing his train near Shenyang.

The Japanese Army considered him not only anti-Japan but also too weak to prevent Chiang Kai-shek's Nationalist Army from advancing into northern China, thereby jeopardizing Japan's interests in Manchuria. The Kwantung Army wanted to have Zhang Zuolin replaced with his son, Zhang Xueliang, an opium addict and womanizer and considered to be more easily manageable.

However, Zhang Xueliang, angry with the Japanese for murdering his father, became more anti-Japanese than his father was, and threw his lot in with Chiang Kai-shek, the head of China's Nationalist government. In April, 1931, he and Chiang Kai-shek held a conference in Nanjing and decided to firmly oppose the Japanese in Manchuria.

Alarmed and infuriated by this new development, the Kwantung Army decided to launch a preemptive strike and occupy entire Manchuria militarily. As a pretext for an all-out invasion, Lieutenant Kawamoto Suemori, in the middle of the night on September 18, 1931, exploded a bomb close to the South Manchurian Railway owned by Japan near Mukden (present day Shenyang).

Intentionally, the Kwantung Army chose a little used and unimportant railway section so that its reconstruction expenses in the aftermath would be minimal. In fact, actual damages to the railway were minimal and did not interrupt the regular train traffic.

Accusing local Chinese elements of the bombing incident, the Kwantung Army launched its planned invasion on a massive scale and within five months occupied all of Manchuria's three provinces, Liaoning, Jilin, and Heilongjiang.

From Nanjing, Nationalist China's capital, China's Foreign Ministry strongly protested the Japanese invasion and demanded immediate cessation of the Kwantung Army's military operations. On November 16, the League of Nations adopted a resolution demanding the withdrawal of Japanese troops within three weeks.

On January 7, 1932 Henry Stimson, U.S. Secretary of State, announced that the U.S. would not recognize any government established by Japan in Manchuria. Japan rejected all these demands, and on March 1 established the puppet state of Manchukuo with Puyi, the last emperor of China, as its head.

With the invasion of Manchuria, Imperial Japan plunged itself into political chaos through the 1930s and also gave impetus to the rise of the unstoppable militarism and fascism leading to its attack on the Pearl Harbor.

It was in the shadow of these ominous events that Masako gave birth to her second son, Yi Ku, on December 29, 1931. Masako had waited for this day for almost ten years since the death of Jin. For her the baby was the most precious gift. She had been willing to have him even if she had to give up her own life.

"Oh God, thank you, thank you, and thank you!" she repeated quietly.

A few minutes after the baby was born, Yi Eun, who had been waiting anxiously outside, entered the room. "Thank you for all your hard work," he said, holding Masako's hands tightly, overcome by joy and gratitude. Without saying a word, Masako and Yi Eun just looked at each other and into each other's eyes, sharing unspeakable joy and happiness.

When the baby was laid next to her, all cleaned and washed, Yi Eun looked at him with proud and happy smiles. Masako was deeply gratified and thankful.

Undoubtedly, Yi Eun would have been anxious about his future succession, but in all the years since Jin's death he had never even so much as mentioned the subject.

Once again, Masako's home came alive with the sounds of baby cries. In his cooing and crying Masako felt her own life, alive and well. And her mind was all on the baby's wellbeing.

One day, holding her newborn baby tightly to her chest, she said to herself with a firm resolve, "My baby, grow healthy and strong. When you have grown big, I will let you visit Korea. Until then, I promise, I will not take you to Korea no matter what." Masako's thoughts were back in Korea on the fateful day ten years ago when little Jin died, poisoned by someone.

Masako with Yi Ku, c.1935

Daily, Masako concentrated her time and energy on her baby, feeding, washing, and giving it baths herself. There was nothing she would hesitate on or spare if it was for her baby.

No matter how physically exhausted she was, she refused to place the baby in the hands of others, including her household servants. She rarely left the baby and seldom left her house except for obligatory formal events in the Imperial Palace.

Whenever Yi Eun came home, he would hold the baby in his arms in a playful mood, singing or baby-talking. Normally of few smiles, Yi Eun would break out in laughs, totally lost in the happiness of his new son.

On August 14, 1933, Princess Deok-hye gave birth to a baby girl. She was named Masae.

Masako was very happy, hoping that the baby would give the princess a new meaning and a reason to be healthy and to keep dreaming for a bright future.

And on December 23, Empress Nagako, the wife of Emperor Hirohito and Masako's first cousin, had her first son, Akihito. Like Masako, Empress Nagako had long been childless. Having personally experienced the agonies associated with barrenness, Masako was happy for the Empress.

In the spring of 1934, Masako went to Seoul, this time alone, because Yi Eun was busy with military training and exercises. She wanted to visit little Jin's grave among other royal duties.

She wanted, more than anything, to show off Yi Ku, now two and half years old, to his older brother, Jin, who would have become 12 years old. But she shook her head, gritting her teeth.

Standing before Jin's grave, she said, "My dear Jin, please wait until your brother has grown big enough to decide by himself to come here and see you. Please forgive me." She did the same before the graves of Gojong, Sunjong, and Lady Eom, Yi Eun's mother and Yi Ku's grandmother.

To Masako, Yi Ku was not just her son. He was the prince of the Yi Royal Dynasty, destined to succeed Yi Eun as its 29th king. She would protect him with her life and every ounce of energy she had in order to help him fulfill his duty, in place of Jin.

At this time, there was a severe economic decline in Japan especially during 1930-32. Agricultural and textile prices fell 40% and 50% respectively.

Among the causes of the decline were partly America's Wall Street crash (Black Thursday) of October 1929 and the Great Depression that followed, and partly Japanese government's adoption of the gold standard and a deflationary policy.

In rural Japan of the 1920s, impoverishment was common, and in time would be further aggravated by the great famine of 1934. In some rural areas, starving farmers were selling their daughters to brothels. These rural crises turned Japan's popular sentiment against the government and the large corporations.

The Japanese public was thoroughly disenchanted with the party governments that had begun during the Taisho democracy of the 1920s and, though normally anti-military, was now turning to the military for national salvation.

Riding on the wave of such public sentiments, right wing nationalists and the military became increasingly bold and assertive. In 1932, the so-called League of Blood Association, a violent ultranationalist group, decided to assassinate 20 prominent businessmen and liberal politicians of Japan.

On February 9, 1932, they gunned down Junnosuke Inoue, a prominent financier and former finance minister, and on March 5, they fatally shot Dan Takuma, Director General of the Mitsui Corporation.

When Prime Minister Tsuyoshi Inukai sought to impose fiscal restraint on the military and control the military actions in China, he was promptly assassinated by naval officers and ultra nationalists of the League of the Blood Association on May 15, 1932.

On February 24, 1933, the League of Nations Assembly, by a 42-1 vote, censured Japan for its invasion of Manchuria and recommended that it withdraw its troops from the occupied areas and restore Manchuria to Chinese sovereignty. Infuriated, Yosuke Matsuoka, the Japanese representative, walked out of the Assembly in arrogant defiance.

Thanks to an economic recovery begun in 1933, the violent incidents subsided for a time. But rural poverty was still rampant. Right wing extreme nationalism was still alive, though largely underground, and the military remained disenchanted with the civilian government.

The Kwantung Army in Manchuria had been restless following its spectacular victories against the Chinese forces in September, 1931. Violence could erupt again any moment. But the momentary calm gave Masako and Yi Eun a window of opportunity for one of the happiest days in their life.

In the summer of 1935 Yi Eun was promoted to full colonel in the Imperial Army, and soon he received a new assignment as commander of the 59th Regiment stationed at Utsunomiya. Accordingly Masako's family moved to a new place near Utsunomiya, a picturesque town outside Tokyo.

Masako loved the country atmosphere. She felt liberated from the hustle and bustle of the city life and didn't have to worry about all the rules of propriety that had to be kept in the Imperial household.

Her house was a simple cottage, and for the first time she felt part of normal, ordinary society. And she thought it was a perfect place for Yi Ku to spend his early life.

From time to time, Masako visited nearby farmers' homes with Yi Ku. After watching rabbits and chickens on a farm they would come home with fresh eggs and vegetables they had bought from the farmers. Living in the country seemed to help Yi Ku grow even more healthily.

Sometimes, young officers would show up in their cottage without notice, demanding something or anything to eat. They were all happy and cheerful young men.

"They kept me frantic, but my cottage was filled with joyous laughter and an air of happiness," she recalled. "They seemed to genuinely like my husband, so I was happy to see them, and their visit delighted me immeasurably."

Yi Eun also was happy, living in the country. "These days I am really enjoying life," he would say. "It is such a good feeling to live in a free and pleasant atmosphere."

Utsunomiya was surrounded by high mountains, and during the winter some of them became ski parks. During the summer and the fall the family would hike, and in the winter they learned to ski. This was the beginning of Masako's life-long love affair with the mountains.

"No thrill was greater than the thrill experienced standing on the top of a high mountain looking into the distant horizon," she remembered, "and no joy was greater than the joy experienced while sliding down the mountain on the snow."

While living in the country cottage, Masako also enjoyed her favorite hobbies such as embroidery, calligraphy, and composing waka poems. Life in Utsunomiya offered some of Masako's happiest and most romantic days, and she used to say, "It was another honeymoon for us."

Even as Masako relished her happy memories of the Utsunomiya days, however, she was also philosophical about the ephemeral nature of all things, including happiness. All things, she believed, are transitory. Like the morning dew, they are here, and then they are gone. "During our life time, happiness comes only for a moment at a time. It is not something that continues forever," she mused.

"Our life in Utsunomiya was one of such happy moments. We three were truly happy. So I can never forget Utsunomiya. Even after I left there, I often thought of it."

True to Masako's musings, her happiness at Utsunomiya was only momentary. As the year of 1936 commenced, right wing nationalism lifted its head, decrying long-persistent rural impoverishment and rampant political corruption. A large number of the Japanese army's enlisted men, coming from the impoverished rural areas, were becoming disenchanted with Japan's party politics in cahoots with the *zaibatsu* (big business and financial corporations)

At the same time, many young officers were unhappy with their politicians' guarded approach to foreign military expansion, especially in China. Generals were upset with the government for reducing the military budget.

On February 26, 1936, more than 1500 soldiers (20 officers and 1528 NCOs and privates), mostly from the elite 1st and 3rd Infantry Regiments and the Imperial Guards, all stationed in Tokyo, decided to overthrow the civilian government of Prime Minister Okada Keisuke.

In the rebellion, this group quickly seized the central district of Tokyo as well as the Diet building, Army Ministry Headquarters, and Tokyo Metropolitan Police Headquarters.

They also killed several prominent leaders in the government, including Finance Minister Takahashi Korekiyo, Lord Keeper of the Privy Seal Saito Makoto, and Inspector-General of Military Education General Jotaro Watanabe. Prime Minister Okada Keisuke was one of the primary targets for his anti-military posture, but he escaped death when the assassins killed his brother-in-law by mistake.

The rebel objective was to create a new government, headed by a general, devoted to repairing the nation's troubled economy, actively supporting the military's aspirations—especially the conquest of Asia and most of all devoid of political wrangling and corruption.

Emperor Hirohito was enraged at the rebellion, declared martial law, and ordered the rebels to surrender. Various army units, including the 59th Infantry Regiment under Colonel Yi Eun's command at Utsunomiya, were ordered to surround the rebels and crush the rebellion.

Yi Eun's troops gathered in the Yasukuni Shrine near the Imperial Palace and awaited its attack orders.

After four days of armed confrontation with the government the rebels surrendered, with several of their leaders committing suicide. Yi Eun returned to Utsnomiya with his 59th Infantry Regiment. In March the following year, he received an appointment on the faculty of the Imperial Japanese Military Academy.

Leaving the simple and pleasant country life at Utsunomiya, Masako was again back in the hustle and bustle of Tokyo life. In April, Yi Ku began kindergarten.

In those days, anti-Korean sentiments were part of the rising Japanese nationalism. "Korea is our pain. Exterminate Korea and the Koreans," people shouted. They also bitterly complained about the special status the Yi royal families were accorded by the Japanese government.

Undoubtedly, Japan's right wing nationalists were targeting Yi Eun and his family as well as other Yi royal family members, such as Yi Gang, Yi Geon, and Yi Woo, who had been officially incorporated into the Japanese imperial system in accordance with Emperor Meiji's annexation decree of 1910.

Equally vehement were the cries of Korean nationalism, now active globally in Manchuria, mainland China, the Soviet Union, Europe, and the United States.

"Japan is our mortal enemy!"

"Japs are thieves and murderers!"

"Annihilate the Japanese!

Korean nationalists shouted and vowed solidarity with each other in their hideouts, in their secret gatherings, and on their guerilla battle fronts. And indeed, as early as 1907, at the Harbin train station in Manchuria, Ahn Joong-geun shot to death Ito Hirobumi, the father of modern Japan and mastermind behind Japan's smothering of Korea's independence. In 1920, Korean anti-Japanese guerrilla fighters operating along the Korean-Manchurian border routed and/or slew thousands of Japanese troops.

On May 14, 1928, Jo Myeong-ha, an avowed Korean nationalist, stabbed Prince Kuniyoshi, the father-in-law of Emperor Hirohito and Masako's uncle, with a mortal wound. The knife used in the attack was poisoned, and a few months later Kuniyoshi died of high fever. At his funeral, Masako mourned with deep sorrow and a heavy heart.

On December 28, 1926, Nah Seok-ju, an agent of the Korean Provisional Government in Shanghai, bombed Japanese companies engaged in systematic economic exploitation of Koreans and killed many Japanese company officials.

After Manchuria came under Japanese control in 1931, Korean independence fighters joined various Chinese anti-Japanese fighters, including Mao Zedong's Communists.

On January 8, 1932, Lee Bong-chang, another agent of the Korean Provisional Government, threw a bomb at Emperor Hirohito as he was entering a gate of the Imperial Palace in Tokyo. The bomb missed its target, and the emperor survived.

On April 29, 1932, Yun Bong-gil, another agent of the Provisional Government, threw a bomb into a party in the Lu Xun Park, Shanghai that was celebrating Emperor Hirohito's birthday. It killed General Shirakawa Yoshinori, former commander-in-chief of the Kwantung Army and current commander-in-chief of the Shanghai Expeditionary Army, and Kawabata, President of the Japanese Residents Association in Shanghai.

Yun also wounded Vice Admiral Nomura Kichisaburo, the commander of the 3rd Naval Fleet, General Ueda Kenkichi, Commander of the 9th Infantry Division, and Shigemitsu Mamoru, Japanese Ambassador to China, who lost his right leg. (In September 1945, Shigemitsu was on the American battleship USS Missouri signing Japan's surrender document.)

In June 1937, Kim Il-sung, as the leader of about 100 anti-Japanese guerrilla fighters in Manchuria, attacked Japanese troops, killing seven and gravely wounding seven. He would kill many more Japanese in Manchuria before he joined, early in 1940, the Soviet Far East 88th International Brigade as a captain (later major) of the Soviet Army.

Kim Ku, as the head of Korea's Provisional Government, supported and trained armed agents such as Nah Seok-ju, Lee Bong-chang, Yun Bon-gil, and others to assassinate high ranking Japanese officials and military leaders. In 1940, he organized the Armed Forces for Korean Independence among Korean youths abroad and declared war on Japan on December 9, 1941.

Syngman Rhee, a Harvard and Princeton educated Korean independence fighter, was deeply involved in broadcasting on the radio passionate speeches exposing the evils of Japanese rule in Korea and appealing to the free world for support of Korean independence from Japan.

At a more personal level, Korean nationalists denounced the marriage of Masako and Yi Eun. On May 8, 1920, *The Independence Daily*, the official newspaper of the Korean Provisional Government, the political center of Korean nationalism, had scorned and reviled Yi Eun for "marrying a woman of the enemy" and denounced him as "a low-grade animal." *The Daily* closed with a warning that someday Yi Eun would be "tried and punished for his sins and crimes."

Knowing that such sentiments were shared by most of Korean nationalists, Masako pondered with the disconcerting thought, "What will happen to us?"

Masako was thinking about the future of her husband and their son as well as about her own life in the days to come.

Even though it failed, the February 26, 1936 Incident, as Japan's military rebellion came to be known, it provided further impetus to Japan's march toward wider and more devastating wars than it had ever known in its history.

Civilian and elected officials were now too intimidated to oppose the growing demands of the military. A few days after the incident, Okada resigned. Hirota Koki, who succeeded him as the new prime minister, decided to placate the military to avoid further domestic violence by restoring an older Cabinet system in which only a general and an admiral on active duty could serve for the War and Navy departments. From that point on, no political or budgetary agenda could pass the Cabinet without the consent of the Army and the Navy.

In November, Hirota signed a pact with Hitler's Germany (and a year later with Italy) to collaborate against the Communists globally.

In June 1937, Fumimaro Konoe became the new prime minister. It was believed by Japan's elder statesmen that he could rein in the military. Within a month, however, he yielded to the Kwantung Army, which launched an all out war in northern China using as a pretext an incident at the Marco Polo Bridge near Beijing on July 7, 1937.

Konoe aided the Kwantung Army by sending three additional divisions. In August he sent two more divisions to Shanghai to defend Japanese interests there.

In December, the Imperial Army General Headquarters, operating independently of Japan's elected government, ordered Japanese troops to assault Nanjing, China's capital at that time. This became the infamous rape and massacre of Nanjing. All of China was now engulfed in a terrifying war, with casualties mounting on both sides.

In December, 1938, Yi Eun was promoted from Colonel to Major General. (There was no intermediate rank of Brigadier General in the Japanese Imperial Army.) At the same time he received an order to go to the Chinese front. Masako was stunned and afraid.

"Has the military now decided to send His Highness to the battle front in order to get him killed?" Masako muttered in anger. "Have they finally decided to eliminate the last heir to the Yi Royal Dynasty of Korea?"

Fuming, Masako wanted to see the Emperor and plead with him to cancel the military order. Yi Eun, however, sternly said, "No. I forbid you." "Since my childhood, I have been exploited by them without end. I know about Koreans' anger and criticism against me. They keep asking why I don't defect from Japan and instead keep living under Japanese protection."

"What will happen to the Koreans if I defect and run away? The Japanese will surely rule them even more harshly and may even decide to eliminate the Yi Royal families altogether. That is what Japanese nationalists are demanding anyway."

"If I go to China, I can help Korean youths who have been forced into the Japanese army. I will do whatever I can to protect them.

Though in name only, I am their king, and they are constantly on my mind."

Masako was stunned. For the first time she heard Yi Eun revealing his innermost thoughts. He was indeed the king of Korea, she said to herself. She was sorry that she had known her husband only partially.

In fact, Yi Eun often invited new Korean recruits in his regiment to his home. Over dinner he would ask them about life back in Korea, always conversing in Korean. He would encourage them, telling them to come and see him if they had problems. The young Korean soldiers were surprised to find Yi Eun, long away from Korea, speaking Korean better than they did. They thought Yi Eun was like their father in a foreign land.

On December 18, 1938, Yi Eun left for the China front. Thinking that he might not return alive, he taught his eight year old son the sacred ancestral rituals of the Yi royal family, which he, as the representative of the Yi royal family, was required to perform annually at the Jongmyo Grand Ancestral Hall in Seoul.

In case he might be prevented from going to Seoul by the expanding wars, Yi Eun even created an exact replica of the Ancestral Hall in his own house in Tokyo.

Eight months later, Yi Eun safely returned to Japan and became the commander of the 2nd Brigade of the Imperial Guards. And in June, 1940, he was appointed commander of the Reserve Army Division in Osaka.

In that year, Yi Eun paid special attention to the plight of Korean students in Japan, who were often discriminated against by the Japanese. First, he persuaded the Tokyo office of the Yi Royal Household Administration to turn one of its buildings into a dormitory for Korean women students. Eleven students moved in during the first year. Then, firmly believing that the future of Korea depended on well-educated young men and women, he established an endowed scholarship fund for Korean students who were bright but poor economically.

In the 1940s Japan's preparations for armed conflicts was intensified. And during his second term as Prime Minister (July 22, 1940-Oct. 16, 1941), Fumimaro Konoe became even more supportive of the military, by choosing Matsuoka Yosuke, a loyal friend of the Army, as the new Foreign Minister.

Together, Konoe and Matsuoka decided to adopt the concept of a Greater East Asia Co-prosperity Sphere, a master plan which the Army had drawn up for a new world order, as a blue-print for Japan's national and foreign affairs agenda. The Co-prosperity Sphere, under Japan's domination, would include Japan, China, Manchuria, Indo-China, and the East Indies.

On September 27, 1940, against the wishes of some prominent leaders, including Prince Saionji Kimmochi and Yonai Mitsumasa, former prime ministers of Japan, Konoe and Matsuoka also signed the Tripartite Pact. This pact brought Japan, Germany, and Italy into the so-called Axis alliance and in time emboldened the Japanese militarists to challenge the U.S. and England in the Asian and Pacific regions.

On April 13, 1941, Matsuoka also signed Japanese-Soviet Union Non-Aggression Pact in Moscow with Stalin. This pact freed Japan from fear of a possible attack from the Soviet Union in the event of a war with the U.S.

Masako was deeply troubled by these rapidly developing events. Instinctively she felt that Japan was taking a self-destructive path from which it could not return.

"Is there no able diplomat in Japan?" she pondered. "Is there no brilliant statesman in Japan? Japan desperately needs Prince Saionji to save it from the impending catastrophe."

Prince Saionji Kimmochi, educated in law at the Sorbonne in France, was a friend of Emperor Meiji and one of the most respected statesmen in early 20th century Japan. Valuing freedom, liberty, and human rights, he detested militarism, always seeking to curb the power of the military.

Saionji opposed Japan's alliance with Germany and Italy and pushed for friendly relations with the United States and the Great Britain, but he died on November 24, 1940 at the age of 92 with his hopes unrealized.

As Masako feared, on July 28, 1941, Japanese forces moved into Indo-China in pursuance of their plan for a Greater East Asia Co-Prosperity Sphere.

The governments of the United States, Great Britain, and the Dutch East Indies froze Japanese assets in their countries. The U.S. also placed a total embargo on oil and gasoline exports to Japan, which had depended on the U.S. for more than 80% of its oil needs.

The United States demanded that Japan withdraw completely from China and recognize China's independence. Konoe wanted to negotiate with the U.S. to avoid a war. The military, however, saw no option but war.

On October 17, General Hideki Tojo, the war minister in the Konoe cabinet, became the new prime minister. He vigorously advocated Japanese advances in Manchuria, the China mainland, and Indo-China. He also believed that the war with the U.S. was unavoidable because of America's continuous interference with Japan's grand plans in Asia.

Along with General Hajime Sugiyama, Chief of the Imperial Japanese Army General Staff, and Admiral Osamu Nagano, Chief of the Imperial Japanese Naval General Staff, Tojo convinced the Emperor that Japanese forces were capable of inflicting a decisive, mortal blow that would eliminate the major Western powers (U.S., England, and Holland) in the Pacific.

In their self-confidence Japanese generals and admirals were deluding themselves with their self-made myth that Japan was a divine nation led by a living god and a million Shinto deities and therefore invincible. Japan's invincibility, they assured each other, was proven in their spectacular victories over China and Russia. Japan, they believed, was destined by the will of their Shinto deities to defeat Western powers and become the supreme ruler of Asia and the Pacific region.

On November 2, 1941, Tojo Hideki received Emperor Hirohito's consent for war with the U.S. And On December 7, Japan attacked Pearl Harbor.

On the eve of the Pearl Harbor attack Masako and Yi Eun were in Korea. On December 5, they had gone to Seoul to pay homage to the tombs of Gojong, Sunjong, and Lady Eom and also to visit Jin's grave.

Returning to Tokyo by plane on December 11, Masako saw in the waters off Kyushu Island a fleet of Japanese aircraft carriers and battleships. They were getting ready to depart for battles in the South Pacific, she thought.

Once again, events beyond her control put Masako in a mood of deep apprehension and uncertainty about the future of Japan as well as that of her own family. The waves of the sea below were turbulent, and her plane was shaking violently in the stormy air. It seemed a portent of things to come.

For a few months following Japan's spectacularly successful surprise attack on Pearl Harbor and other victories in the South Pacific, all Japan was caught up in excitement and celebrations. Students daily paraded on the streets, beating drums and singing victory songs.

With other members of the Imperial families, Masako also joined in the victory celebrations and went to the Meiji Shinto Shrine to pray for the safe return of soldiers from various battle fronts.

At the same time, Masako, along with the entire Japanese population, was obligated to serve Japan's war efforts under the National Mobilization Law enacted in 1938, following Japan's invasion of mainland China.

Masako reduced her family's daily food consumption, often to mere potatoes and noodles. Sometimes she would collect supplementary wild greens in the fields. One day she even cooked wild clover plants but found them too coarse to swallow. She discovered that foods animals ate were not always suitable for humans.

Masako also simplified her clothing by adopting the baggy *mompei*, the national war-time uniform demanded by the government for all women.

Masako making bandages at a local Red Cross station in Tokyo

On April 18, 1942, American bombers appeared for the first time in the sky above Tokyo. In a raid planned and led by Lieutenant Colonel James Doolittle of the U.S. Army Air Forces, 16 B-25B Mitchell bombers flew from the U.S. Navy aircraft carrier, Hornet, in the Western Pacific to drop bombs on the city.

Even though the Doolittle raid caused very limited material damage, it seriously affected the morale and self-confidence of the Japanese military and general public. The Japanese mainland, they realized, was vulnerable.

In addition, the air raid placed all Japan and its entire population on a 24-hour alert against American bombing. The government ordered construction of bomb shelters and subjected the population to all kinds of physical drills, including hiding in bomb shelters, fire-fighting, and treatment of the wounded.

Masako was not exempted from such war-time drills. Dressed in soiled and crumpled *mompei*, she participated in exercises carrying water buckets and providing emergency medical care to the wounded.

On many a day she would also visit military hospitals to comfort wounded soldiers returned from battlefields and visit women workers in factories.

In June, 1942, Yi Eun was transferred to the First Air Command Headquarters. As he flew daily in a military plane to visit various airfields Masako could not help worrying about his safety. When the weather was bad all the more she feared for his life, spending sleepless nights.

As the war continued, life in Japan became increasingly dire. To supplement her groceries, Masako dug up her family tennis court to plant corn and potatoes. Many times, her family dinner consisted of corn and buckwheat flour. Sometimes, she boiled grass she picked in her garden to make vegetable porridge.

Under the strict censorship of the military, the public knew little of what was actually happening on the battle fronts in China and the Pacific. But by mid-1943, they began to sense that things were not going well for Japan.

On May 21, 1943, the government announced that Admiral Yamamoto Isoroku, commander of the Combined Fleet of the Imperial Army and Navy, had been killed in the South Pacific.

Admiral Yamamoto was Japan's greatest naval strategist and one of its most revered commanders. He had masterminded Japan's devastating attack on Pearl Harbor, and all Japan had hoped that he would help Japan win the war against the Americans. The news of his death, therefore, sent shock waves throughout the nation.

Actually, one year earlier, on June 4-5, 1942, the U.S. had achieved a decisive victory in the battle of Midway, destroying four Japanese aircraft carriers and a cruiser and severely damaging two destroyers. The Midway victory had already turned the tide of the Pacific war against Japan, but it was to drag on for two more disastrous years.

In the South Pacific, on August 8, 1942, U.S. Marines captured an unfinished airfield on Guadalcanal from Japanese troops, and after many fierce battles they took complete control of the strategic island in early February, 1943.

Then on April 18, 1943, eighteen U.S. P-38 fighter planes shot down a Japanese bomber carrying Admiral Yamamoto near Bougainville in the Solomon Islands, mortally wounding him.

Amidst these ominous events, Masako, on June 14 went to Hokkaido to spend time with Lady Park Chan-joo. She was the wife of Yi Woo, who was Yi Eun's nephew and a colonel in the Imperial Army. Lady Park was visiting women farm laborers there to raise morale at the request of the Imperial Palace.

Masako and Lady Park were not only in-laws but also firm friends. They spent a long night talking about the war, their fears, and their worries about the future. One thing they were already certain about—Japan was losing the war and life would get only tougher and more precarious.

Lady Park concluded: "This war is going to end soon. Until then we must stay alive. At all cost we must safeguard the life of everyone in our families for the sake of our future."

Lady Park spoke with such firm conviction and fervor that Masako was deeply moved, and resolved that she would not allow herself or anyone in her family to become a sacrificial victim of a war that could have and should have been avoided and was now failing.

That night the two women made an oath to each other—that they would stay alive at any cost and would do their utmost to help as many family members as possible to come out alive from the war.

In the midst of overwhelming uncertainty Masako had a premonition that Japan's defeat in war might make it a long time before she could visit Seoul again. So, on June 28, while it was still possible despite the tense war-time atmosphere, she made a hurried trip to Seoul to visit Jin's grave and also see the widowed Queen Yun, who had been kind and gracious to her as her Korean sister-in-law.

When they met, Masako and Queen Yun held hands and shared tears.

"Please take good care," Masako kept repeating, as it came time to bid farewell.

"I hear that Tokyo has become dangerous under American bombing. Please be careful," Queen Yun replied holding Masako's hands tightly. "Especially, please look after Yi Ku and safeguard his life." The queen spoke firmly: "He is the most important member of our Yi royal family, for he is next in line to carry on our royal family lineage."

For Masako, leaving Queen Yun's residence at Changdeok Palace was unbearably painful. She promised the queen she would come back to see her again, but she had no confidence in her own promises.

Even more painful was her having to say good-bye to Jin. She had visited Jin's grave almost every year. During each visit she was comforted and felt she had comforted Jin. The thought that Jin would be left alone now overwhelmed her with sadness.

For years Masako treasured her last sight of Jin's grave, where she was leaving him alone on a lonely hillside.

On July 20, 1943, Yi Eun was promoted to the rank of Lieutenant General and appointed as commander of Japan's First Air Force. The promotion, however, did not please either Yi Eun or Masako, for he was being assigned to a dangerous task as the war entered the most difficult phase.

As fighting continued, hospitals throughout Japan were becoming crowded with wounded soldiers from various battle fronts, and the numbers of dead troops kept mounting.

"In the third year of the war, 1944, Japan entered a state of utter desperation," Masako reminisced. "There was starvation. Deaths were everywhere. Even people around us were becoming 'the dew of battle fields' one by one."

"We did not see again many of the young and cheerful officers who used to visit our home. So many of the bright young men, so close to us, were dying in faraway places without any good purpose or meaning," Masako recalled.

On February 25, 1944, Count Otowa, an imperial family relative and the second son of Prince Asanoka, perished on Jarin Island, and on June 8, Colonel Iriye, a family friend and a frequent visitor to her home, died in Burma.

Whenever Masako learned that a friend or relative had died on a battle field she could not sleep, overcome with sadness. It was unbearably painful for her to think that she could never see again the happy smiling faces of the young men who had come to say good-bye on their way to the battle front.

In those days, as most of Japan's able bodied adult men were sent to the battle fronts, the government put young school boys to work on farms and in factories. Even Yi Ku, Masako's 13-year old son and the grandson of imperial prince Nashimoto Morimasa, could not escape it. He was sent to work in the Odawara Electric Machinery Company as a "wartime laborer."

When she watched her son come home exhausted late at night she could only pray for the quick ending of the war.

The government kept promising "a victory at the end," but Masako, like most Japanese, didn't believe it. Her only hope was to somehow come out alive from the ashes of the war.

Beginning in the summer of 1944, life in Japan turned even more bleak and dire under America's new weapons, the terrifying B-29 bombers. In June they dropped bombs on the steel works at Yawata. On November 24, two dozen B-29s bombed the Nakajima aircraft factory near Tokyo.

Air-raid warnings often sent the Japanese to underground shelters. On January 1, 1945, imperial families held their New Year ceremony in the palace air-raid shelter. Gakushuin, the imperial peers school, was closed, and its students were evacuated to the countryside. Yi Ku was sent to Nikko.

On February 25, a flight of 174 B-29s dropped incendiary bombs on Tokyo, destroying about one square mile of the city. On March 9-10, a squadron of 279 B-29s dropped 1,700 tons of bombs, turning 16 square miles of Tokyo into ashes and killing about 100,000 people. As a single event, this firebombing was deadlier than the atomic bombings of Hiroshima and Nagasaki.

In late May American bombs dealt deadly blows to Japan's imperial families. Beginning on May 24th, about 500 B-29s rained fire bombs on areas around the Imperial Palace for three days, destroying the homes of many imperial families, including those of Prince Jichibu, Emperor Hirohito's brother, Prince Nashimoto, Masako's father, and Princess Noriko, Masako's sister.

Masako's own house caught fire, but it was put out by the quick actions of her residential guards.

As soon as the bombing ended on May 26th, Masako and Yi Eun rushed to Prince Nashimoto's Palace. On the way they saw countless numbers of charred corpses lying on the streets, some with burst abdomens and others without limbs.

"In normal times, I would have been utterly shocked and terrified, but on that day I was in a daze and feeling numb," she recalled her personal reactions to the war's cruelties.

Her parents' palatial residence had gone up in flames, and all that remained was ashes. Prince Nashimoto and Itsuko, his wife, were standing at the entrance of their family air-raid shelter, stunned and dazed. Without a word, they gave a ghostly look at Masako and Yi Eun.

Masako escorted her parents to her home, and at the same time invited her married sister, Noriko and her family to live with her.

It had been a long while since Masako's families were together, but their future looked only bleak and uncertain.

Beginning in November 1943 under General Douglas MacArthur's Operation Cartwheel (the so-called "island-hopping strategy"), American forces had begun to push across the central Pacific. Following spectacular successes at Tarawa, Kwajalein, and Saipan, they captured the islands of Tinian and Guam by the end of August 1944.

On March 3, 1945 American troops liberated Manila, the capital of the Philippines. After capturing Iwo Jima on March 25-26 they advanced toward Okinawa, killing tens of thousands of Japanese defenders. By June 21 Okinawa, the southernmost island of the Japanese archipelago, was in the hands of American forces.

Following the disastrous defeat on Okinawa, the Japanese public was engulfed in utter despair. Hope for a better day and the courage to hang on completely evaporated, even among the imperial families.

"Only a feeling of resignation and hopelessness was in the air," Masako said as she recalled the mood among her imperial kin.

The ultimate terror hit Japan when the first atomic bomb exploded over Hiroshima on August 6, and three days later the terror was repeated over Nagasaki. Among the tens of thousands of Hiroshima victims was Colonel Yi Woo, the husband of Lady Park Chan-joo, Masako's Korean niece-in-law and a trusted friend.

Yi Woo was the second son of Yi Eun's elder half-brother, Yi Kang. He was a handsome and dashing young man. In accordance with the Japanese policy required of all children of the Yi Royal families, Yi Woo came to Tokyo as a boy to be Japanized, and like Yi Eun, his uncle, he graduated from Gakushuin, the Peers School, and the Military Academy.

Atomic explosion over Nagasaki on August 9, 1945,

Also, as with Yi Eun and Princess Deok-hye, the Japanese government expected him to marry a woman of the Japanese nobility, but Yi Woo adamantly defied the government.

Even though he was educated to become a Japanese and an officer in the Imperial Army, Yi Woo hated and despised everything Japanese. He dreamed of the day when Korea's Joseon Kingdom would be revived and the Yi Royal Families restored to their proper place.

In his heart Yi Woo was a Korean and a member of the Yi Royal Families, and he had resolved early in his youth that he would marry a Korean. To that end, he secretly courted Park Chan-joo, a Korean student in Seoul, and soon the two fell in love.

So when the Imperial Household Ministry started to put pressure on Yi Woo to marry a Japanese, he announced in the media that he was already engaged to Park Chan-joo. This set off a four year-long battle between Yi Woo and the Japanese government.

When threats and cajolery in every form failed to persuade Yi Woo to change his mind, the government finally gave in, and on May 3, 1935 Yi Woo and Park Chan-joo had their wedding.

At the news of Yi Woo's death, Masako was deeply saddened. "He fought so hard to marry Park Chan-joo," she thought to herself, "and they were so deeply in love. Why did he have to become a victim of the world's first atom bomb?"

Masako also remembered the time she had spent with Lady Park in Hokkaido two years before and the pledge they had made to each other then in behalf of their loved ones, that they would strive to keep each other alive at any cost.

"She is only 34 years old, too young to become a widow," Masako lamented. "What is now going to happen to her and her two little children?" she wondered, feeling the fear and the shock that Lady Park would be undergoing.

On August 12, the Imperial Palace held an emergency meeting of all imperial families in the palace's underground air-raid shelter. Everyone was gloomy and depressed. No one spoke and no one stirred. Amidst a stifling silence, they were waiting for the Emperor.

Finally, Emperor Hirohito entered all alone, haggard and tired. In a sullen voice, he revealed his willingness to surrender unconditionally to the Allied Forces. No one among the imperial families raised an objection. Exhausted and hopeless, they were all yearning for peace.

Masako realized that what had to happen came to pass at last. She was both sad and grateful. She was sad because of all the damage, death, and suffering caused by the war, and she was deeply grateful for the Emperor's decision for peace.

It was a sultry day on August 15. Exactly at noon, Emperor Hirohito's surrender speech, sullen and teary, was carried on radio to every home throughout Japan.

Even as the Emperor praised the loyalty and patriotism of his subjects, feelings of shock, dismay, sadness, anger, and relief were gripping the nation.

For Masako, the situation was even more foreboding, uncertain, and complex than for most Japanese.

The empire of Japan had offered her as a sacrifice on the altar of its imperialistic ambitions. That empire and all its ambitions were now in tatters. The union of Korea and Japan, which her marriage was to enhance and symbolize, was broken.

"What is going to happen to us now; to me, to my husband, and to our son?" She pondered.

Most of all, she was worried about her husband, once the crown prince of Korea, now a member of the Japanese nobility and a lieutenant general in the Imperial Army, and the king of Korea's Joseon Kingdom, though in name only.

She was afraid that he would be rejected by his own people of Korea and suffer grave harm because of his marriage to her, a Japanese.

"Your Highness, please do not worry because of me," Masako said to Yi Eun who was absorbed in deadly silence. At the moment she could find nothing else to say in the way of encouraging her husband.

"Please do not worry, my dear," Yi Eun responded in his usual gentle voice. "You are my wife, and Yi Ku is my son. I am no longer the king of Korea. I am a free man. Even if I return to Korea, I will refrain from all political activities. I will live simply as an ordinary husband and father." Yi Eun was firm and resolute. He had already considered and pondered on the eventualities and decided that he would live out the rest of his life as an ordinary citizen.

Fifteen days after Emperor Hirohito's surrender speech, General Douglas MacArthur, Supreme Commander of the Allied Powers, landed at Atsugi Airport in his triumphal entry into Japan. Two days later, on September 2, he formally accepted Japan's surrender on the battleship USS Missouri anchored in Tokyo Bay.

CHAPTER 11

KOREA DURING WWII

In August, 1936, Minami Jiro, former Minister of War in Japan's Wakatsuki Cabinet (1931) and Commander-in-Chief of the Kwantung Army (1934-1936) arrived in Korea as the new Governor General and ruler of Korea.

Calculating and ruthless, General Minami of the Imperial Japanese Army intended to turn Korea's material and human resources into an essential and vital component of Japan's imperialistic war efforts in Asia. To achieve his objective he pushed twin policies of forced assimilation and forced mobilization.

Convinced that a nationalistic and patriotic mind-set would be prerequisite to Koreans' loyal service to Japan and its war efforts, Minami sought to transform Koreans culturally, mentally, and spiritually; that is, he sought to turn Koreans into loyal and patriotic Japanese. To achieve this transformation, Minami first increased the number of elementary schools (grades 1-6) throughout the Korean peninsula in order to brain wash as many Korean children as possible.

Next he prohibited Korean students from using the Korean language in the study and general instruction. Three years later, he would banish the use of Korean language altogether from all schools. He also ordered that only Japanese be used in public offices. "To turn Koreans into Japanese, make them think and speak in Japanese," was his motto.

At the same time, he enforced with vigor an order enacted by the Government General in 1935, which required Korean students and government employees to worship at Japanese Shinto shrines. As all Koreans had venerated the spirits of their ancestors as the most sacred family duty, this move struck at the very heart of Korean spirituality.

The forced Shinto worship was especially traumatic to Korea's Protestant Christians numbering more than 500,000 or about 2% of the Korean population during 1930-1940, for it was compelling them to violate the first two of the Ten Commandments fundamentally important to their faith. Minami took a hard stand against them also because Korean Protestant churches had been actively involved in independence movement.

Under increasing threat of imprisonment and church closure, some gave in, while others, including Pastor Joo Ki-cheol, a prominent Presbyterian leader, chose prison rather than bow down before Shinto deities. Pastor Joo died in prison after five years of imprisonment.[12]

After 1937, Minami also abolished freedom of association among Koreans. Trying to prevent Koreans from forming any groups—cultural, educational, labor, or political—which might oppose his policies, he forced the entire Korean population into mass organizations under his direct control.

These included the Korean Federation of Youth Organizations, various Children's Organizations, the All Korea Writers Federation, the Korean Labor Federation, and the Korean Defense Association, among others.

With direct and tight control of the Korean population through these mass organizations, Minami attempted to mobilize Koreans for Japan's war effort, particularly for labor and military recruitment.

In July, 1939, as Japan began to suffer a manpower shortage with its expansion of warfare on the China mainland, Minami proclaimed the Korean National Draft Order, under which able-bodied Korean males were forcibly sent to work in coal mines, in hydro power dam construction, in railroad and highway projects, and in various war material factories throughout the Japanese islands.

In November, Minami did the unthinkable in an effort to assimilate and destroy the Korean identity. With the so-called Name Change Order, he required all Koreans to Japanize their surname as well as their personal names.

For example, Kim, one of the most prominent Korean surnames, would become Kanemoto, and a Korean given name such as Jeong-wung would become Masao. Consequently, Kim Jeong-wung would become Kanemoto Masao.

Koreans were commanded to comply with the Name Change Order by August 8, 1940. Those who refused the Order would be prevented from entering schools and applying for employment in public offices. Those already working in government offices would be dismissed.

In addition, Koreans without Japanized names would be refused services at all public offices. They would be barred from receiving food and clothing rations from the government. And no mail would be delivered to them.

The Name Change Order was the ultimate insult to Korean identity. Some chose suicide rather than subjecting themselves to the humiliating forced extinction of their cherished personal identity as a Korean.

In 1940, Minami organized Korean schools into semi-military organizations by ordering students to undergo regular military exercises and also to wear green fatigues and a combat hat instead of the customary school uniform and school cap.

Along with militarization of the Korean schools, Minami organized the entire peninsular population into 350,000 Neighborhood Patriotic Associations. Each association, consisting of ten households, became the basic unit for all forms of government-directed activities, including the collection of goods for war purposes, mobilizing labor for public projects, and food rationing.

The same year, Minami issued Rice Regulation Order. First, Korean farmers were strictly forbidden to trade rice in the open market. Secondly all Korean farmers were required to hand over to the government their entire yearly rice production, at a dirt cheap price set by the government. The consequence of the Rice Regulation Order was starvation among farmers, many of whom tried to survive on grass and tree bark.

Also in 1940, Minami abolished freedom of expression among Koreans by shutting down all Korean language newspapers.

In 1941, Minami turned Korean schools into semi-work camps. Students were required to spend half of their classroom hours on labor in public construction and on farms.

Utilizing Neighborhood Patriotic Associations, in June 1941 Minami decided to collect as much metal as possible by ordering Koreans to donate whatever metal they had in their work places and homes.

Along the way, Koreans were also forced to give up even their gold and silver jewelry as well as brass tableware handed down over many generations as family heirlooms.

In May, 1942, General Minami was replaced by Koiso Kuniaki, another Japanese army general. As the new Governor General of Korea, Koiso's mission was to exploit Korea and Koreans ever more effectively in support of Japan's expanding war in China and the Pacific.

In March, 1943, Koiso proclaimed a Military Conscription Order requiring all able Korean males to register for military service.

Soon thousands of Korean young men were sent to various battle fronts in China and the South Pacific. During 1944-45, some 209,279 Korean youths were inducted into the Japanese army to serve as frontline soldiers, prison guards, and sentries as well as laborers in the battle zones.

Even in the battlefields, Koreans were harshly discriminated against. On Tinian, for example, Japanese soldiers massacred five thousand Korean laborers on the eve of an expected major American assault because they feared that the Koreans might attack them from behind while they were fighting American troops.

Because of the discrimination as well as other reasons, Korean draftees defected almost from the beginning. As early as March 1944, those stationed in China deserted their units and turned their guns against the Japanese in solidarity with anti-Japanese resistance forces in various parts of China. Others, after defecting, disappeared into thin air.

In July 1944, Abe Nobuyuki, another Imperial army general and the former prime minister of Japan (August 1939-Janury 1940), replaced Koiso.

As soon as he arrived in Korea, Abe proclaimed Women Mobilization Order to recruit young Korean women from rural locales, 12-40 years old, to serve Japan's war efforts. In the course of a few months, Japan forcibly shipped more than 200,000 of them to various battle fronts to serve Japanese soldiers as sex slaves, the so-called "comfort women." Some of them had been recruited with the promise of a well-paying factory job while others were forcibly kidnapped from streets and even from their homes.

Such forcible kidnapping of Korean women by Japanese authorities had actually begun as early as in 1943. In his interview with the *Dong-A Ilbo* on November 11, 1991, Yoshida Seiji, one of the official Japanese "Korean women hunters" who was directly involved in such kidnapping, made a tearful confession that from 1943 to August 1945, under the order of Japan's Imperial Army and the Japanese government, he himself kidnapped more than 1000 Korean women and shipped them to the battle fronts. He said,

> "I would surround Korean villages with the help of armed Japanese police, whom I led from Japan and snatch the Korean women, mostly young mothers of three or four year-old children, from the hands of their desperately crying children . . . They probably never came home."[13]

The "Comfort Woman" statue
Representing all Korean young women whose lives were destroyed by
the Japanese during WWII, the statue sits on a chair in front of the
Japanese Embassy in Seoul with a sorrowful gaze toward the Embassy.

By the end of World War II, more than four million Koreans were dispersed throughout Asia and the Pacific under Japan's war mobilization, working in mines and factories, building air fields, roads, harbors, and dams, or fighting an unwanted war in foreign lands. More than 70,000 of them perished in Hiroshima and Nagasaki alone.

On the other side of this picture, at the same time, Korean nationalists and patriots were pursuing Korean liberation movement against the Japanese. Driven out of Korea by the repressive Japanese Government General police forces, most of the resistance forces had their operational bases abroad.

In China, Kim Ku's Korean National Party and Kim Weon-bong's Korean Revolutionary Party formed a united front, and after 1937 joined the Chinese Nationalists in their war against the Japanese.

Members of the Korean Communist Party, formed originally in 1920 in Shanghai, largely worked against Japanese forces in alliance with Mao Zedong's Chinese Communist Party in North China, under the leadership of Mu Cheong.

In 1940 Kim Ku, Jo So-ang, and Lee Cheong-cheon, the leading figures of the Korean Provisional Government, at that point, formed the Korean Independence Party, and soon thereafter established a united resistant front called the Korean Restoration Army. Emerging as one of the largest Korean military forces in China, with about 3000 troops, the Korean Restoration Army worked with Chang Kai-shek's Nationalists. It also cooperated with the U.S. military, providing assistance in intelligence gathering, espionage, propaganda activities, and guerrilla warfare, among other things.

In the Soviet Union, Kim Il-sung, a former anti-Japanese guerilla fighter in Manchuria, was working with the Soviet Far East Army and patiently waiting for the day of Japan's defeat and of his return to Korea.

In the United States, Syngman Rhee, a graduate of Harvard and Princeton and a revered Korean patriot in exile, had been waging an anti-Japanese campaign for 35 years, and in anticipation of Japan's collapse, was laying ground work for the establishment of an independent, democratic nation in Korea.

In the Korean peninsula itself, by the middle of 1944 Koreans were sensing that Japan's defeat was certain and that Korea would soon be liberated. In this atmosphere, a number of anti-Japanese elements fled into Korea's rugged mountains, where they organized armed resistance groups. Their primary target was Japanese police stations in rural locales, much hated by Korean farmers. Also, some of Korean youths about to be inducted into the Japanese army escaped Japanese authorities by joining resistance forces in the mountains.

In August 1944, Lyuh Un-hyeong, a highly respected Korean patriot and a prominent leader of the Korean independence movement, secretly formed the Korea Reconstruction Alliance. Comprised of various leaders of farmers, young laborers, women, young students, and teachers, the Reconstruction Alliance's primary aim was to gain full and complete liberation from Japan in cooperation with victorious Allied Powers and to secure the freedom and independence of Koreans in accordance with democratic principles.

The Alliance launched anti-Japanese sabotage operations behind the line within Korea, disrupting the movement of war materials and urging Korean youths to escape military conscription at all costs. With the Allied victory over Japan in 1945, all these forces emerged as major players in Korea's post-war reconstruction.

CHAPTER 12

KOREA AFTER LIBERATION

Emperor Hirohito's unconditional surrender to the Allied Powers on August 15, 1945, brought tumultuous jubilation to Koreans everywhere. People of all walks of life, young and old, men, women and children, flowed into public squares and streets, shouting "Liberation! Liberation! Liberty! Freedom!" and waving the Korean flags long banned by the Japanese Government General.

In the morning of that same day, Korean independence leader Lyuh Wun-hyeong received a call from the Government General asking for a meeting, in which a Japanese representative pleaded for Lyuh's cooperation in protecting Japanese citizens and enabling their safe repatriation to Japan.

In response, Lyuh demanded that the Government General free all political prisoners immediately, guarantee a three months supply of food for all Koreans, and absolutely refrain from interfering with Korean political activities aimed at creation of a free and independent nation in the peninsula.

The Government General, in a desperate situation, agreed, and immediately Lyuh Wun-hyeong and his compatriot, Ahn Jae-hong, formed a Korea Reconstruction Preparation Committee (KRPC) comprised of prominent Koreans. Overnight its branches called "people's committees," sprang up everywhere throughout the peninsula, taking control of local administrations.

In the meantime, earth-shaking decisions far beyond the control of Koreans had already been made in faraway places, which would affect their future and their nation. In February 1945, at the Yalta Conference dealing with future international issues, Franklin Roosevelt, Joseph Stalin, and Winston Churchill agreed to put the Korean peninsula under an international trusteeship for up to 30 years. Also, Roosevelt, in his ardent desire to hasten Japan's surrender, ill-advisedly invited Joseph Stalin to belatedly declare war on Japan. Stalin accepted the invitation in return for occupation zones in Manchuria and North Korea, and promised to attack Japanese forces in Manchuria and Korea within two to three months after Germany's defeat was sealed.

The American invitation of a Russian advance into Manchuria and Korea was a major American blunder and a golden opportunity for Stalin to realize Russia's long-held dream to have a foothold in that region. Accordingly, on August 9, sixty Soviet army divisions crossed Manchuria to attack the Japanese Kwantung Army, and the following day Russian forces landed at Unggi and Najin, port cities in northern Korea.

While Soviet forces were establishing themselves as the new occupiers of northern Korea, American forces were still on Okinawa, 600 miles away.

Suddenly, becoming gravely concerned about rapid Soviet advances in East Asia and about the possible fall of the entire Korean peninsula to the Russians, the United States government decided to stop the Russian advance with a specific demarcation line.

Hastily charged with the task of devising a plan to divide Korea between Russian and American occupation zones, two U.S. Army colonels in the War Department, Charles H. Bonesteel and Dean Rusk, took only 30 minutes to decide on the 38th parallel which ran roughly between the cities of Pyongyang and Seoul (according to an old map in National Geographic magazine).

The line was approved by the Joint Chiefs of Staff and approved by President Truman on August 14. Two days later, Stalin agreed to the American proposal, and the Russian southward advance stopped at the 38th parallel.

It was one of the worst and most ill-fated decisions in human history, not only for Korea and the Koreans but also for America, for within a few years that decision would cost Korea the lives of 3 million men, women, and children, and America more than 36,000 young American lives.

On September 8, nearly three weeks after the Soviet occupation of the North was completed, American troops finally arrived at Inchon, and on the following day they formally accepted Japanese surrender in Korea and simultaneously established the United States Army Military Government in Korea (USAMGIK).

When the American soldiers landed in Inchon thousands of Koreans lined up along streets to give them a rousing welcome, for they believed that the Americans were their liberators.

To Koreans' utter dismay, however, General John R. Hodge, commander of the U.S. occupying forces, announced that the Japanese Government General would be kept intact in Korea. Furthermore, he informed his officers that Korea was an enemy of the United States. At the time, Washington knew very little about Korea and Korean feelings and aspirations, and American involvement in the Korean peninsula thus began with grave missteps.

Three months later, on December 7, the Allied foreign ministers met in Moscow and decided to place the Korean peninsula under an international trusteeship for five years. They also agreed to a joint U.S.-U.S.S.R. commission to help organize a provisional government for all Korea.

Amidst these events, Korea was torn in myriad ways—socially, economically, and ideologically, with antagonism, open as well as hidden, between the anti-Japanese elements and former collaborators, between landlords and tenants, between the haves and the have-nots, between conservatives and liberals, between capitalists and socialists/communists, between pro-American and pro-Soviet factions, and between anti- and pro-trusteeship elements, among others.

On the top of it all, Japan's 40-year rule and its forced Japanization attempts had wrought havoc on Korean national and cultural identity.

In this disarrayed and conflicted situation there emerged many politically ambitious men vying for recognition and leadership.

Lyuh Wun-hyeong, working tirelessly since August 15, was leading the Korea Reconstruction Preparation Committee (KRPC), comprising multitudes of factions including peasants and workers' unions. On September 6, delegates of the Committee decided to establish the People' Republic of Korea (PRK) and hold national elections for all Korea. Even though Lyuh himself was not a communist, he was willing to help create a coalition government, with leaders from the right as well as from the left, and including communists, for the sake of national unity.

Following its formation, the PRK and its branches began to remove the vestiges of Japanese rule including former collaborators, further enhancing social turmoil of southern Korea.

Working semi-underground, Park Heon-yeong, a long-time communist leader, was busily organizing communist cells among Korean workers, farmers, young men returning from war fronts, school teachers, and even members of the Constabulary, South Korea's security forces.

In reaction to PRK's high-handed tactics and its close ties with communists, wealthy landlords, businessmen, and former Japanese collaborators joined hands to organize a conservative political party. On September 16, it officially became the Korean Democratic Party (KDP) and immediately denounced communism and communist activities in the South. Its members also worked closely with USAMGIK.

On September 25, Kim Il-sung, a 33 year old anti-Japanese guerilla fighter in exile in Russia arrived in Pyongyang. Five months later, in February 1946, he formed the Interim People's Committee, a *de facto* provisional central government in Pyongyang, with Stalin's approval and himself at the top. He also created the People's Army.

On October 12 Syngman Rhee, with the help of General Douglas MacArthur, returned from his 30-year exile in the U.S. MacArthur considered Rhee to be the only viable leader of the Korean people and asked General Hodge to support him for that role. On October 20, USAMGIK duly presented him to the Korean public amidst great welcoming fanfare.

Kim Il-sung   *Syngman Rhee*

Source: public domain

Rhee's primary goal was to establish a free, independent, and democratic government in Korea, and to achieve his objective, he organized his political supporters around the conservative Korean Democratic Party.

As a staunch anticommunist, Rhee denounced not only all Korean communists and their sympathizers such as Lyuh but also the Soviets who were giving support to them. He also disdained moderate leaders such as Song Jin-woo and Jang Deok-soo, and came into conflict with Kim Ku, who, upon his return from China, sought to have opposing factions unified.

Buried among the communists, the right wing advocates, and the middle of the road factions were a few loyal remnants of the old Yi Joseon establishment seeking to restore the Joseon Kingdom dead since 1910.

Meanwhile, USAMGIK, under Washington's order to cooperate with the Soviets, sought to create a centrist coalition government around Lyuh Wun-hyeong, finding both Syngman Rhee and Kim Il-sung too extreme. In the atmosphere of polarized politics of Korea, however, USAMGIK's efforts were hopelessly stymied. Simultaneously, by early 1947 Soviet intentions in Eastern Europe convinced Washington that the communists were on a march for world conquest and had to be stopped.

Washington's new perspective on the Soviets gave birth to the Truman Doctrine, first revealed on March 12, 1947. It warned the American public and the free world of "domino effects" and called for active resistance against communist advances.

And in order to stop further Communist advances in the Far East, Washington sought to create a separate government in the South to counter Kim Il-sung's provisional central government in Pyongyang. This would result in a permanent division of the peninsula, a home of a unified nation for over a thousand years. The U.S. plan, therefore, was not a propitious beginning for the newly liberated post-Japanese Korea.

On November 14, 1947, with US endorsement, the UN General Assembly passed a resolution to create a UN commission to facilitate a fair and open election in Korea in order to create a free and independent government.

When the Soviets and Pyongyang refused to recognize the UN commission, however, South Korea, on May 10, 1948, held a general election under the supervision of United Nations Temporary Commission on Korea (UNTCOK), to choose members of the National Assembly.

Two months later, on August 15, the Assembly adopted a constitution and established the Republic of Korea with Syngman Rhee as its first president.

Kim Il-sung responded by holding elections in the northern half of Korea on August 25, and 15 days later, on September 9, established the Democratic People's Republic of Korea with himself as the head.

With two separate governments in the peninsula, the division of Korea and its people became permanent. It was a moment of gargantuan national tragedy inasmuch as the geo-political division would soon bring about a civil war, destruction, and carnage with more than three million Korean military and civilian population perishing.

If there was any small consolation to Koreans in those fateful days, it was a report from Tokyo that the International Military Tribunal for the Far East had tried Minami Jiro and Koiso Kuniaki, the ruthless wartime Governor Generals of Korea, as Class A war criminals and sentenced them to life imprisonment.

The geopolitical division of the peninsula became a cursed nightmare for all Koreans. Every Korean wished and longed for quick reunification. And no Korean was more eager and determined to achieve it than Kim Il-sung, regardless of the cost.

In March 1949, less than 6 months after the division was established, Kim Il-sung travelled to Moscow to ask for Joseph Stalin's permission and support to invade the South and reunify Korea by military means. Having secured a firm promise of military support from Stalin, in April 1950, Kim Il-sung launched a massive surprise attack against South Korea three months later.

In the early morning of June 25, some 231,000 well-trained North Korean troops crossed the 38th parallel at all major fronts, on land and in the air, equipped with Soviet war-machines including 200 artillery pieces, 274 Soviet-built T-34 tanks, 250 Yak fighters and attack bombers, and 35 reconnaissance aircraft. An ill-equipped and ill-prepared South Korean force of 65,000 combat troops, with no tanks and no air force, collapsed and retreated. President Harry Truman of the United States, determined to stop the communist advance, immediately ordered General MacArthur to help Syngman Rhee of South Korea in repelling the invaders.

On the same day, the UN Security Council met and unanimously condemned the North Korean invasion with its Resolution 82. Two days later, on June 27, the Security Council issued Resolution 83, recommending that UN member states provide military assistance to the Republic of Korea (South Korea) in repelling the invaders and establishing peace and security in the peninsula.

By then, the Red Army of North Korea was capturing Seoul, the South's capital, and racing down the peninsula.

By early September, more than 180,000 UN troops, nearly 90% of whom were Americans, were on Korean battle fronts around the Pusan perimeter, a small piece of land around Pusan and Taegu in the peninsula's southeast corner bounded by the Naktong River.

In the course of two months, the war had turned much of Korea into piles of ashes and rubble. Millions of Koreans became refugees, and untold numbers of Koreans were dying, military and civilian alike.

Women of Hamheung City searching for relatives
killed by North Korean Communist troops during the Korean War
Source: US Army Photo, public domain

On September 15, with General MacArthur's spectacular success in the Inchon landing, between Seoul and Pyongyang near the 38th parallel, the tide of the war turned against the North Korean communist invaders. UN and South Korean troops marched north all the way to Korea's Yalu River boundary with China, only to be ambushed there by Chinese communist soldiers sent by Mao Zedong.

Under heavy casualties the UN and South Korean troops retreated once again, all the way to Daejon in south-central Korea. On January 4, 1951, Seoul fell once again to communist forces.

With a massive counter offensive, UN and South Korean troops pushed the Chinese Communists back across the 38th parallel, where the war remained stale-mated for nearly three years until the warring parties signed a cease-fire treaty on July 27, 1953.

In the end, Kim Il-sung achieved nothing except destruction and the immense suffering of the Korean people for decades to come.

CHAPTER 13

MASAKO IN POSTWAR JAPAN

Following their unconditional surrender, the world, as the Japanese had known it, came to an end.

No longer was there the mighty Japanese empire that had extended all the way from Sakhalin Island in the north to the islands of Java, Timor, and New Guinea in the South Pacific. And no longer was Emperor Hirohito a living god guiding Japan's destiny.

Japan was now under a blue-eyed foreign ruler, an American shogun in the name of General Douglas MacArthur, Supreme Commander for Allied Powers (SCAP), who formally accepted Japan's surrender on September 2, 1945 in Tokyo Bay on board the battleship USS Missouri and became the *de facto* governor of Japan.

General Douglas MacArthur and Emperor Hirohito, 1945
Source: US Army Photo, public domain

As for the Japanese people, with their empire in tatters and many of their cities laid in ash and rubble, they were utterly demoralized psychologically and spiritually.

The heavy wartime bombing had destroyed 40% of Japan's 66 major cities and rendered about 30% of their populations homeless. In Tokyo, 65% of all residences were destroyed. In all, nearly 9 million people were homeless throughout Japan in 1945.

The dire situation was further aggravated by millions of dispirited and exhausted soldiers returning from the war fronts. Nearly 4.5 million servicemen demobilized at the end of the war were identified as either wounded or sick.

Every major city was filled with demoralized ex-soldiers, war widows, orphans, the homeless and the unemployed. The whole nation was plagued with poverty, hunger, alcoholism, drug addiction, prostitution, and diseases including a high rate of tuberculosis, as well as violent and non-violent crimes.

In the midst of such social turmoil, General MacArthur, the new ruler of Japan, began to issue a series of decrees intended to dismantle the socio-cultural and political edifice of old Japan and remake it entirely new. His ultimate aim was to demilitarize and democratize Japan.

One of MacArthur's first decrees was an edict that prohibited prominent military, political, and business leaders, numbering about 200,000, from holding a public office. This included most of the male members of various imperial families, who were high ranking officers in Japan's Imperial Army.

And beginning on September 11, 1945, SCAP began to arrest thousands of Japanese suspected of war crimes, sending them off to Sugamo Prison in Tokyo, built in the 1920s to house political prisoners.

Among them was Masako's father, Prince Nashimoto Morimasa, a retired field marshal in Japan's Imperial Army and the chief priest of the Grand Shrine of Ise (1937-1947), the holiest state Shinto shrine in Japan.

On December 3, an American military police jeep arrived outside the home of Prince Nashimoto. The military police came to pick up the 72-year old prince for the Sugamo Prison. It was a cold frosty morning. As her aged, frail father was driven off, holding in his weathered hands a pair of underwear to keep warm in the prison, Masako wept aloud.

Among all the members of Japan's Imperial families, Nashimoto was the only one arrested and sent to prison, suspected of war crimes. Masako was dumbfounded.

"He was retired from the military long before the war," she said to herself. "He had nothing to do with the Pearl Harbor attack. Why is he arrested? What did he do wrong? How could he survive in the prison under this cold, freezing temperature?" she wondered.

A few days later, Masako went to the prison to visit her father but was forbidden to see him. American guards at the prison even refused to accept the food she took for him. With no communication from him, Masako and her family could only worry and imagine the worst possible outcome.

One day, a Mr. Nakamura, an official from the Japanese Foreign Ministry, came to the house with a report that Prince Nashimoto was suffering from frost bite. Masako and her family could imagine what life in prison was like and the hardship he was undergoing, but there was nothing they could do to help.

Prince Nashimoto was released without charges four months later, on April 13, 1946, but his imprisonment in the middle of the freezing winter was an inexplicable part of the agony and misfortune visited upon Masako and her family in the aftermath of Japan's demise.

To make things worse for Masako, her financial resources dried up.

Until the end of the war, Yi Eun was "the king of Joseon Kingdom" and at the same time a member of Japan's Imperial Household, according to the Imperial Household law, revised soon after Korea's annexation. As such, the Yi Royal Household Administration in Seoul bankrolled Yi Eun, covering all of his financial needs through the Imperial Household Ministry in Tokyo. All that automatically ended as Korea's annexation was annulled with Japan's unconditional surrender to the Allied forces.

On August 15, 1945, Yi Eun suddenly became a hapless Korean citizen living in Japan as an alien like so many other Koreans who had come to Japan in pre-war days. With Korea severed from Japan and the Yi Royal Household Administration abolished, Yi Eun's financial resources completely dried up.

Recalling the crisis situation, Masako said, "Now that all relations between Japan and Korea were severed, we became international orphans, completely uprooted in Japan as well as in Korea. Our immediate problem was how to survive physically."

Having been born and raised in royal families, Masako and Yi Eun knew nothing about finance or business matters. They had no understanding of how money was made or how it was spent. These matters were all handled by their staff.

Yi Eun had spent all his adult life in the military; consequently, outside military circles he had no friends. Having no close friend or acquaintance in the business world for advice, he felt helpless, and each day he sank deeper and deeper in despair.

His cousin, Prince Yi Keon, a former officer in Japan's Imperial Army, had decided to open a red bean porridge shop on a street corner of Shibuya market. He looked pathetic and lowly but had no other choice to make a living.

Masako and Yi Eun considered returning to Korea as part of the tens of thousands of Korean repatriates leaving Japan. They were somewhat encouraged by the news that some loyal remnants of the old Joseon Kingdom were eagerly waiting for Yi Eun's return.

That thought, however, was short-lived. Reports arrived from Korea that some of the radical political groups were calling for trial and punishment of Yi Eun "as a traitor, who lived in luxury under the protection of the Japanese." One Korean leader, Park Keon-wung, was even demanding that Yi Eun "commit suicide for his traitorous acts."

Yi Eun had already been suffering inside with a deep sense of guilt about his protected life in Japan and his military career, rising ultimately to the rank of lieutenant general in Japan' Imperial Army.

The reports from Korea only deepened his sense of guilt. For days, he could not sleep, nor could he eat.

As long as Masako had known him, Yi Eun had been a proud and self-reliant man. He was always self-confident and excelled in all things he undertook. He was a model student and model officer, commanding respect from his fellow officers. He was also a good father, teaching his son in all things proper.

As she watched Yi Eun now languishing in despair, guilt, and helplessness, Masako became frightened. She sensed that her family was falling apart in the midst of events beyond their control.

Alarmed, Masako said to herself, "I cannot allow this to happen. I know that in difficult times families are torn, and personal happiness is trampled upon. But I will not let my family become a victim of these hard times. I must save and keep my family at any cost!"

To keep her family—Yi Eun, Yi Ku and herself—together, Masako would endure and undergo any hardship. "Especially for Yi Ku's sake," she said to herself, "I will endure all things."

On December 29, Yi Ku, now 14 years old, came home from his place of wartime refuge in mountainous Nasu, north of Tokyo. Seeing her son, Masako was resolved to do everything in her power to hold her family together and, most of all, to safeguard Yi Ku's wellbeing and his future. To Masako, however, the world waiting for her was raw and wild, often a brutally cold and unkind place.

For 45 years, the princess had lived a sheltered life among Japan's imperial families. She had never ventured out alone. She did not even know how to use money, buy a city bus ticket, or ride a bus. Nor did she know the streets of Tokyo. She was always accompanied by personal aides and guards who did everything for her.

In prewar times, a 30-member staff assigned from the Yi Royal Household Administration ran her household. When the war ended, the staff was reduced to eight, and now there was only one frail old maid.

Suddenly Masako found herself doing daily chores including cooking, cleaning, and even grocery shopping in open street markets. To her the markets, noisy with hawkers, peddlers, and crowds milling and pushing, were intimidating.

In her first awkward and timid shopping trips, with no experience in haggling, she would pay whatever price the vendors would name, and often became an easy target of cheaters and swindlers.

Sometimes, lost in the crowds or on unfamiliar streets, she wondered in circles for hours. One day while returning home from the market, she boarded a street car only to discover that the car was heading into a wrong direction. As she nervously struggled to get off, holding her grocery basket with both hands, a thief ran away with her purse.

Terrified, Masako could not move except for shaking and crying. And for days afterwards she was afraid to go out.

Masako's father, once a dignified Field Marshal in Japan's Imperial Army, changed drastically since his release from Sugamo Prison. During the four months imprisonment, he had aged and become weak beyond recognition. Frail and exhausted physically and mentally, he just stayed in the house.

In the spring of 1946, SCAP issued an order requiring all imperial families to pay capital property tax. Initial taxes were imposed on 70 to 80% of the assessed value of all their real estate. For Masako and Yi Eun, with no source of income and little cash at hand, the SCAP order presented them with their first major family crisis.

Learning about their quandary, the chairman of the House of Councilors (the Upper House) in Japan's Parliament, offered to rent their Akasaka mansion to be used as his official residence.

With little choice, Masako and her family moved into a one-room apartment behind the mansion, once used as maids' quarters.

The chairman, Masako soon learned, had no intention to actually live in the mansion, but he was only trying to help Masako and Yi Eun in their dire straits.

When their property taxes were paid with the rental money, not much was left for living expenses, with inflation sky-rocketing continuously.

They sold their villas at Oiso and Imaihama, southwest of Tokyo along the coast. For Masako, the Oiso villa was a special place with many unforgettable memories. There she had spent some of the happiest days of her early life as a young girl. There she first learned about her betrothal to Yi Eun, and there she and Yi Eun discovered that they were deeply in love with each other, sharing their most romantic moments.

After the villas, Masako sold her long cherished furniture items and personal valuables collected through her life time. It was the only way they could survive.

The same things were happening at the home of Prince Nashimoto and Princess Itsuko, Masako's parents. First, they had sold what had been left of their grand mansion after the massive B-29 bombings of May 1945: an empty piece of land. Then they sold their two villas and finally their furniture. To make things worse for them, robbers broke into their house not once but twice, stealing all their clothes.

Having learned of their plight, Emperor and Empress Hirohito personally sent clothes to help the Nashimotos to get by through the winter.

This was the fallen status of Japan's imperial families at the end of the war. They were all in the same boat, lost and stumbling around in the dark trying to make a living.

Prince Kan'in Haruhito operated a hardware store and tour business, while Prince Higashikuni Naruhiko, Masako's uncle, who was a former premier and a general in Japan's Imperial Army, operated a noodle shop and a used goods store in Tokyo. All alike, in their naiveté about ordinary matters, they became easy targets of cheaters and swindlers in the cunning world of business.

General MacArthur resolutely pursued his goal of democratizing Japan, and most fundamental in the process was the adoption of a new constitution guaranteeing civil and human rights and democratic principles and institutions.

In consultation with Japanese lawyers, political leaders, and constitutional scholars, MacArthur's staff drafted a new constitution in February 1946.

Following reviews and some revisions by Japanese government officials, the new constitution was approved and adopted by the Diet on October 6-7, and was signed by the Emperor, the Prime Minister, and all members of the Cabinet on November 3. On May 3, 1947, it went into force.

As a revision of the Meiji Constitution, the new constitution, under Article 1, specified that the sovereignty of the nation resided not in the Emperor but in the people of Japan and that the Emperor was merely a symbol of the state willed by the people.

Under Chapter IV, the sovereign powers of the nation would be exercised by representatives in the Diet, elected by the people. Under Article 9, the Japanese people would forever renounce war as a sovereign right of the nation and the threat or use of force as means of settling international disputes.

Particularly prominent in the new constitution, as specified in Chapter III, were guarantees of individual rights to "life, liberty, and the pursuit of happiness," equality before the law, and freedom of speech, assembly, and association. Chapter III also outlawed discrimination based on race, creed, sex, social status, family origin, education, property, or income.

Directly affecting Masako and her family was Article 14 under Chapter III forbidding the Japanese government from recognizing peers and peerage. No honors could be hereditary or granted as a special privilege.

Accordingly, as of October 14, 1947, only Emperor Hirohito and his immediate family and kin (his wife, his widowed mother, five of his six children, his three brothers and their wives) would keep their imperial status and titles. All eleven branches of the imperial family, including that of Prince Nashimoto Morimasa, and the Yi Royal Family, would be demoted to the status of common citizens and required to register as such at their local city office.

More than one thousand Japanese families of prewar Japan's exalted peerage system lost their titles and ranks of nobility, be it prince (or duke), marquis, earl (count), or baron along with every special privilege—social, political, and economic—associated with their status as peers.

Thus, Princess Masako and Yi Eun became common citizens. As for Yi Eun, he was now not only a common citizen but a Korean and a foreigner residing in Japan.

When the Japanese government ordered all foreigners in Japan to register with their local administrative office, Yi Eun did so on October 14, 1947 as a Korean resident in Japan. At the same time, by virtue of her marriage to Yi Eun, Princess Masako registered herself as Yi Masako.

Under the new democratic constitution, the fabric of old imperial Japan was thus torn asunder, and a radical opening up of Japan's social structure was initiated. The imperial and peerage families which had served as the social and political elite of Imperial Japan were no more, and it was Japan's common citizenry that was now taking charge.

This was made clear on the night before the old peerage system would effectively end. Matsumoto Jiichiro, representing in the Diet the Eta people, the lowest social class in old Japan, stood up and made the fateful announcement. Matsumoto's act was a powerful symbol of Japanese society becoming radically new.

In the evening of October 17, Emperor Hirohito gathered all 51 members of collateral branches of the Imperial Family, who had become commoners just three days before, for "the last supper."

After drinking a glass of wine with the guests, the Emperor solemnly but emotionally announced: "This is your last gathering as Princes and Princesses." He then thanked them for their loyal service and expressed his utmost hope that they would endure and rise above the hard and difficult days lying ahead with wisdom and dignity.

Gone with the Emperor's farewell was the world in which Princess Masako had lived and had her being. Facing Masako now, the wife of Yi Eun, a former Korean king without a kingdom, was a world full of uncertainty and apprehension.

CHAPTER 14

FROM REJECTION TO A TASTE OF HAPPINESS

In the Korean peninsula, meanwhile, the chaotic social and political turmoil among many rival factions finally resulted in the creation, in August 1948, of two separate governments: Kim Il-sung's People's Democratic Republic of Korea in the north supported by the Soviets, and Syngman Rhee's Republic of Korea in the south, supported by the United States.

As relative calm was established under the new government, Masako and Yi Eun thought about visiting Seoul. It was five years since they had last visited their son's grave, too long for Masako to bear. She also deeply missed Queen Yun, to whom she had made a promise in June 1943 to visit again soon.

On his own, Yi Eun was also pondering his future in Korea, not in politics but simply as a common citizen. Having learned about all the political fights and threats against his person he had absolutely no desire to become involved in Korea's politics.

After all, Korea was his home. He went to Japan not of his own volition but as a political hostage against his will. During his life of exile, he shed tears more than once as he longed for his home, his parents, and his friends. Most of them were now gone, but his heart was still in Seoul and especially in the gardens of Deoksoo and Changdeok Palaces.

He also wanted to meet and congratulate Syngman Rhee on his election as the first president of the Republic. He believed that Syngman Rhee, with his illustrious educational background in

America, his unquestioned patriotism, and recognized leadership in Korea's independence movement, was exactly what Korea needed to grow and develop as a free and democratic nation.

He was especially pleased that Syngman Rhee was one of his own kin. Yi Eun and Syngman Rhee were of the same Jeonju Yi Clan that had established the Joseon Kingdom.

Eager to visit Korea, Yi Eun and Masako contacted the Seoul government through Korean representatives in Tokyo seeking Korean passports. Syngman Rhee's government, however, made no response.

Instead, Syngman Rhee demanded that Yi Eun and Masako turn their Akasaka Mansion in Kioicho over to Korean representatives in Tokyo to be used as their mission office.

"We are barely surviving with rental money from the property." Masako sighed, "We would have no place to go if we lost it."

Syngman Rhee, Masako thought, was downright cruel and insensitive. The Akasaka mansion was not even a Korean government property. She and Yi Eun had received it in 1930 as a gift from Japan's Imperial Household Ministry. As such, they considered it their own personal property.

In February, 1950, Masako learned from the Office of Korean Diplomatic Mission in Tokyo that Syngman Rhee was coming to Tokyo to meet General MacArthur. Rhee wanted to thank the general for the support he had given to Korea and to him personally in the process of establishing the Republic of Korea.

Still eager to visit Korea, Masako and Yi Eun asked to see the president and make an appeal for help directly in person. At the Diplomatic Mission, they were cordially led to Rhee by Dr. Shin Heung-woo, head of the Mission. The president was surrounded by several high government officials from Seoul, including his secretary of foreign affairs.

After exchanging formal greetings, Masako and Yi Eun mentioned their desire to visit Korea and appealed for his help.

"As the president responded, he didn't even look at us." Masako recalled. "With his face turned toward the window, he said in a blunt tone, 'If you desire to come to Korea, come.'" He then went silent. Not a word of welcome or encouragement. Syngman Rhee was as cold as ice. So were the officials, staring down with a blank look.

Yi Eun was confounded. With nothing more to say, Masako and Yi Eun thanked Rhee for seeing them and left the room.

Masako and Yi Eun were greatly disappointed by President Syngman Rhee's brusque treatment. As the president of Korea, however, Rhee had his own reasons. He was one of Korea's most ardent nationalists of the time, and for nearly 40 years he had lived in exile, fighting for Korean independence and exposing Japanese atrocities in Korea.

Rhee knew all about Yi Eun's misfortunes and had sympathy for him, but at the same time he, as most Korean nationalists, had long resented Yi Eun's leading a comfortable life under Japanese protection, at the expense of the Korean treasury.

Syngman Rhee's new Republic of Korea was in financial desperation, and Rhee believed that Yi Eun should atone partly by gifting his mansion to Korea to be used as Korea's Diplomatic Mission in Tokyo.

While the conflict between Syngman Rhee, Yi Eun, and Masako continued, Korea was suddenly engulfed in a war on June 25, 1950 with the North Korean invasion of South Korea.

As well-armed North Korean Communist troops swiftly marched across the 38th parallel and reached the outskirts of Seoul in just two days, General MacArthur's office in Tokyo was quietly considered calling Yi Eun into active duty in the Korean defense forces.

At that particular time, no officer in the Korean army had as much training as Yi Eun in military science, and none of them had achieved the rank of lieutenant general in Japan's Imperial Army. Yi Eun, therefore, became a person of great interest among Americans in Tokyo as Syngman Rhee's troops were collapsing all over the battle fronts.

A rumor began to circulate among desperate Koreans that General Yi Eun was on his way to Korea from Japan to help repel the communist invaders and that he would soon become Korea's defense minister. Amidst such rumors, remnant old Joseon Kingdom loyalists were organizing welcoming parties for Yi Eun.

When Syngman Rhee learned of these developments he was enraged and ordered everyone around him not to even mention Yi Eun's name.

In truth, however, the subject of Korea's military defense system had long been one of Yi Eun's foremost interests.

Early in his life of exile, he became painfully aware that his Joseon Kingdom suffered its tragic fate because it had failed to develop a strong military defense system. Consequently, he wanted to learn all about the military and hence welcomed opportunities of attending military schools in Japan—to prepare himself for the day that his father had admonished him to wait for, with patience.

Yi Eun hinted this in a conversation he had with a Korean young man who came to visit him on August 15, 1945. The young man had been an officer in the Japanese Imperial Army but was now on his way back to Korea following Japan's defeat. During their visit Yi Eun said to the young Korean officer, "When I look back to my childhood life in Korea's royal palace, I remember the overwhelming number of scholar officials in the palace and royal court. For centuries, Korea had emphasized pen over sword, deemphasizing the importance of the military."

"Consequently," he continued, "when Japan, with its strong military, encroached upon our nation, Korea could not defend itself. Korea became easy prey to the Japanese aggression . . .

In my situation there is little I can do now, but when you return to Korea, build a strong military defense for the new Korea to withstand any future aggressor . . ."[14] Yi Eun thus challenged his Korean guest.

The young Korean officer thus being admonished by Yi Eun, a Lieutenant General in Japan's Imperial Army, was Captain Lee Hyeong-geun.

Upon his return to Korea, Captain Lee helped establish the Korean Defense Force. His army identification number was #1. In time, he became a four star general and served as chief of staff of the Republic of Korea's Army.

In light of the restored Korean nation's needs, especially during the Korean War, Yi Eun could have become an indispensible asset not only to Syngman Rhee but to his nation. Unfortunately, personal feelings and politics stood in the way.

In the chaos and confusion of Japan's postwar days, Yi Ku, the only son of Masako and Yi Eun, had been finding his way and was slowly but firmly building his future independently.

Handsome and delicate, like his mother, Yi Ku was also bright and sensitive. When he saw Japan in tatters in the aftermath of its humiliating defeat at the hands of Allied Powers he quickly sensed that his future lay not in Japan but in America. Especially so, now that he realized he was neither Japanese nor Korean.

Yi Ku's admiration for America grew as he made friends with Americans. At 15, while working as a leader of his high school Boy Scouts group he met a Mr. Fisher, an American from Kentucky who was in charge of Tokyo Boy Scouts activities. Through him Yi Ku not only learned all about America and the great opportunities it held for his future, but also improved his English.

As days went by Yi Ku and his best friend, Fushimi Hiroaki, a former prince but now a commoner like Yi Ku, became increasingly determined to go to America, most of all, for their college education. That was Yi Ku's dream even as his parents were struggling just to survive.

In March 1950, now 18, he found a clerk's job at an American store in Shinbashi during his last year of high school. Mr. Roger

Williams, the store owner and manager, was kind and offered to help him earn money for his passage to America.

Also, with the help of Mr. Fisher, Yi Ku and his best friend, Hiroaki, received a letter of admission from Center College in Danville, Kentucky, along with scholarship aid from the Japanese Scholarship Society. They would sail for America on August 3, 1950.

Masako and Yi Eun were delighted to see their young son finding his way and taking initiatives on his own behalf in the midst of family hardships. Yi Ku rarely complained about the various ill fortunes visiting upon his family and himself. He was brave and acting like a fearless pioneer!

But when Masako learned about his wish to go to America, she was startled and couldn't help grimacing. "He is our only son, and still so young," Masako thought to herself. "How can we bear the thought of his living in America all by himself, so far away from us? And how can we live here without him, by ourselves? We will be too lonely."

But that was only momentary. To Masako's surprise, Yi Eun was happy, and with great enthusiasm welcomed his son's plan to go to America.

"Since I was 11 years old," he uttered, "I have lived as a prisoner like a bird in a cage. I have not been allowed to make decisions for myself or my life. The same fate must not fall on our son. He should be free, and we must let him be free to live as he wishes!"

"It appeared," Masako recalled, "as if all of His Highness' rage pent-up since he was brought to Japan as a hostage was exploding."

Masako had always assumed that she understood her husband's innermost thoughts and feelings, and for the first time realized that she had failed to grasp something hidden deep in his heart: anger strong enough to risk losing his son so as to help him become free.

Feeling shame, she made a firm resolve. "From now on I must be strong for the sake of my husband, to help him live out his life in peace and quiet. I myself will face and fight anyone seeking to hurt us!" The resolve gave her a new courage and freed her from all worries and misgivings about her son's future.

Yi Ku's American dream, however, was beset by unwelcome road blocks. As a Korean resident in Japan he was required to secure a Korean passport to travel to the United States. The Seoul government under Syngman Rhee, however, refused to issue him the travel documents.

In desperation, Yi Ku turned to the Japanese Foreign Ministry, which issued him an emergency passport. Upon learning of this, Kim Yong-ju at the Korean Mission in Tokyo and a friend of Yi Eun's was upset, and without higher authorization issued a Korean passport to Yi Ku to be used in case of exigency.

Yi Ku understood the delicate nature of the issues between his parents and Syngman Rhee, but the passport fiasco was the first of much heartache he would have to endure along the way in his relations with Korea.

As the day of their departure neared, Yi Ku, Masako, and Yi Eun went to Hayama, where Emperor and Empress Hirohito were spending their summer. As Yi Ku told about his impending travel to America for study, Emperor was pleased and encouraged him to study hard.

The following day, Yi Ku and his friend Hiroaki went to visit Crown Prince Akihito, who was two years their junior in Gakushuin. They shared their memories of old school days and said difficult good byes.

Finally on August 3, 1950, Yi Ku and his friend boarded a trans-Pacific ocean liner, the General Gordon, at Yokohama Harbor. This was their first time away from their homes and their parents, but they were excited and full of hope and dreams.

Standing on the pier, Masako wept as she and Yi Eun watched two tiny frames quickly disappear among other tall passengers, American and European. Her tears were those of joy and happiness, as well as sadness.

As the General Gordon gradually disappeared from her sight, Masako said a quiet prayer, "My son, be strong, and be free. Follow your dreams as far as you can and as high as you can. Fly, fly like a bird, and soar into the sky like an eagle . . ."

After Yi Ku was gone, Masako and Yi Eun felt only emptiness. Sometimes it was unbearable. Each day, they waited for a letter from America.

And to their joy, Yi Ku wrote often, describing his new life in an American college. He thanked his mother for all the things she had taught him early in life, including cleaning his own room and doing other chores, which made his dormitory life so much easier.

Like many American college students, he even worked at a local restaurant as a dishwasher or a waiter to earn money for personal expenses.

On October 20, which was Yi Eun's birthday, Yi Ku sent a package containing a pair of socks. For Yi Eun it was the first present from his son and the greatest among all the presents he had ever received.

Two weeks later, on her birthday, Masako received from her son a beautiful birthday card along with a pair of gloves. For her also, it was the most precious gift she had ever received. She knew that Yi Ku bought it with the money he earned as a dishwasher. Holding it tightly to her heart, she cried.

In the early morning of January 1, 1951, Masako received word that her father had passed away. Since he was released from Sugamo Prison five years ago, he had been living a quiet secluded life. After selling everything of any value, he and his wife had been living in poverty in a tiny house next to a pond.

When Masako reached the house, she found her aged mother, Itsuko, weeping all alone. Together, they set up an altar in an empty spot near a shed and held a simple funeral service,

Meanwhile, Syngman Rhee's government continued to make demands on the Akasaka mansion. When Masako and Yi Eun refused to yield, officials of the Korean Diplomatic Mission in Tokyo offered to buy the mansion for $400,000, which was much lower than the market value. The Korean Mission would pay $200,000 immediately and the rest later.

The transaction would require that Masako abrogate the existing rental contract with the chairman of the House of Councilors.

When the Japanese government learned of the Korean offer, it made its own offer to buy back the said mansion at a fair market value. It explained that inasmuch as the mansion was a gift from the Emperor it would be only proper for it to be returned to the Japanese government.

After pondering the matter, Yi Eun said to Masako, "As long as our (Korean) government wishes to use the property, we should not sell it to another government. Even if we end up receiving only $200,000 it is only proper that we sell our property to the Korean government."

Masako agreed, and they promptly cancelled the existing rental contract with the chairman of the House of Councilors.

For six months they waited, but there was no more word from the Korean Diplomatic Mission. Consequently, they lost even the $800 rental money they had been depending on, resulting in further hardship on their life.

As they learned later, Syngman Rhee was adamant in his belief that the Akasaka mansion was a property of the Korean government and that not a penny should be paid for it.

The Korean Mission was being instructed to confiscate it by any means. Finding itself in a quandary, the Mission simply went incommunicado.

Finding themselves in a destitute situation, Masako and Yi Eun sold everything of any value among their possessions.

In the end, Yi Eun had to give up even his beloved orchid plants. Growing orchids with many colors in a green house was his cherished hobby. When he sold the beautiful plants which he had personally tended like his babies Masako was deeply sorry and sad.

The biggest problem for Masako and Yi Eun was the enormous debt which they had been accumulating. In order to pay capital taxes they kept borrowing money, and recently even from money sharks charging exorbitant interests. By early 1952, they owed over $100,000 to various creditors.

With little or no regular income, the checks and promissory notes they issued were bouncing, to their embarrassment. Masako's financial distress inevitably became a topic of gossip within Tokyo social gatherings, and their Akasaka mansion became a target of some greedy businessmen. Hoodwinked by clever middlemen, Masako and Yi Eun ended up selling the mansion for less than half of its real value of nearly $300,000.

When Masako paid off their debts with money from the house sale, they had only about $7000 left, with which they bought a small cottage near Denenchofu station.

On April 28, 1952, the American occupation of Japan ended as the San Francisco Peace Treaty signed on September 8, 1951 went into effect. Japan once again became an independent country.

As its own leaders took charge again of their governmental and financial institutions, some of Masako's and Yi Eun's old friends and acquaintances offered material help, which gave them a little breathing room.

Among them were Emperor Hirohito, Prime Minister Yoshida Shigeru, and Uemura Kentaro, a high ranking officer in the Japanese government.

It was, however, during Japan's economically difficult times, and even the Emperor's pocket was severely limited. All he could do for Masako was sharing a portion of his monthly allowances, about $250 per month.

Friends' help enabled Masako and Yi Eun to meet their daily needs including groceries, water, and electricity, and they were deeply grateful. At the same time, they could not escape deep feelings of discomfort. This was particularly so with Yi Eun, once the proud crown prince of Korea, a king, and a general in Japan's Imperial Army.

For most of his life he had never suffered want. The treasury of the Yi Royal Family Administration was his personal bank, supplying him all of his material needs. But now, he was in poverty, rejected by his own country and a recipient of other people's sympathy.

When walking along Tokyo streets, he felt as if people were jeering at him. "Look, there goes the crown prince and king of Korea, once rich but now in poverty and disgrace, almost a beggar!"

Submerged in embarrassment and self-pity, he holed himself up in his house in deafening silence. As days went by, he was becoming increasingly dispirited and depressed.

The situation made Masako want more than ever to return to Korea and help Yi Eun live out his remaining life with honor. The Korean government of Syngman Rhee, however, showed no interest in their coming.

Aggravating their already dire condition, the Korean government in 1954 nationalized the entire property of the old Joseon Kingdom and Yi royal family. For Yi Eun, the last crown prince of the Joseon Kingdom, there was nothing to claim as his own from the vast holdings of the now extinct Yi Royal Dynasty.

Following the nationalization, the Korean government decided to pay monthly allowances to living members of the Yi Royal Dynasty including Queen Yun.

Masako and Yi Eun hoped they too would be included among the recipients, but the government simply ignored them.

Even though he was slighted by the government of his own country time and time again, Yi Eun never complained. "All I want is for Korea to prosper and for Queen Yun to be well," he would say.

Ever since he learned that Queen Yun had been forced to move out of the Nakseonjae in Changdeok Palace during the Korean War and had been living in a humble cottage on the outskirts of Seoul, Yi Eun had been concerned about her and her well-being.

Whenever he saw a visitor from Seoul, he would say, "I have no concern for myself. Please take care of Queen Yun. Do everything possible to safeguard her well-being."

One day, a prominent Japanese lawyer came to Yi Eun and encouraged him to sue the Korean government for refusing to give him allowances to which he was entitled as a living member of the

Yi Royal Dynasty. The lawyer was convinced that Yi Eun would win and offered his assistance free of charge.

To the lawyer's surprise, however, Yi Eun refused. "Thank you for your good will and generosity," he said. "But this is a matter between me and my country's government. And no matter how dire my personal situation may be, I will not bring a suit against my own country's government." He was firm in his reply.

For a moment Masako was a bit bewildered, unable to understand why her husband, living in poverty, refused to fight for his rights, but she knew it would betray his character. And once again, she marveled at Yi Eun's noble spirit. Her respect and appreciation of him grew even deeper.

In June, 1953, Yi Ku graduated from Center College in Kentucky and was admitted to the architectural engineering department at Massachusetts Institute of Technology (MIT) in Boston.

Masako and Yi Eun were proud of their son and filled with joy. Like other parents, they would have been delighted to attend Yi Ku's graduation and rejoice and celebrate with him for the joyous events happening in his life.

But in their personal circumstances, they could only dream and fantasize their son marching in a gown and receiving his hard-earned college diploma.

In January, 1954, Masako had an unexpected visit from Lady Park Chan-joo, the widow of Prince Yi Woo, who had died in the Hiroshima atomic bombing. The last time they saw each other was during World War II in June, 1943, when they made a firm promise to each other in Hokkaido that they would defy the war and stay alive at all cost.

They did survive the war, but the new world which they faced was full of uncertainty and apprehension, and they had to go through untold hardship each in their own way. While Masako, as a common citizen, was struggling to survive in the turbulent years of postwar

Japan, Lady Park Chan-joo had to cope with her new life as a young widow with two children during Korea's chaotic days following its liberation and the trauma of the Korean War. Reminiscing about their past they stayed up all night, often in tears.

Lady's Park Chan-joo's son, Yi Cheong, had grown to be of college age. He had a striking resemblance to his father, the handsome and debonair Prince Yi Woo. Like his father, he was tall, handsome, and strong. Suddenly, Masako felt as if she were seeing Prince Yi Woo, whose tragic death at Hiroshima had long grieved her. And in a small measure she was comforted.

In times when their old friends rarely came to visit, seeing Lady Park Chan-joo was, for Masako and Yi Eun, like coming upon an oasis in the middle of a desert.

Most of the time, however, they felt unsettled and uneasy about their life. They had no jobs and no office to go to. They were earning no money, not even a penny. They were just spending up what little they had. And increasingly they were feeling useless.

To find some freedom from their stifling predicament Masako and Yi Eun decided to keep busy and occupied. "We can't be just sitting around doing nothing," they said to each other. So they joined a painting club organized by Inokuma Genichiro, the famous Japanese painter of the day. The club members met on each Sunday for fellowship and for sharing ideas on the history of art. Sometimes, they made trips to scenic places to make drawings, guided by Inokuma himself.

Beginning in April, 1954, Masako also became active in the Buddhist Women's Association of Japan as vice chairwoman. Meeting once a month, often in Kyoto or Kamakura, the Association members exchanged their thoughts on Buddhism.

At the famous Zen Buddhist temple of Engakuji in Kamakura they spent time in Zen meditation and in listening to Zen masters' lectures.

Masako kept herself busy with various events, including bazaars intended to raise funds to help the needy. Occasionally, Masako also attended informal gatherings of old imperial family members, visiting over refreshments with relatives, including Emperor and Empress Hirohito.

In spring of 1955, Masako also decided to establish an art academy called *Academie Beaux Art* for the purpose of offering private lessons on cooking, flower arrangement, tea ceremony, and sewing. Because she had no fund, she used the upstairs of a Mrs. Yoneyama Hisako, a member of the Buddhist Women's Association, and her friends and acquaintances, skilled in various arts, volunteered as instructors. The academy became so popular with local women that Masako had to add evening sessions.

These activities, and especially the monthly bazaars, kept Masako busy, but her greatest joy was always receiving a letter from her son, Yi Ku, telling her about the things happening in his life. Yi Ku was a wonderful and dependable son. He would write every week, and nothing gave Masako and Yi Eun a greater sense of joy, pride, and satisfaction than reading their son's weekly letter.

As soon as they finished reading his letter they were waiting for the next one, and the time till the next one was like an eternity. Even without their conscious knowledge, their son had become their only hope, their joy, and their life.

On New Year's Day, 1957, Masako and Yi Eun were full of excitement and anticipation. This year Yi Ku would graduate from MIT. For seven long years he had been putting himself through college in America, doing all sorts of odd jobs along the way. And finally, the fruition of his hard work was just around the corner.

Masako and Yi Eun could hardly contain themselves as they pictured their son marching proudly in his graduation gown to receive his hard-earned diploma from one of the world's most prestigious universities.

"This time," Masako said to her husband, "we shall go to America and see our son no matter what the cost . . . even if we have to sell everything we have." "Yes, yes, of course!" Yi Eun replied without a moment of hesitation.

They had been selling one thing after another to make ends meet, and the only thing left of any value was a small cottage at Nasu village, which they had used for vacations in the past. They had been trying to sell it, but it became hopelessly tangled up in disputes among potential buyers.

This time, they decided to dump the cottage even for little profit. They would be happy if they could get just enough money for their travel to America. As Masako contemplated selling her last material possessions, she mused on the meaning of happiness.

"Happiness," she said to herself, "is a matter of the mind."

"There is no end to desire. There is nothing more important than inner tranquility and inner joy," she mused.

"When a person is happy inside, she/he is grateful even for a small thing. She/he bothers no one and troubles no one."

"Happiness," she was convinced, "is all a matter of one's mind. Depending on the state of one's mind, one can find happiness or lose it."

Traveling to America required a passport, so they went to the Korean Diplomatic Mission in Tokyo to apply for a Korean passport, only to be rejected once again. The Mission's response was that they received no permission from the Seoul government. Through their friends they learned that Syngman Rhee, the president of Korea, still resented them and refused to allow them to travel either to Korea or to America.

Yi Ku's graduation date was approaching, and they became anxious. In desperation, they turned to Japan's Imperial Household Agency for help. When the Japanese foreign ministry learned of their plight, it issued them a temporary passport.

As Masako and Yi Eun realized that they could soon see their son, who had been away for longer than seven years, they danced and exulted with tears of joy.

"Oh, at last we are going to see our son, our dear son! Oh, how we have longed for him!" They felt like floating above the clouds. About the same time, the Nasu cottage was finally sold. The money from the sale was just enough for them to buy one-way airplane tickets to America and cover other necessary travel expenses.

On May 18, 1957, Masako and Yi Eun left Haneda International Airport in Tokyo. "We were so happy and excited that we could not even eat," Masako recalled.

This was before the days of fast-flying jet passenger planes. The trans-Pacific flight from Tokyo to America's west coast involved two stops for refueling, first at Wake Island and then at Honolulu.

Thanks to the good will of friends in Honolulu, they were able to spend a few days touring the island of Hawaii, but their heart was already in Boston with Yi Ku. An hour was like a day, and a day like an eternity as they could not wait to see their son.

At last, on May 23, their plane landed in San Francisco. At the magnificent sight of the Golden Gate Bridge through the plane's window they knew that they were really coming to America, the land which had given their son a new life and new hope, the land which they had only dreamed about.

In one of his letters, Yi Ku had asked his parents to arrive in Boston just a day or two before his graduation ceremony. Due to his busy schedule he would have no time to spend with them if they arrived too early. So to kill a few days, they decided to travel by train from San Francisco to New York.

The vast American continent, seen as they traveled through the lofty mountains and desert and across the endless plains, impressed them with the beauty and the grandeur of America. The endless rows of oil pumping machines, the city of Chicago with its towering sky scrapers, and giant industrial towns along the way awed them. They wondered how Japan, a tiny island country, had dared to attack and fight such an immense and mighty nation.

In New York, they were met by Rev. Robert M. Kamide, a long-time Japanese-American Christian minister in New York and a personal acquaintance, who had been looking after Yi Ku like a member of his family. After settling in for the night at the Kamide's, Masako called her son in Boston.

As she heard Yi Ku's voice, tears of joy burst, choking her in her throat. Yi Ku told her that she would come to New York the following evening. Next day, Rev. and Mrs. Kamide gave the Yis a personal tour of New York City, from the Statue of Liberty to the United Nations headquarters and the Harlem District. But their minds were all on the long-awaited evening event, seeing their beloved son.

A little after seven o'clock, following their evening dinner, Masako heard the sound of footsteps approaching the house. Holding their breath, she and Yi Eun stood by the entrance door, left slightly open. Suddenly standing before them was a handsome young gentleman with the look of a distinguished scholar.

With no word, Masako held her son's firm hand, placing her face to his, reminiscing about the long lonely eight years that had gone by. There were proud, approving, and satisfied smiles on Yi Eun's face too.

Instantly, Masako saw a hapless father finding new strength and new hope in his son who had grown up and was on his way to achieving his American dream.

Encouraged, Masako said to herself, "Until now my feeble hands have been the only support His Highness has had. From now on, we will move as three, with our son as the main pillar. Together we shall move forward through the rough storms of life."

Next day, they found an apartment in the Park Hotel on Park Avenue, and for the first time in eight years, the three—father, mother, and son—were together as a family again.

It was Masako's first taste of true happiness in many years.

On June 6, Rev. Kamide, Masako, and Yi Eun travelled to Boston to attend Yi Ku's graduation ceremony on the following day.

On the morning of June 7th, Masako, Yi Eun, and Rev. Kamide headed to the campus of MIT and to the open court where the commencement was to be held. Upon arrival, they found it already full of people, including parents, relatives and friends of graduating students. They could feel joy and excitement thick in the air.

"I feel so happy and pleased that we decided to come," she thought to herself, taking a deep breath of relief and satisfaction.

"How lonely it would have been for Yi Ku," she mused, "if he walked in the procession with no family member rejoicing and congratulating him in this once-in-a-lifetime event! And what a lonely way it would have been for him to start his new professional life!" Masako felt a chill going up her spine.

As MIT's 91st commencement ceremony began, several hundred graduating students from various departments, moved in procession toward the platform, all in joyous smiles. From a far corner of the open court, Masako spotted Yi Ku, walking slowly in a black gown toward the University president to receive his diploma. Warm tears welled in her eyes.

Yi Ku's personal journey to that platform had not been an easy one. Born as a prince of imperial blood of Japan and Korea, he was once among the most privileged in the world.

Yi Ku at MIT graduation, June 7, 1957

Losing all in the aftermath of Japan's surrender to the Allied Powers, however, Yi Ku became nobody, neither Japanese nor Korean. Lost in the ambiguity of his personal identity, he decided on his own volition to come to America to begin a new life. He put himself through college and MIT, doing odd jobs to earn school and living expenses. And thanks to the kindness and good will of many friends along the way, he was fulfilling his dreams.

Masako was grateful and prayed quietly, "O Lord, thank you for Yi Ku, and thank you for his good friends. May my son, and all these young men and women from all over the world become instruments of blessing, peace, and happiness here and everywhere."

Following the ceremony, Masako met another Korean graduate. Holding his hands firmly, she blessed him and his future as he was returning to Seoul to help rebuild his war-torn homeland.

Yi Ku had wanted to stay in America following his graduation from MIT, so with the help of his American friends he had applied for and received permanent residence. He was also hired by I. M. Pey and Associates, an architectural firm in Manhattan, New York City, and on June 10th, Yi Ku began his full-time professional career at his new office as a promising architectural engineer. And, with a Japanese-American architect friend, George Stanicci, Yi Ku rented an apartment near his office.

In their burning desire to stay near their son, Masako and Yi Eun located themselves at Hotel Paris on the Riverside Drive, close to the Hudson River, moderately priced and popular with tourists.

After his work, Yi Ku would drop by at their place and the three would have dinner together. Afterwards, they would take a walk along the Hudson River or spend a quiet evening, sometimes reminiscing about days gone by.

Masako was blissfully happy to see her son daily and spend time together as a family. "O, how long have I yearned and longed for such a moment!" she said to herself. "If this is not heaven, what is it?" she mused, overcome by feelings of euphoria.

Even more so was Yi Eun. He looked as if all of his burdens had dropped from his shoulders. As with most aging Asian fathers, he was already leaning on his son. Yi Ku was becoming his hope, his security, and his life.

By coincidence, Masako's friend, Inokuma Genichiro, the artist, was also in New York at that time. He maintained an art gallery in the city and made frequent trips to America. So, in the daytime, while Yi Ku was working in his office, she, Yi Eun, and Inokuma would visit museums, art galleries, and other cultural attractions.

Also, by another coincidence, Dr. Suzuki Daisetsu, her old acquaintance and a famous Zen scholar, was giving lectures at Columbia University on Zen Buddhism. Masako and Yi Eun met him several times and listened to his talks on Zen meditation.

Completely happy and content, Masako and Yi Eun did not want to return to Tokyo, so with Rev. Kamide's assistance they received a six-month extension of their tourist visa from the U.S. Immigration and Naturalization Service.

More than anything, Masako wished to live together in a quiet place just with her family. After some searching, they found an apartment in the town of White Plains, a quiet and lovely town, about 35 minutes by train ride north of New York City. And on September 8, they moved to the new place.

When Yi Ku left for his work in the morning, Masako and Yi Eun took a walk. They also went to a local high school's trade classes to learn skills on pottery and leather goods making, which would become invaluable in Masako's later life.

On the weekends, Masako and Yi Ku would go shopping at a local grocery store. Walking home with her son side by side, holding grocery bags, Masako would mumble to herself, "O, this is so wonderful! O, I love living like this! This is heaven!"

Masako's happy days in America

For the first time in all their lives, Masako, Yi Eun, and Yi Ku were leading their lives without someone interfering or watching over them. And for them, living in true freedom was overwhelming.

Painfully aware of how precious freedom is, Masako and Yi Eun had made a firm resolve to let their son live as freely as he wished. They would not interfere with his decisions be they about work, profession, or marriage.

So, when Yi Ku revealed to his parents, on the New Year's Day of 1958, that he was in love with an American girl of Ukrainian parentage and planned to marry her, they welcomed the news and freely gave their blessing, even though they had hoped that he would find a Korean or a Japanese for his wife.

"If you have found a person to be your lifetime partner," Masako said to Yi Ku, "you must love and respect her with full commitment and responsibility. We bless you and pray for your happiness."

Julia Mullock was a lovely and highly cultured young woman, one or two years older than Yi Ku. As a graduate of New York Fine Arts School with a major in interior decoration, she had much in common with Yi Ku. They had met while working at the I. M. Pey architectural firm.

On Sundays, Julia came over to Masako's apartment for dinner and a visit. She was impressed by Julia's warm personality and homey demeanor. Each visit brought the two closer to each other, and extra joy to Masako's happy days in New York.

As the winter was gradually pushed away by the warm spring air of 1959, Masako knew that her happy days in America were also coming to an end. They had stayed in America for one year and a half, and their tourist visa was running out.

Yi Eun, however, was in no way ready mentally to return to Tokyo. He was just happy to be with his son. One day he asked Masako if there was any way he could extend his stay in America. Could he find a job or anything that might help extend their visa?

They racked their brains and talked with friends, but having already extended their visa several times they found no solution.

Money was another problem. Having extended their stay by many more months than originally planned they had run out of cash to the point of worrying about their return passage.

One day in March, their artist friend, Inokuma Genichiro, dropped by their apartment. Placing an envelope in Masako's hands, he said, "This is from Mr. Nakata Masaichi in Tokyo." Inside the envelope Masako found a $5,000 cashier's check!

"What is this? It's a huge amount of money. Who is Mr. Nakata?" Masako reacted, completely bewildered.

"Mr. Nakata is the president of Daieisha Motion Picture Company of Japan. He is also a very generous man," Mr. Inokuma explained.

"During my recent trip to Tokyo, I told him about your present financial plight—that you are kind of stuck in New York, unable to buy your return passage. He has long known of you and held you in high respect. In shock he said, 'This cannot happen.'"

"But we don't even know Mr. Nakata," responded Masako. "How can we take money from a stranger? Besides, we are in no position to pay back this kind of money. Please return the money and thank Mr. Nakata on our behalf."

"Please kindly accept Mr. Nakata's good will and generosity. It comes from his heart. Perhaps, someday you can pay him back," Mr. Inokuma pleaded.

They had been trying to find money for their return passage, so Masako and Yi Eun decided to accept the money for now, firmly determined to return it as soon as they were able to do so. They would depart for Tokyo in the first part of April.

Then, suddenly in the middle of the night of March 26, just a few days before their planned departure, Yi Eun found himself partially paralyzed. On the way to bathroom he fell and was unable to walk.

The following day, doctors examined Yi Eun and diagnosed that he had suffered a stroke. His blood pressure was over 200.

Throughout the month of April, Yi Eun stayed in bed under his doctors' care. And by the end of the month, he had recovered enough strength and was able to walk even if he dragged his feet slightly. With his weakened health, however, Yi Eun dreaded the thought of returning to Tokyo. He just wanted to stay near his son.

New York, however, was for working people and those with money. There was no place in it for poor foreigners like themselves. So, in consultation with Yi Eun's physician, Masako and Yi Eun decided to return to Tokyo sometime in the middle of May.

Finally, on May 17, they flew from New York to Los Angeles, where they boarded a cargo ship operated by Hanno Maritime Shipping Company. They were placed in one of two or three cabins on the ship, with special care provided for Yi Eun by the ship's medical personnel.

Before the parents left New York, Yi Ku and Julia decided to become formally engaged, with a plan to marry in the fall.

Back in Tokyo, Masako found herself once again back in a life beset with the same mundane anxieties that had long plagued her.

Her household still had no income, and there was no prospect of things improving in their favor.

Having lost his old physical vigor, Yi Eun was easily depressed. He even lost interest in the things he had enjoyed so much, such as golf and photography. Most of the time, his mind was far away with his son in New York.

On October 25, a beautiful autumn day, Yi Ku and Julia were married in a small church in New York, in the presence of a few close friends. Afterwards, they celebrated their wedding at their new apartment in Brooklyn with the cutting of a cake.

O, how dearly Masako and Yi Eun wished to be at their beloved son's wedding! And how excited they would have been to share the couple's happiness! But it was not meant to be. From far away, across the ocean, they prayed quietly, sending their heart-felt blessings. But for the aged father and mother it was a sad and lonely day.

By the end of the year, Yi Eun's longing for his son had become an obsession. Becoming increasingly aware that his life was gradually slipping away under his deteriorating health, he was thinking only of his son. And he pleaded with Masako to help him visit him once again.

Masako felt a sense of urgency as she realized that Yi Eun's worsening health might prevent him from making another trip to New York, and she was determined to help Yi Eun fulfill his wish.

On June 6, 1960, to save money she and Yi Eun boarded the Hikawago, an old transpacific ocean liner, at Yokohama, arriving in Seattle 16 days later. The following day, they flew from there to New York.

Even as Yi Eun saw Yi Ku from a distance he was acting like an excited little boy unable to contain himself. "This may be his last visit," Masako whispered to herself. "How glad I am to have made this trip."

They checked into a hotel across from Yi Ku's apartment. In the evenings they would walk over and have dinner with Yi Ku and Julia.

It was the first time for them to be treated so loyally by their new daughter-in-law. And once again, life was blissfully heavenly.

Unlike the last time, however, Yi Eun had no desire to go outside for long walks. He wanted just to stay in the house. Increasingly, he was dependent on Masako. And he was acting helpless without Yi Ku.

Masako now became worried for Yi Eun. She sensed that his physical and mental health was declining rapidly. Fearing that their presence was becoming a heavy burden to Yi Ku and Julia, she decided, holding back her tears, to leave New York. By August 12, they were back in Tokyo.

CHAPTER 15

COMING HOME AT LAST

In the meantime, earthshaking events had been underway in Korea's political scene.

On April 19, 1960, about 30,000 university and high school students, angry with rampant frauds in national elections, rose up against the government of President Syngman Rhee. Soon, ordinary citizens joined the students.

As tensions between the populace and the government continued to rise, President Rhee resigned on April 26, ending Korea's First Republic. The political crisis was the culmination of an internal socio-political upheaval that had been plaguing the fledgling Republic for more than a decade.

From the moment of its inception, the Republic of Korea faced existential threats from various groups opposed to its creation, most notably from communists in sympathy or alliance with Communist North Korea.

On October 19, 1948, just two months after the first Republic was established (on August 15), Communist elements in the 14th Army Regiment, stationed in Yeosu City on the south coast, defied the new government with a bloody insurrection. Through guerrilla operations closely coordinated with various local Communist groups, the rebels plunged much of South Korea's countryside into a social and security crisis.

There was a real possibility that the life of the new-born Republic of Korea could be snuffed out before it was even on its feet if opposing forces went unchecked. As the supreme leader of the Republic, President Syngman Rhee became more determined than ever in his anti-Communist posture.

On December 1, the National Assembly enacted the National Security Law (NSL) for the purpose of identifying and rooting out all Communists and other seditious elements within South Korea.

Communist North Korea's devastating invasion 18 months later, on June 25, 1950, further reinforced Rhee's resolve to stamp out all elements opposed to the Republic. He also became convinced that he alone in the Republic had the will, determination, and leadership skills necessary to succeed in the war against the Communists.

With the National Security Laws as his primary weapon, Rhee unleashed the National Police and others loyal to him in crushing "the Republic's enemies" and also in consolidating his personal power.

In 1951, to secure his power base Rhee created the Liberal Party, consisting of wealthy businessmen, property owners, and other privileged citizens opposed to Communism.

In 1952, as his first presidential term was ending, Rhee persuaded the National Assembly to adopt constitutional amendments to elect Korea's president by popular vote rather than by the National Assembly, now beset with partisan politics.

The Korean War was still raging, and North Korea's Kim Il-sung was still determined to destroy the Republic, now with the massive support of Chinese Communist forces.

In the face of his nation's continuing existential crisis, Rhee was not willing to allow the presidency to fall into the hands of another.

By 1954, the Liberal Party became the majority force within the National Assembly, and with its support Rhee got new laws passed: first, to have an iron tight control of Korea's Communist elements, and second, to establish himself as the absolute power. Rhee achieved the latter by persuading the National Assembly to remove the constitutional two-term limitation on presidential tenure.

By the end of the 1950s Rhee had no political rivals on the left or right. All political institutions—the National Assembly as well as the entire government bureaucratic apparatus—existed to serve him.

The Korean War had ended seven years before, and with the U.S.-Korea Mutual Defense Treaty signed in 1953, the Republic of Korea was no longer under its existential threat. Rhee, however, kept all political opposition under tight control through the National Police and the National Security Laws.

While there was a semblance of peace and order in the nation, however, Korea was in a dismal state economically. Per capita income was only $100, an equivalent found in only the poorest countries of Africa or Southeast Asia at that time.

Korea's economic base was predominantly agricultural, with no meaningful industry. Its infrastructure, including highways, railroads, harbors, and electric power, was in a woeful state.

Food was scarce. In spring-time, many farmers scoured hillsides to find edible roots and spring greens.

Between 1948 and 1960 the number of colleges and universities had doubled, but more than 60 percent of their graduates could not find employment, resulting in anger and frustration on the part of the general public.

By 1960, on the eve of his fourth presidential term, Rhee was 85 years old, considered by the public as too old to govern, and his Liberal Party was far more interested in perpetuating its monopoly of power—often through intimidation, fraud, and election rigging—than in the welfare of the nation. Finally, public anger and frustration erupted on the streets in March, 1960, when Rhee's Liberal Party was suspected of massively rigging the national elections on March 15.

On April 11, a young student's body was found floating in Masan Bay on the southern coast, apparently killed by police during a street demonstration against the fraudulent elections. The news spread like wildfire throughout the nation, and tens of thousands of students, supported by a sympathetic public, forced Rhee's resignation on April

26. Thus finally ended the political dominance of President Syngman Rhee and the Liberal Party as well as the First Republic.

Syngman Rhee lived a simple and austere personal life, even going about in old worn-out socks repaired by his wife, Franzisca. He disdained bribery and personal profiteering. He was Korea's undisputed patriot and would be justly known in Korean history as the George Washington of the Republic of Korea. But in his old age he became a hapless victim of the greed and ambition of the political "friends" and "supporters" that surrounded him, pulling the wool over his eyes.

Rhee's resignation on April 26, 1960 was the beginning of a new day, not only for Korea but also for Masako and Yi Eun. The one person who had kept them from returning to Korea was now gone.

In the aftermath of the revolution, an interim government was quickly established to help pave the way for democratic reforms. On June 15 a new constitution was adopted, creating a bicameral parliamentary government centered on a prime minister and a cabinet responsible to the National Assembly. The presidency was now largely ceremonial.

Six weeks later, on July 29, new elections were held, in which the Democratic Party won the majority. Jang Myeon, who had served as prime minister (1950-52) as well as vice president (1956-1960) during the First Republic, was chosen as the first prime minister of the Second Republic.

Soon thereafter, a Korean official came to the home of Masako and Yi Eun with a letter from Prime Minister Jang Myeon. In the letter, the prime minister expressed sincere apologies for the way he and Masako had been treated by the First Republic. The letter was also an informal invitation for Yi Eun to serve as Korean ambassador to Great Britain.

Yi Eun was deeply grateful for Prime Minister Jang's good will and his gracious offer but firmly declined to be involved in any political or governmental matters, citing his ill health.

In truth, he did not feel comfortable about Korean politics. Many waters had passed under the bridge since he was Korea's crown prince.

Yi Eun's longing for his homeland, however, was just as deep and intense as ever. Going home to the land of his birth and early childhood was something he had been longing for more than 50 years, often with tears and agonizing pain.

Masako knew Yi Eun's innermost thoughts as well as his life-long dreams. She knew how he had longed to return to his old home and live out his life quietly among the rocks and the trees which were part of the world in which he grew up.

"Yes, this we shall do," Masako pledged to herself. "We shall return to our home, and there we shall live out our lives, in peace and quietude."

From the outset, Prime Minister Jang Myeon's government and his Democratic Party were beset with endless factionalism, bordering on political chaos.

If Syngman Rhee's First Republic was too harsh with political dissent, Jang Myeon's Second Republic was the opposite. Suddenly released from a decade of suppression, there was an explosion of unconstrained in-fights and rivalries among aspiring Korean politicians.

Plagued by schisms and disunity, Jang Myeon's government was quickly paralyzed. Cabinet members were replaced on the average every two months. There were no coherent reform strategies, nor were any effective measures taken to improve the nation's social and economic conditions. Corruption ran rampant at the highest level.

Amidst the political paralysis, leftists (and Communists) emerged from their underground hideouts and organized masses of students for street demonstrations that called for unification with Communist North Korea.

In the eyes of many thoughtful citizens, democracy was the problem rather than the solution for Korean society. Alarmed by the social and political chaos plunging their nation into a dark age, a group of young army officers decided to take over the government.

On May 16, 1961, under the leadership of Major General Park Jung-hee and Lieutenant Colonel (ret.) Kim Jong-pil, they succeeded in a coup-d'e-dat, that swiftly brought an end to civilian rule. Korea now was ruled by the Supreme Council for National Reconstruction, with General Park Jung-hee as its Chairman.

Masako and Yi Eun received the news of these tumultuous events with sadness and distress. "When will the Koreans ever live in peace and tranquility?" they wondered.

Even since Japan began its aggressive encroachment in the late 19th century, Koreans never had a moment of peace. Forty years of brutal Japanese rule was followed by the chaos of post World War II days, then by the division of their country, by the devastating North-South war of three years, the 12-year dictatorial reign of Syngman Rhee, and now by a military dictatorship!

Masako and Yi Eun wept for Korea and the Koreans. More immediately, they wondered what was going to happen to them. Could they ever go home to Korea and to Yi Eun's old home in Seoul?

Then, as if fate was entirely against them, Yi Eun's illness got worse. He was now having trouble in walking and speaking, and was often confused and incoherent. All the mental stress and anxiety over the political turmoil in Korea, and his premonition that he might never be able to return to his homeland, were a bit too much for him to bear.

Then one day in July, the Korean Diplomatic Mission in Tokyo telephoned Masako to convey a personal message from General Park Jung-hee, Chairman of the Supreme Council for National Reconstruction, sending his best regards to Yi Eun.

This was followed by the arrival of two special envoys from Seoul. They informed Masako and Yi Eun that henceforth the Korean government would assume all of their living expenses as well as their medical bills.

BEAUTIFUL AS THE RAINBOW

One of the two envoys was Eom Ju-myeong, who had accompanied Yi Eun to Japan in 1907 during the latter's voyage as a hostage, and became Yi Eun's conversational companion during his lonely days of exile in Tokyo. Later he returned to Korea and served as an officer in the Korean army, rising to rank of brigadier general.

The other envoy was Kim Eul-han, a reporter for the *Seoul Daily* who was stationed in Tokyo. His wife had been a classmate of Princess Deok-hye, Yi Eun's half sister, while they were little girls growing up in Seoul. Having long been interested in the welfare of Yi Eun, Kim Eul-han had contacted General Park Jung-hee and informed him of the plight of Yi Eun and Masako and their longing to return to Korea.

Unlike President Syngman Rhee, who had spent most of his life in exile fighting for Korean independence from Japan, Park Jung-hee had volunteered to serve in Japan's military, even graduating from its elite Military Academy as did Yi Eun.

When Park Jung-hee was only a first lieutenant in Japan's Imperial Army during World War II, Yi Eun was a general. Lieutenant Park had looked up to General Yi Eun with the highest esteem and admiration, and still did.

But Park also knew about the tragic story of Korea's last crown prince—the person who just might be in his position had things worked out differently. He was shocked by Kim's report. "This cannot be," Park shouted. "If Yi Eun dies in Japan without proper medical care for lack of money it will go down in history as a national disgrace!" Immediately General Park ordered his secretary to tell the Korean representative in Tokyo to place Yi Eun in the best hospital with all expenses to be assumed by the Korean government. And he sent the two men to Yi Eun to deliver his personal message of help.

On August 3, Masako took Yi Eun to St. Luke's Hospital. On the way she explained to Yi Eun that the new Korean government had come to their rescue, but Yi Eun had no understanding of what was happening.

On the one hand, Masako was happy, but on the other hand, she was sad because Yi Eun's life-long dream was finally being fulfilled—he had gained acceptance by his people, but was not even aware of it.

After a month of care in the hospital Yi Eun's condition improved. He still could not speak but he understood words.

Masako told Yi Eun about the good will and kindness of General Park Jung-hee. Yi Eun just kept nodding his head, indicating he understood, with tears of gratitude rolling down his cheek.

By unfortunate coincidence, unknown to others including Yi Eun, Masako was suffering from a breast cancer at that time. She had known about it since May, but preoccupied with Yi Eun's deteriorating condition she had been ignoring her own problem. Besides, with no money for a surgery, she had left her own life to fate.

Fortunately, the cancer was in its early stage, and in September, with the improvement in Yi Eun's condition, she finally went to a hospital and had a tumor in her right breast removed.

Two months later, on November 12, 1961, when General Park Jung-hee stopped in Tokyo on his way to a summit meeting with President John F. Kennedy in Washington, D.C., he sent a bouquet of flowers to Yi Eun still at St. Luke's Hospital. Yi Eun and Masako were overwhelmed with feelings of gratitude.

General Park's schedule was tight with no minute to spare. In addition to a meeting with Japan's Prime Minister Ikeda Hayato, he had to attend a state banquet hosted by Japanese dignitaries. As soon as the banquet was finished he was to fly to America.

Nevertheless, the general informed Masako that he would find a time to see her. At four o'clock in the afternoon, immediately before the banquet, Masako was escorted to a VIP room where Park Jung-hee was waiting.

"Thank you from the bottom of our hearts for all your good will and kindness shown to His Highness," Masako whispered to the general.

Masako meeting General Park Jung-hee
June 16, 1962

"Please don't mention it," replied the general with a smile. "It is something the Korean government is obligated to do. We are delighted to offer our help."

"We are ready to welcome you back to Korea anytime," the general continued. "We will take care of your Korean citizenship and all your living and other expenses. Come home, whenever you wish."

The kind and gracious words of the general overwhelmed Masako with indescribable gratitude and joy, instantly releasing her from all the frustration and hopelessness that had been plaguing her and Yi Eun.

"What an incredible irony!" she thought to herself. "President Syngman Rhee was from the same Yi clan as Yi Eun. They had much in common in their kinship heritage, and yet it is the young army generals, with no relationship of any kind, who are helping His Highness come home."

In the course of the visit, Masako mentioned the plight of Princess Deok-hye.

"Who is Princess Deok-hye?" asked the general.

Ever since she, like Yi Eun, was taken to Japan as a hostage and later forced to marry a Japanese, Princess Deok-hye's life had been a series of tragic events. Along the way she went insane and was sent to the Matsusawa Mental Hospital, where she had been confined to a lonely life for more than a dozen years. From the beginning of her arrival in Japan, Masako and Yi Eun had stayed close to her. In recent years they had been paying for her hospital expenses out of their own limited income.

Upon hearing the story, General Park said, "This is the first time I have ever heard about the princess. Of course, she too should return to Korea, and we will make all necessary arrangements for her speedy return."

On January 26, 1962, 38 years after she had been forced to come to Japan, Princess Deok-hye was taken to Haneda International Airport to be flown to Seoul. Her old Japanese classmates at Gakushuin came to say tearful farewells, holding bouquet of flowers, but the princess was lost in another world, unable to speak or recognize anyone. She didn't even know she was going home at last.

When the plane carrying the feeble princess arrived at Kimpo International Airport in Seoul, she was met by a 71-year old Ms. Byeon. In the early 1900s Byeon had served as a member of the Yi Royal Court staff, looking after the princess as her nurse mother when the princess was a child.

Seeing the princess again after nearly 40 years, the old nurse mother broke down in loud wailing, overcome by joy and sadness. All the bystanders also wept. The princess was taken to Seoul National University Hospital and placed in the care of Ms. Byeon, her childhood nurse mother.

Within a few weeks Princess Deok-hye's condition improved. For years she had been only staring into a bare wall in a mental hospital, but she now seemed as if she were waking up from a long sleep. One day she took out a piece of paper and on it wrote a letter of greeting to Yi Eun, her beloved half brother, and Queen Yun, who had loved her as her own daughter when she was a child.

Queen Yun had been sent to live in a village outside Seoul in a forced exile during the war days and thanks to General Park Jung-hee's kindness, had just returned to the Nakseonjae, her former residence within the Changdeok Palace grounds.

Even though most of her formal education took place in Japan, in the Japanese language, Princess Deok-hye wrote her letter in Hangeul, the Korean alphabet, which she had learned as a child before she was taken to Japan.

"Such is the power of love and affection. It works miracles!" Masako mused as she learned about the positive changes in the princess.

After Princess Deok-hye's return to Korea, Masako's mind was now all on Yi Eun. "Korea is ready to welcome him with open arms, but *he* is not ready," she sighed daily while waiting patiently for even a slight improvement in his condition.

Suffering from a cerebral thrombosis, Yi Eun could not speak or stand on his own feet. Most of the time, he was essentially bed-ridden with his mind gone blank.

When he would recognize Masako for a short moment, she would try to encourage him, "My dear, it's time to go home. Korea and all your people are waiting for you." Yi Eun would reply: "I do not wish to go home in the hands of doctors and nurses. I will step on the soil of my homeland with my own feet, so that I can see the rivers and the mountains of my land with my own eyes on my feet."

Masako, however, knew that this was an impossible dream. Yi Eun's condition was only deteriorating with no hopeful signs. The plan would have to change.

"Yes, my dear," Masako whispered to herself, "we *will* go home, even if I must carry you in my arms."

On June 13, 1962, Masako was on a plane for Seoul. She wanted to make advance preparations for Yi Eun's return.

It was her first trip to Korea in 20 years. Before the war, she and Yi Eun often travelled together, but this time she was alone. "When my plane was approaching Seoul, I thought I was dreaming," she recalled. But she also felt feelings of sadness churning.

From the airport Masako went straight to the Nakseonjae to see Queen Yun. The queen was now 70 years old but still vigorous and dignified. Holding each other's hands, Masako and the queen wept. During her last visit with the queen Masako had promised her to see her again soon. But 20 years had passed. So many things happened during those long years and they had much to talk about.

But their conversation was mostly about Yi Eun, whom the queen held in highest esteem and affection.

When told that Yi Eun was unwilling to return to Korea while bed-ridden, the queen jumped in consternation. "No, no! His Highness must come home," she countered. "This is the land of his parents," Queen Yun continued. "He may come in any form, in bed or on a person's back; it does not matter. I am old and do not know how long I will be around. Before I die I want to see His Highness. So he must come. Go back and convey my words," the queen insisted.

Masako understood how deeply Queen Yun had been longing to see Yi Eun, and she became resolved more firmly than ever that she would help Yi Eun come home no matter what.

For two days afterwards, Masako spent her time visiting various government officials including General Park Jung-hee. She also met representatives of three schools: Jin Myeong Girls High School, Sook Myeong Girls High School, and Yangjeong High School, which Yi Eun's mother, Lady Eom, had established at the turn of the 20th century. Masako and Yi Eun had been considering devoting their life to educational work, if they ever returned to Korea, along with other services beneficial to Korean society.

From the moment of her arrival in Seoul, Masako wanted to run to her son's grave at Cheongyang-ri, in the eastern outskirts of Seoul.

She had been longing to do it for 20 years. Finally, on her third day in Korea she went to the Yeonghui and Soongin Royal Tombs, where Lady Eom and Jin were buried.

The tombs had suffered the devastations of the Korean War. Once beautiful, the hillsides were now in a state of ruin, riven by landslides and shorn of trees and vegetation. Wartime refugees had moved into the cemetery compound, pitching tents at the very bases of the tombs.

Jin would have been about 40 years old at the time of her visit, had he lived. Placing Yi Eun's photo in front of Jin's tomb, Masako said, "My dear son, here is your father's picture . . . Your father has been longing to see you for these 20 years. O, how he has wished to come here if only he could fly like a bird or on a cloud. But this time, I came alone . . ."

Unable to control the tears rolling down her cheeks, she suddenly heard footsteps around her. Half dozen Korean women from a nearby village were standing next to her, paying homage to Jin.

As she greeted them with deep gratitude, an old woman approached Masako and said in broken Japanese, "Welcome. Welcome home. Next time, please come with His Highness, King Yeongchin. And please, from now on, make your home in Seoul." (King Yeongchin was Yi Eun's official title as known to Koreans.)

Deeply moved by the old woman's sincerity, Masako replied in her halting Korean, "Omony, Gamsa Hamnida. Gamsa Hamnida." (Omony is the Japanese pronunciation of *eomony*, Korean word for "mother," or "dear Mom." *Gamsa Hamnida* is Thank you.)

While in Seoul, Masako still worried about Yi Eun. So, on June 18, she rushed back to Tokyo. Yi Eun recognized Masako. As she related all the happenings in Seoul, he listened quietly but uttered not a word.

The only thing Masako could do was to pray and hope for the better. But regardless of any progress in Yi Eun's condition, Masako decided that she and Yi Eun would return to Korea by the following year.

While waiting for Yi Eun's recovery, Masako gave her time to various women's groups that were raising money to help orphans, lepers, mental patients, and paraplegics, in whose welfare Masako had for some time maintained a keen interest.

She organized a charity organization called Jikokai (Charity Works Association), to raise funds for the handicapped and disabled people, and in this effort she put her cloisonné craft skills to work.

Undoubtedly, Masako's personal concern for the plight of society's neglected people was heightened by the tragic life of Princess Deok-hye, who came into Masako's own life as a bright and happy little princess during her first trip to Korea back in 1922.

In the course of 40 years, Masako saw joy and laughter being gradually snuffed out of the life of the princess by society's unreasonable demands. As the process unfolded she witnessed a happy human being become helpless and locked away to vegetate in a mental hospital. As Masako suffered with the princess, so her heart went out to others like her.

Then, Yi Eun's stroke and its devastating consequences further brought home to her the perils and sufferings of the handicapped and the disabled.

Masako had sought whatever help she could find in dealing with her disabled husband's problems, and before long she became a part of various women's groups helping such people.

"My heartfelt wish," she recalled, "was that all the physically and mentally handicapped children had a nice facility where they could receive love and care and in return become useful and productive members of their community."

In anticipation of her return to Korea, Masako was giving serious thought to devoting her life to such services there along with educational work that had been begun by Yi Eun's mother, Lady Eom, six decades before. Such were Masako's dreams and hopes.

But they all depended on Yi Eun's condition. She prayed that Yi Eun could at least recover his mental abilities, if not his physical strength. She could only wait with patience.

By May, 1963 nearly a year had passed since Masako's trip to Korea, but there was no sign of improvement in Yi Eun. Then on May 7, his condition turned for the worse. Suddenly, his facial appearance changed. His hands and fingers shook in spasms, and he had difficulty in breathing. Every 30 minutes these symptoms would recur for a period of 15 minutes. After an examination his doctors concluded that Yi Eun had suffered another serious hemorrhage in his brain.

A week later, Yi Ku and Julia arrived in Tokyo and headed straight to the hospital. Bending over Yi Eun's face, Yi Ku cried, "Father, I have just arrived. Your son, Yi Ku, has come. Can you recognize me?"

Watching Yi Ku overcome with grief and helplessness, Julia knelt on her knees beside him and cried out, "O father, dear father, do you recognize me?"

There was a slight smile on Yi Eun's face. He appeared to have recognized Yi Ku. Then again he stared into the ceiling with a blank expression.

"Poor Father! He is so helpless!" Yi Ku kept murmuring, unable to control his tears. Yi Ku concluded that his father should be placed in a hospital close to Masako's house, and after consulting his doctor, Yi Eun was moved to Sano Hospital, just a ten minute walk from her house.

Every morning Masako, Yi Ku, and Julia went to visit Yi Eun with fruits and jelly, Yi Eun's favorites. Masako was happy to be with her family once again, but they could not escape a melancholy atmosphere.

At the best, Yi Eun's condition was stabilized without further deterioration. Yi Ku's presence seemed to help Yi Eun's spirit.

While Yi Ku and Julia were in Tokyo, Masako suggested that they visit Korea, and they agreed.

When Yi Ku was born in Tokyo 32 years before, on December 29, 1931, Masako had firmly resolved that she would never allow him to step on the soil of Korea until he had grown up and could make his own decisions. She was then still grieving the untimely and horrible death of her first son, Jin, in Korea. Yi Ku was now an adult, and Masako thought he and his wife should visit the land of his father and his royal ancestors of Joseon Kingdom.

Yi Ku and Julia visiting Queen Yun: June 16, 1963

Upon their arrival in Seoul on June16, 1963, Yi Ku and Julia went to the Nakseonjae to pay respect to Queen Yun. Holding Yi Ku's hands, the queen cried. Afterwards, Yi Ku and Julia went to the Soonginweon Royal Cemetery, to pay homage to Jin, his deceased elder brother. Yi Ku had never known him, but he wept.

During their five day stay in Seoul, Yi Ku and Julia met government officials and representatives of the Jeonju Yi Clan.

Yi Ku also paid homage to his royal ancestors at the Grand Jongmyo Ancestral Hall, where all the past kings of the Joseon Kingdom were memorialized. With the official act, Yi Ku became

216

ritually initiated into the lineage of the Joseon Kingdom monarchs. A few days later, they returned to Tokyo.

As Yi Eun continued to languish in the hospital into the summer, Masako feared the worst—that Yi Eun might die without ever seeing his homeland again.

Thus early in July, Masako invited Drs. Seo Seok-jo and Kim Hak-joong of St. Mary's Hospital in Seoul to come to Tokyo for consultation. In a joint meeting the Korean doctors, Japanese physicians from Sano Hospital, and Masako concluded that Yi Eun could be flown to Seoul if he were placed securely in a stretcher and attended by a medical team.

Masako chose November 22, 1963 as the D-day. Yi Eun would finally go home on that day.

As the word of Yi Eun's impending departure spread, his Japanese acquaintances of many decades held farewell gatherings. Sadly, the gatherings were bereft of the usual laughter and biddings of bon voyage.

On October 7, 1963, Masako invited about 100 old friends to a farewell party for Yi Eun at the New Japan Hotel. Many of them had been helpful to her over the years, and she wanted to thank them.

With Yi Eun in the hospital, however, an atmosphere of melancholy hovered over the guests. Conversation was no more than sad comments such as "What a tragic and lonely life he has lived!" With tears, Masako's mother murmured, "How sad that he has to return to his home in this condition!"

A few days before Yi Eun's departure, Emperor and Empress Hirohito invited Masako and Yi Ku to the Imperial palace to bid their personal farewell. In a constrained atmosphere, the Emperor offered his good wishes: "I sincerely pray that His Highness will soon recover fully and spend his remaining life in peace in his beloved homeland."

For several nights before their departure, Masako sat alone beside Yi Eun "conversing with him" deep into the night, though he heard nothing and said nothing. She shared with him her fears as well as her hopes and aspirations for the days to come.

"When we go to Korea," she whispered to Yi Eun, "I want to devote myself to something beneficial to Korea and the Koreans, starting in a small measure, step by step. This is what we have been wishing and dreaming for."

As part of her aspirations, she thought about working with like-minded women at the Korean Red Cross to help physically and mentally disabled children, providing facilities for their care as well as training in trade, drawing on her experiences from her Jikokai (Charity Works Association) in Tokyo.

In order to make such social services possible, Masako was even thinking about introducing cloisonné craft to Korea, which she had mastered in Japan while raising money for women's charity groups. She was pondering the use of her own personal craft skills to raise money for Korea's unfortunate children.

Then, during the night before their departure, Masako's heart became unbearably heavy. "What will happen to me if His Highness dies?" she wondered. At the possibility of her being all alone in Korea she shuddered and cried through the night.

Finally, the D-day arrived on November 22, 1963. That morning Masako spoke to Yi Eun as she used to in the old days when he was strong and healthy.

"Your Highness, let us go to Korea, to our home. I will accompany you," she said.

Masako thought she heard him respond: "Really? Are we really going home to Korea?"

"Yes, Your Highness, we have waited so long. Haven't we?" she said.

"Now, you can go home and rest comfortably."

Again, Masako thought she heard Yi Eun: "Ah, finally, our long, long waiting is ending."

"Yes, Your Highness, at last." Masako whispered, looking at Yi Eun's expressionless face.

On their own Yi Ku and Julia had been pondering their future in light of the new developments unfolding in his family, and after much thought they decided to join Yi Eun and Masako. They were willing to give up their promising careers in America and begin a new life in Korea. Yi Ku hoped and believed that even as he helped his parents, he could become an asset to Korea in its post-war rebuilding effort. When told by Yi Ku and Julia about their decision, Masako was ecstatic. Nothing ever gave her greater happiness and joy than being with her whole family. "Surely, this is a blessing . . . ," she thought.

In a special ambulance sent by the Imperial Household Agency, Masako, Yi Ku, Julia, and Yi Eun arrived at the Haneda International Airport. There they boarded a Japan Airlines charter flight paid by the Japanese government. Yi Eun was borne in a stretcher.

When the plane landed at Kimpo Airport in Seoul an hour and a half later, thousands of people were waiting to welcome Yi Eun. As Masako stepped out of the plane, she found herself buried among bouquets of flowers and shouts of welcome.

An ambulance took Yi Eun to Seoul's St. Mary's Hospital. The Catholic hospital was chosen not only because of its excellent medical staff and facilities but also because Yi Eun had been baptized as a Catholic while staying at St. Luke Hospital in Tokyo. His given baptismal name was Joseph.

He was placed in Room # 616. "When someone said to Yi Eun, 'Your Highness, you have come home, to your homeland,' Yi Eun let out three loud wailings," recalled Dr. Kim Hak-joong. Unable to express his innermost joy with an intelligible word, Yi Eun just wailed in the realization that he was home at last.[15]

Yi Eun had originally gone to Japan in silence, constrained by forces beyond his control, and 56 years later he returned to his homeland in silence, again constrained by forces beyond his control.

Yi Eun at St. Mary's Hospital in Seoul, 1964

CHAPTER 16

AN ANGEL FROM THE LAND OF SAMURAI

Masako in the garden of the Nakseonjae,
her new home in Korea

With the Korean government's assistance Masako, Yi Ku, and Julia took up residence at Oegukin Apartment in Hannam-dong on the south side of the Namsan Hill in Seoul. From there, Masako would commute daily to the hospital to help care for Yi Eun.

Within a week color returned to Yi Eun's face and he could even smile. Encouraged by the sudden improvement, Masako hoped that he could leave the hospital in a month or two and move into the Nakseonjae, where he had spent his childhood days.

It was, however, only a fleeting fantasy. Even though Yi Eun was mentally conscious and could even watch television, his physicians concluded that he had to remain at the hospital for around-the-clock observation and care.

Within three months he was able to sit in a wheel chair by the window, looking at the buildings and hills outside. As the prominent Namsan Hill at the south end of downtown Seoul came into his view, Masako said: "That is the Namsan Hill. You remember it. Don't you?"

After gazing at the mountain for a good while, Yi Eun said, "Oh, Namsan Hill!" He was crying with tears rolling down his cheek. He recognized the Namsan Hill, which he used to see every day while growing up in Deoksu Palace nearby. He seemed to have truly realized at last that he was back in his homeland.

Such a positive turn, however, was only momentary. Over a period of several years, he kept reverting back to a vegetative state that prevented him from leaving the hospital.

While keeping herself busy between the hospital and her other daily chores, Masako volunteered at the office of the Korean Red Cross. Also, she joined the Korean Rehabilitation Association of the Physically Disabled, serving as its vice chairperson.

At the same time, in accordance with Yi Eun's life-long wishes and dreams, Masako and Yi Ku sought to promote educational services for Korea's youth.

In this endeavor, Masako and Yi Ku hoped to use as their operational base Sookmyeong Women's University (formerly Sookmyeong Girls High School), which Yi Eun's mother, Lady Eom, long ago, had helped establish with personal funds and with which Yi Eun and Masako had maintained a close supportive relationship for many decades. They believed, as Yi Eun did, that they had a rightful stake in the University. Even the government, especially the Ministry of Education, concurred and was willing to lend its supportive hand.

To achieve their goal, Masako and Yi Ku first sought to gain leadership in the University's governing board. Fearful of losing their control, however, the old managers of the University and certain members of the governing board became adamantly opposed to Masako and Yi Ku, taking the matter to the court. Sook-jong Lee, Chairman of the Governing Board, representing the opposition, stated that Lady Eom's financial contribution was "a gift without any condition." Therefore, he declared that "no one, including even Yi Eun, could claim a stake in the University."[16]

As the issue became heated up, the government stepped in with increasing pressure against the opponents. Amidst the ongoing conflicts between pro- and anti-factions, Masako and Yi Ku became targets of an ugly anti-Japanese outburst.

As part of their political strategy, the opponents instigated some of the University students to hit the streets with anti-Japanese slogans. Simultaneously, they used friends and relatives in the media to attack Masako and Yi Ku. In doing so, they were resorting to exploit Koreans' anti-Japanese sentiments always simmering just below the surface.

One jeering sign said, "You, Jap squaw, go back to your country!" Another taunted, "You, Jap gook, get out of our country!"

By "Jap squaw' and "Jap gook" the angry crowds meant Masako and Yi Ku. Yi Ku was a Korean as Yi Eun's son, but he was also a Japanese as Masako's son.

This was in the days when Korea was under military dictatorship whose high-handed tactics many civilians and private institutions resented, and when the government became involved in the matter, the University management and its friends rebelled. In an atmosphere of suspicion and mistrust, there was probably a serious breakdown of communication as well.

In another time, things might have been different, and with their extensive social contacts, both in Korea and Japan, Yi Ku and Masako would have greatly enriched the University and Korean higher education at large both as managers and benefactors. Masako and Yi Ku's dream of advancing educational services in Korea, however, was dashed to pieces by the angry opposition.

Masako was deeply hurt by the poisoned arrows directed to her. But she grieved even more over the pain and hurt meant for Yi Ku.

Since his birth, Korea had done absolutely nothing for Yi Ku. If anything, it had rejected and ignored him even when he sought for its help for securing a Korean passport needed for his travel to America. And yet, he gave up a promising career in America as an MIT trained architect intending to become a useful citizen in his father's homeland, and Masako felt deeply sorry for the cruel hurt he had to endure.

Masako was hurt but not resentful. She was taunted and told to go back to her own country but was not deterred. She was now a Korean, and Korea was her land also. She was thankful that Yi Eun knew nothing about the incident, and for his honor's sake she was even more determined to live out her life as a Korean in Korea. She and Yi Eun had already made a solemn pledge to each other that they would live out their remaining life as Koreans in Korea and for Korea and that in the end they would be buried in the Korean soil next to each other.

Masako was resolved to give her life to something else in the way of blessing Korea. She would devote her whole being—her mind, soul, and body—to the care of Korea's neglected and forgotten children— those with physical handicaps and mental disabilities. This was her hope and dream the night before she and Yi Eun left Japan.

In January, 1966 while living on modest financial support provided by the Korean government, Masako rented a small room in Donggyo-dong near the Han River and founded Charity Works Association (Jahaenghoe), similar to Jikokai which she had previously founded in Tokyo.

Its founding members included wives of prominent Korean business leaders as well as performers well-known to the public, among whom were Mrs. Nam Gung-yeong, Myeong Kye-choon, and Miss Han Ki-joo.

Initially, the Charity Works Association began by helping one child with a mental disability, which she found by running an ad in a local newspaper. In the Korean society of the time, families regarded handicapped and mentally disabled children as a family disgrace, and they were customarily kept inside the house, hidden from the public. Within one year, however, as the word about the Charity Works Association spread, the number of handicapped children under Masako's care increased to ten.

"An angel is among us," people were murmuring to one another. "She is searching for the paraplegic, the blind, the deaf, and other handicapped children and youth to help and teach them to read, write, and make things with their own hands," they whispered to their neighbors incredulously.

An angelic savior, they thought, came to their land to rescue its forgotten, despised, and dejected.

Masako was a highly gifted artist, excelling in cloisonné, calligraphy, floral drawing, and ceramic art, and in order to supplement the Association's operational funds Masako opened a cloisonné craft shop to make glass-glazed broaches, beads, pendants, and other jewelry of exquisite beauty.

Masako in her cloisonné workshop
Source: Myeonghui-weon

Every piece of cloisonné jewelry had to be made by hand, and many a time Masako's hands were so swollen and painful that she could not hold an object and had to stop. For ceramic baking, she used a burner requiring a foot-operated bellows. For an old woman of 66, it was physically exhausting, but worse, her feet would be frequently swollen and painful. Also, in the steamy hot summer climate of Korea, the heat from the burner would turn her workshop into an oven, drenching her in sweat from head to toe.

Then suddenly, Masako had to undergo another painful sadness with the death of her beloved Queen Yun.

No one in Korea was more excited by Yi Eun's return than Queen Yun. She had pleaded with Masako to help Yi Eun return to Korea in any way possible in a stretcher or on someone's back. From the moment Yi Eun arrived in Seoul, Queen Yun could not wait to see him, but the hospital staff would not allow it, fearing that the meeting might cause Yi Eun a fatal emotional shock. Consequently, Masako and the doctors kept postponing the meeting. Then, on January 3, 1966, the queen suddenly died.

Queen Yun had entered the Joseon Kingdom's palace at 13 to become the wife of Sunjong. She became a widow twenty years later at the young age of 33 when her husband died in 1925 without a child. For more than 40 years after that, with no close kin, she had held affectionate feelings for Yi Eun and Masako and was comforted by her thoughts of them. Masako too had been loved and comforted by her genuine affection and support. Queen Yun's death, therefore, left a sad, empty spot in her heart.

After Queen Yun's death, Masako, Yi Ku, and Julia moved into the Nakseonjae. When Yi Eun was a child, he had lived there and had many fond memories of the royal residence. Therefore, Masako hoped more than anything for Yi Eun to return to the Nakseonjae and live out his life there in peace and quiet.

Early in October, 1967, Masako founded another charity organization with the help of the Seoul YMCA for the primary purpose of caring for those with sight, hearing and speech impairment as well as polio victims.

The Seoul YMCA had been operating a charity agency called Borin-weon (Neighborhood Assistance Association) since 1922 to help the poor and the needy, and in 1967 it decided to place the agency under Masako's care, also appointing her as its first Board President.

In honor of Yi Eun, whose pen name was Shining Light (Myeonghui), Masako and YMCA leaders renamed it Shining Light Association (Myeonghui-weon) on October 20, Yi Eun's 70th birthday.

On the day of her inauguration as board president, she was so happy she could hardly sit still. She kept thinking about her beloved husband. "How wonderful it would be if we worked together. We would have already accomplished so much . . ." she mused.

Still holding a bouquet of flowers presented to her during the ceremony, she rushed to see Yi Eun at the hospital to share her joy and happiness. "Oh, how excited and pleased he was . . ." she told a reporter afterwards about her imaginary conversation with Yi Eun on that happy day.

Yi Eun too had a special place in the history of the Seoul YMCA. When it was first established in 1903 Emperor Gojong, Yi Eun's father, had taken a deep interest in it believing that the future of Korea depended on its youth.

Accordingly, when the first YMCA building was constructed in central Seoul in 1907, Gojong donated substantial funds and sent Yi Eun, recently chosen as the Crown Prince, to attend the dedication ceremony. Yi Eun personally wrote "1907" in the building's corner stone.

In her inauguration address as the first Board President of Shining Light Association, Masako thanked everyone involved and shared her dreams and hopes: "Thank you for graciously remembering and honoring His Highness, King Yeongchin (Yi Eun's official name as known by Koreans)."

"Since long before I came to Korea, it has been my utmost wish to care for physically handicapped and mentally disabled people . . . Thank you for your support in helping me fulfill my wish with the expansion of Borin-weon's charity work to include those with sight, hearing and speech impairment as well as polio victims."

"Beginning next year," she continued, "we will provide these children with training in various skills so that they can lead independent lives as proud citizens. We will also secure workshops, a dormitory, and garden plots . . ." Masako was not a young woman any more. Soon she would be 70 years old, and yet she was thinking like a youth full of hopes and dreams.

Immediately, Masako turned an available space in the YMCA building into a classroom for training of the handicapped in sewing, embroidery, weaving, and carpentry.

On October 20, 1967, Masako, Yi Ku, and Julia celebrated Yi Eun's 70th birthday in his hospital room. They prayed that the next birthday celebration would be held at the Nakseonjae with friends, supporters, and guests from all sectors of Korean society.

Masako with her new students in 1968 Source: Myeonghui-weon

April 28, 1970 was the golden anniversary of Masako and Yi Eun's marriage, and Seoul YMCA held a magnificent party, regrettably without Yi Eun's presence.

During the celebration, Masako reminisced about her silver anniversary 25 years before celebrated in a Tokyo bomb shelter in 1945 beneath American fire-bombing. It was simple and awkward. "How wonderful it is for us to celebrate our golden anniversary here in Korea at the YMCA with so many well-wishers," she mused.

But, with her husband still confined in a hospital room, Masako was sad and prayed silently, "We do not need such celebrations. The only thing we need is His Highness' recovery. His health is our only wish and hope."

Ever since Yi Eun returned to Korea, Masako had visited him every morning at the hospital, rain or shine, to encourage and help, sometimes feeding him, sometimes holding his hands, sometimes combing his hair, sometimes talking to him in silence, sometimes massaging his paralyzed hands and legs, and sometimes just sitting next to him.

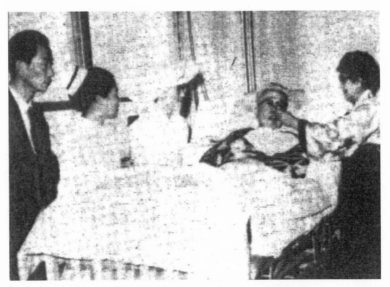

Masako nursing Yi Eun at St. Mary's Hospital

Four days later, on May 1, 1970, at 5 o'clock in the early morning, Masako received an urgent call from St. Mary's Hospital. Yi Eun's condition, the caller said, was critical. When she and Yi Ku rushed to the hospital, Dr. Kim Hak-joong told them that at 3 o'clock Yi Eun had suffered convulsions and gone into coma. Dr. Kim gave no encouragement about Yi Eun's prognosis.

Believing that Yi Eun should spend his last minutes at his childhood home, Masako had Yi Eun taken to the Nakseonjae by ambulance, still connected to intravenous tubes. Inside the ambulance, Masako desperately wished for Yi Eun to open his eyes just once. She wished to look into his eyes and say her last goodbye.

When they arrived at the Nakseonjae at 7:30 a.m., Masako entreated Yi Eun, "Your Highness, please I beg you, open your eyes just once. You have returned to the Nakseonjae, which you have longed to see for 60 years. Before you go, please look at the Nakseonjae . . ."

Yi Eun never opened his eyes. At 12:30 his blood pressured dropped, and at 1:00 p.m. he stopped breathing.

"Goodbye, Your Highness. Go in peace." Masako whispered. She had a million things to say, but that was all she could manage.

"He came home finally," she murmured, "but he is going away without even seeing his beloved home or touching its soil." The more she thought about the prince's fate, the sadder she became. It was Masako's saddest day since the death of her son, little Jin, 47 years before.

On May 9, following a Catholic requiem mass, a grand funeral was held for Yi Eun, befitting a crown prince, held under the auspices of the Jeonju Yi Clan Association in front of the Daejojeon Hall of Changdeok Palace. Gathered for the funeral were numerous dignitaries of the Korean government as well as an imperial delegation from Tokyo.

Upon leaving Changdeok Palace, the hearse carrying Yi Eun's casket slowly moved through a crowd of several hundred thousand grieving citizens toward the Yi Royal Cemetery of Yeongweon at Geumgok, in the outskirt of Seoul.

Countless mourners watched the funerary procession from roof tops, house windows, and street corners, some sitting and others standing. Their grief was genuine and a comfort to Masako' heavy heart.

"Your Highness, your people love you," Masako said, facing the hearse. "The beautiful, cloudless sky and the warm feelings of your people are guiding your journey . . . If Your Highness can see all these crowds, you will be so pleased and laugh with joy . . . See how dearly your people love you, and now rest in peace."

Masako in mourning during Yi Eun's funeral with Yi Ku and Julia

Yi Eun was buried on a hillside a short distance from the tombs of his father, Gojong, and his half-brother, Sunjong.

"The three of them, a father and his two sons, are together now," Masako mused. "They must have so much to talk about . . ."

Yi Eun was 73 years old when he died, 6 years and 6 months after coming home from his long exile.

Along the way during his exile, Yi Eun might have considered suicide in despair, but he always remembered his father's last advice, "Above all, be patient, and be patient again. Until the right time comes, endure all hardships and obstacles which come in your way." Yi Eun waited and waited for the right time, enduring all hardships and learning things which would be useful when that right time came. It never came.

Following a period of mourning, Masako devoted her mind, body, and soul to the charity work which she had begun while Yi Eun was still living.

First, on May 5, 1971, she received a government approval to incorporate Shining Light Association as a social service corporation. A month later, on June 3, she began construction of a four storey trade school in Insa-dong in the central part of Seoul to expand the educational programs begun by Shining Light Association in the YMCA building four years before. Masako named the trade school Shining Grace Institute (Myeonghye Hoegwan) after Yi Eun's and her pen name, with Shining from Yi Eun's Shining Light (Myeonghui) and Grace (Hye) from Masako's Beauty and Grace (Gahye).

The trade school was built with donations provided by the founders of Myeonghui-weon. They included Lee Yong-seol, chairman of the Seoul YMCA board, Pastor Kim Woo-hyen, former board president of the Seoul YMCA Borin-weon, and Dr. Kim Myeong-seon, the former vice president of Yonsei Christian University.

At the same time, Masako recruited Japanese sponsors for her charity work from among her friends and acquaintances in Japan. Masako's Japanese supporters, numbering more than 200, established a sister organization called Shining Grace Association (Meikeikai). It became Masako's major financial support base.

In the meantime, the number of disabled children being cared for at the Charity Works Association in Donggyo-dong continued to increase, and its limited physical space was becoming a critical problem. So, in October, 1972, Masako built Jahye Hakkyo (Charity and Compassion School) in Tapdong, Suweon City, south of Seoul. It had a spacious playground, classrooms, and skill-learning workshops.

"The handicapped and disabled children," Masako reminisced years later, "had no place to go for physical activities. How tearfully delighted I was to watch them play, study, and receive practical training in various skills with joy and laughter in the new school!"

Masako's journey from a beginning with one disabled child at the Charity Works Association, in January, 1966, to this point was not always smooth. There were disappointments and heartaches. As with most charity works, money was always in short supply. Ever striving to help meet the needs, she tried to save every penny earned through her strenuous labor in her cloisonné craft workshop.

In 1972, Masako began earnestly looking for a piece of land on which to construct a new school for the Charity Works Association, which had been steadily growing in size.

She made a down payment on a lot in Suweon City, south of Seoul, with money she had been saving. A few days later, however, she discovered that she had been swindled by a crook, and she lost all the money she had paid.

When this story appeared in a local daily, a reader offered Masako a large piece of land as a gift. She was overjoyed by the surprise turn of events.

Soon Masako had a personal acquaintance, which happened to be a building contractor, begin construction of the badly needed school on the lot.

When the building was completed, however, the contractor informed Masako that his costs had exceeded the originally anticipated amount and demanded $100,000 more in addition to the money she had already paid.

The school's new semester was to begin in a few days. Desperate, Masako contacted Korea's First Lady, Madame Yook Yeong-soo, the wife of President Park Jung-hee., who had been generously supporting her charity work.

A few days later, Korea's First Lady invited Masako to the presidential mansion and personally placed in her hand an envelope. Arriving back at her Nakseonjae residence, she opened the envelope with Miss Eom Jeong-bok, her assistant, who had been waiting for Masako's arrival nervously.

Inside the envelope was a bundle of cashier's checks, which instantly set the two to screaming and dancing with joy. Madame Yook had given her enough money to pay the contractor and secure the new school building![17]

This was how the Charity Works Association, originally begun with one student, became Jahye Hakkyo (Charity and Compassion School) with more than a hundred disabled students.

Jahye Hakkyo (School) in Suweon, Korea
(completed in 1972)

As her social work continued to expand, Masako wanted to know how other advanced nations were caring for their disabled children. She was curious about their facilities, programs, goals and objectives as well as their support bases. She also wanted to raise funds. With this objective, in September, 1973, she spent a month visiting eight nations: Sweden, West Germany, Italy, France, England, Switzerland, Denmark, and the United States.

In Denmark, Sweden, and West Germany, she found superior programs and facilities well-funded by their governments, and

America impressed her with its ongoing development of various skill training programs for the handicapped and the disabled.

Most significant, she learned that the advanced nations were not simply providing care for the handicapped but were seeking to help them lead independent lives as adults similar to her own goals in Korea.

As one of her fund-raising events, during this tour, Masako held a fashion show exhibiting beautiful court dresses of the Joseon Kingdom that she had collected over the years. Accompanying her for this purpose was a Catholic nun, Sophia (Korean name: Choi Bun-i). Looking much like a male, the nun played the role of Crown Prince Yi Eun walking side by side with Masako, the Crown Princess of Joseon Kingdom.

During the tour Masako could not help reminiscing about her last European travel. She wondered, though in vain: "How wonderful it would be if His Highness also came along to expand our knowledge for the care of our disabled children! We would accomplish so much together."

Three months after returning from Europe, Masako dedicated a girls' dormitory built for the Jahye Hakkyo (Charity and Compassion School) in Suweon City. Among Jahye Hakkyo's disabled students, some were so severely handicapped physically that they could not walk daily to and from the school. So Masako had been dreaming of a dormitory for such children. Help for its construction came from many people and organizations. Rotary Clubs, Lions Clubs, and other service organizations, as well as many individuals in Japan along with Korean supporters, raised money through a fund-raising campaign named "Buy a square foot for Jahye Hakkyo".

While many donors bought one or two square feet of land, others bought larger pieces, bringing Masako's dream for a girls' dormitory to a reality.

To supplement such donations, Masako expanded her art work. In addition to the glass glazed cloisonné jewelry, she produced decorated porcelain, calligraphy writings, and floral drawings.

Her labor was physically demanding as well as mentally exhausting, but many a day Masako worked in the shop 12 or more hours, sometimes in making 20 to 30 items in one day. These she sold through her kiosks at the Lotte Hotel and the Chosun Hotel in downtown Seoul.

She also held bazaars and public exhibitions where people would buy her art products, in support of her social services. In these endeavors, Julia, Masako's daughter-in-law, was most generously helpful with her time and talents. Julia was herself a gifted artist and made many artistically designed clothes, blankets, cushions, and dolls, donating much of the proceeds from the sale of these at bazaars.

Masako at her kiosk featuring cloisonné jewelry
Right: Masako's art productions including calligraphic
works, paintings, and painted vases
Source: Myeonghui-weon

Among Masako's artistic productions her calligraphic art of the Chinese character和 (hwa) was her favorite. Meaning peace, harmony, and friendship it was sought out by many and hangs on the living walls of many Korean homes.

Having personally experienced the pain and heartaches brought upon by political, racial, and cultural conflicts Masako had come to value peace and harmony as precious as life itself. Along with her social work, therefore, she was ever striving to promote for peace, harmony, and friendship in the world, especially between Korea and Japan, the two mortal enemies whose fate was intertwined with her own. For this the Korea University of Foreign Studies honored her with a doctorate in a grand ceremony.

Masako's favorite calligraphic work
Source: Myeonghui-weon

Along with producing crafts, Masako held fashion shows featuring beautiful royal dresses of the Joseon Kingdom. Starting with the dazzling royal wedding costumes which she and Yi Eun wore during their wedding ceremony in Changdeok Palace in 1923, Masako had collected many rare Joseon Kingdom court dresses. No matter how hard Masako labored, however, her art production and fashion shows were insufficient to undergird all of her social service operations.

Another pressing problem was developing for Masako. The physical surroundings of the Shining Grace Institute, located in the central part of Seoul city, were becoming a crowded red light district, posing serious problems for its handicapped children. All concerned concluded that the Institute had to be relocated to a safe place.

In 1974, Masako was 74 years old. Most people would have been by then long retired from their active working life, but Masako was not deterred. She decided to go abroad and appeal for financial donations, and in November of that year, she went to Japan with a group of students from Shining Grace Institute. In appealing for financial contributions from her supporters, she wanted to show the fruits of her labor.

Masako visited Lions and Rotary Clubs as well as Japan-Korea Friendship Associations asking them to display and advertise her art productions. She also visited the offices of all 50 local prefectural governments, appealing for specific donations.

Wherever they went, the students showed off their newly gained skills and put on concerts, drawing praise and admiration from their Japanese audiences. Even in the post-World War II era, many Japanese regarded their Imperial family with a special emotion and nostalgia, and Masako, an imperial princess, was welcomed in Japan warmly with respect and affection, and in many cases with sympathy for her tragic past. And her Japanese supporters responded generously to her requests of help for her students.

Six months later, in May 1975, she made another trip to Japan, repeating her fund-raising circuit. Then, a year later, in 1976, she went to America for a whirlwind visit to Korean-American communities in major cities from Honolulu to Seattle, to Chicago, to Detroit, to Boston, to New York, and to Los Angeles.

Commenting on her American tour, a Korean reporter in Chicago wrote, "Madame Yi Bangja [Korean pronunciation for Masako] . . . albeit her 70 years of personal misfortunes . . . is engaged in a truly noble service. She has come here, carrying her old and aged body, for the sake of the physically and mentally disabled children of Korea . . ."

By 1978, the Korean economy was prospering with massive industrialization and expanding exports. Accordingly, the leaders of large corporations, including Hyundai and Daerim, also became interested in Masako's social services.

On October 20, their financial contributions, and donations from others in Korea and Japan enabled Masako to successfully relocate Shining Grace Institute from the crowded and dangerous central part of Seoul to a spacious location at Cheolsan-ri in Gwang Myeong City.

Shining Grace Institute in Gwangmyeong City
(completed in 1978)
Source: Myeonghui-weon

On November 12, 1981, Shining Grace Institute, now expanded in its educational programs, received a government approval to become a full-fledged school, Myeonghye Hakkyo (Shining Grace School). Consisting of two levels, its Primary Division provided one year of basic education and some practical training to students 13-18 years old. Upon graduation from the Primary Division, the students entered the Practical Training Division to be trained as professional technicians in carpentry, sewing, building design, electronic gadgets assembly, hand weaving, machine weaving, machine embroidery, and other skills.

The students also participated in numerous extracurricular activities including dancing, chorus, bands, sports, typing, and so on. Masako was deeply moved and gratified whenever she saw her students with sight, hearing and speech impairment perform dances, sing in chorus, or play musical instruments. In 1980, she was overwhelmed with an indescribable joy when some students who were polio victims won a gold medal at a Special Olympics held at Osaka, Japan.

The graduates found jobs, and some students married their classmates, starting homes as happy couples.

By 1981, Masako's 15 year labor resulted in the birth of two schools for Korea's physically handicapped and mentally disabled children: Jahye Hakkyo (Charity and Compassion School) in Suweon City and Myeonghye Hakkyo (Shining Grace School) in Gwangmyeong City. In addition, there was Shining Light Association (Myeonghui-weon), a major corporation operating Myeonghye Hakkyo and multiple other social services for adults and children.

Masako was now 81 years old, and she was giving an increasing attention to Yi Ku, her son, and his personal welfare.

Along with her charity work, Yi Ku had been her primary source of pride and joy. She loved him as the apple of her eye and treasured every moment with him. Their living together at the Nakseonjae brought her much comfort and happiness.

When he arrived in Seoul with his parents in 1963, Yi Ku was no longer a mere private citizen. As Yi Eun's son, he represented the Yi Royal Dynasty; accordingly he was required to act as the leader in all Yi Royal Clan ritual matters. In particular, Yi Ku had the responsibility of leading the solemn ritual of paying homage to innumerable ancestors of the Jeonju Yi Royal Clan, especially the deceased kings of the Joseon Kingdom.

Such ancestral rituals entailed traveling hundreds of miles in the course of a year from one royal cemetery to another and from one ancestral shrine to another, bowing down on the knees several times at each sacred place. Some days, Yi Ku bowed down more than a thousand time times in a day, until his knees were bruised and bleeding. He wrapped the bleeding knees with latex pads, which soon became ragged.

At the same time, Yi Ku sought to be useful to Korean society with the architectural engineering knowledge and training he had received in America, and he strove tirelessly in this regard. He taught at Korea's most prestigious universities, including Seoul National University and Yonsei University.

He also did contractual work in architectural design in Australia, Vietnam, and Guam. From each trip abroad he would gain new ideas on marketable crafts for the purpose of developing new Korean export markets. He designed national parks. He even designed the new school building for Shining Light Association. And along the way, he was becoming an invaluable asset and help to Masako's charity work.

But all during this time, Yi Ku had to struggle with three demons constantly plaguing him. First, he became increasingly conscious that in Korea he was like "a drop of oil floating on water." No one, including the officials of the Yi Royal Clan, took him in as a real Korean, and he felt an invisible boundary line between himself and other Koreans. Many a time, he felt like an orphan in his father's land.

Secondly, many Koreans approached him with business proposals, but none of them, he felt, was seeking to become a genuine, trusting partner. All were seeking to take advantage of his social position and especially his princely status.

Thirdly, the Yi Royal Clan did not approve of his marriage to Julia Mullock. As the last living head of the Yi Royal family, Yi Ku had the responsibility of providing a male heir to continue the royal lineage, but Julia appeared to be barren. Furthermore, many influential members of the Jeonju Yi Royal Clan preferred having a full-blooded Korean to continue the royal lineage. Accordingly, they pressured Yi Ku to divorce Julia and marry a Korean woman.

The three demons in time wrought havoc in Yi Ku's life as well as in the life of Julia and Masako.

In 1972, Yi Ku established an aerial surveying business with a partner, but soon he became a target of fraud and exploitation. Despite seven years of tireless effort, his business failed and underwent bankruptcy in 1979. No one in Korea came to the rescue in his desperate days. Korea, he felt, rejected him.

Completely disillusioned, Yi Ku left Korea for Japan in June, 1979. "Korea," he bitterly declared, "is neither my home nor my country . . . I am an orphan without a country of his own." Two years later, he and Julia divorced.

These events devastated Masako, breaking her heart to a million pieces. "It was unbearably painful for me," she said, "to see Yi Ku and Julia divorce." "His Highness and I underwent pain because of our fate beyond our control. Have Yi Ku and Julia been born with a similar fate to face such agonies?" she wondered.

Masako felt that her son never had a fair chance in Korea without genuine friends and supporters, but she was not bitter.

"Yi Ku tried his best," she said, "but his businesses kept failing. To begin with, he was an engineer, and somewhat academic. As such he was not good at handling money. In his businesses, he focused more on technical skills than on management, becoming an easy prey for exploitation by others."

After Yi Ku's departure Masako's health rapidly declined. Unable to eat well, she lost weight and began showing signs of aging. In November, 1983, she was diagnosed with a stomach cancer. Following a successful surgery at Seoul National University Hospital, she recovered and returned home at the Nakseonjae two months later. A week later, however, she suffered side effects from the surgery, going back to the hospital for another seven weeks.

Julia was a strong woman. Even after the divorce from Yi Ku, she continued to live in Korea, operating a gift shop in Seoul. Believing that she had married into Korea, like Masako, she stayed close to her former mother-in-law, helping her generously in myriad ways.

Masako had hoped to spend the rest of her life with Yi Ku close by. Now, she painfully missed him. She was also worried daily about his welfare. She tried every means to persuade him to return to Korea but in vain.

Masako, however, refused to despair. She unwaveringly believed that her son loved her and that he would honor her wish. "I miss him with an unbearable pain in my heart," she wrote in her final autobiography in 1985, "but as his mother I understand his shattered mind and emotions as well as his loneliness" "Regardless of what others may say, I firmly believe that my son loves me, his mother, and therefore will come back to me and stand by my side before I die."

Then, she made a passionate appeal, her first and last, to her fellow Koreans on behalf of her son. "As you have treated me so graciously, please accept my son with kindness. And even after I am gone, please love him as you have loved me. This is my entreat from the bottom of my heart."

Yi Ku, however, did not return. And sensing that she did not have much time to wait, Masako flew to Tokyo in the fall of 1986 to see him. She lived with him for a while, though not always under pleasant circumstances.

A year before she left for Japan, she had entrusted Shining Light Association and Myeonghye Hakkyo (Shining Grace School) to Eternal Help, a Catholic charity organization operated by the St. Mary Nuns Association.

While in Japan, her health continued to deteriorate. All her friends encouraged her to return to Korea, to her land and her home. One year later, Masako returned to the Nakseonjae. Then on October 27, 1986 she collapsed, suffering from severe anemia. She was physically and mentally exhausted.

In the course of recovery, Masako suddenly found a new incentive and a new hope for living. She wanted to create a small art museum on the Bright Sunshine Association campus to display Yi Eun's favorite paintings and thereby commemorate Yi Eun's life.

"I will endure all things until I complete this project," Masako promised herself. She worked on it for two and half years.

Then, on April 11, 1989, Masako suddenly suffered a high temperature and threw up blood. She was taken to the Seoul National University Hospital. Knowing that her death was near, she called Sophia (Choi Bun-i), a Catholic nun and long-time friend. During a fund-raising trip to Europe, Sophia had played the role of Yi Eun, walking side by side with Masako in fashion shows featuring the Joseon Kingdom's court dresses.

Ever since Yi Eun came under the care of St. Luke's Hospital in Tokyo and was baptized as a Catholic, Masako had special feelings for the Catholic community, and along the way she made friends with many priests and nuns. This had continued at St. Mary's Hospital in Seoul. So much so that in 1985 Masako placed Shining Light Association and Myeonghye Hakkyo (Shining Grace School), the loves of her heart, in the hands of the nuns at Eternal Help, a Catholic charity organization.

As Sophia stood next to Masako's bed holding her hand, Masako said, "How happy I am to see you! You were always so wonderful in the fashion shows acting as His Highness. I love you, and I have asked you to come and baptize me. Would you please?"

"Oh, how honored I am! God bless you," Sophia replied placing a gentle kiss on Masako's forehead.

Sophia knew how much Masako loved and missed Yi Eun. After the baptism, she held Masako's hands, frail and weak, and whispered into her ear, "His Highness has been waiting for you for many years. Now, when you go to heaven, please see the love of your life."

"O yes, yes!" Masako replied with a smile.

During the same period, on April 21, Princess Deok-hye, Masako's Korean sister-in-law and best friend, died. Taken to Japan as a little girl and later forced to marry a Japanese, the princess had broken down mentally under the stresses of life in exile. In time, she was taken to a mental hospital, where she languished in a vegetative state.

From the moment of their first meeting during Masako's first Korea trip in 1923, they had been fond of each other, and for 60 years since then Masako loved Deok-hye like a little sister. During the last 20 years of their lives they lived close to each other at the Nakseonjae.

Nine days later, after Deok-hye's death, on April 30, Masako was taken back to the Nakseonjae. Soon after arrival there, she also died surrounded by her loving Korean friends.

Japanese Princess Nashimoto Masako was 88 years old when she died as Yi Bangja, a Korean.

Yi Bangja

EPILOGUE

The Greatest Thing in the World

As I was following Masako through her life's journey a myriad of questions came to my mind, but more than anything, I wanted to know if she ever regretted not having been chosen to become the wife of Emperor Hirohito. Did she ever wish that she had become the Empress of Japan?

In my imagination I heard her reply with a gentle smile, "O yes, of course, but only for a day, just out of curiosity."

Born a member of Japan's imperial family, Masako knew too well that the palace was also a prison shackling its residents, including the Empress, with untold rituals, rules, and protocols controlling every word spoken and every step taken.

For Masako, free-spirited, adventurous, and passionate, the palace life would have been too stifling. Just for one day though, she might have wanted to try the Empress' throne, just out of curiosity.

In fact, along the way, more than once, Masako had much sympathy for the Empress Hirohito, her first cousin. Like herself, the Empress was barren for a long time, unable to bear a prince for the Chrysanthemum throne. It was a burden too oppressive for an empress to bear, and Masako shared that burden. She also shed tears for the Empress during the war and in the days following Emperor Hirohito's humiliating surrender. She knew that the Empress, along with the Emperor, was under unbearable stress, and she felt deeply sorry for her.

From early on Masako was driven by empathy and passion. When she first learned about the misfortunes of Yi Eun, a little lonely

Korean boy at her Imperial Peers school, Gakushuin, ten-year old Princess Masako's heart went out to him. "Poor boy," she thought to herself with heart-felt sympathy. "They say that he has been brought here against his will and that he was not even allowed to see his mother when she was dying! How sad and painful it must have been for the young boy. I am so very sorry."

The Korean boy was only a stranger from a faraway foreign country, but she was emotionally stirred by his plight. When Japan's rulers forced her to marry the Korean boy a decade later as a sacrifice on the altar of their imperialistic ambitions, she fell in love with him and loved him with all passion. She was blissfully happy when she was with him and missed him with pain when separated.

One day, while Yi Eun was away at a military training camp, she wrote in her diary:

> Ah! Today I cannot wait to see him and to visit.
> I so dearly miss him, and I am thinking only of him.
> I am so very happy.
> He is so bright and wise; he is healthy.
> Even though he is from another country there is not a
>   trace of strangeness between us.
> As soon as we say good bye I miss him and I want to see
>   him again.
> While waiting for him eagerly, I forget the passing of time
>   as well as any troubling thoughts.
> A half day goes by quickly as I am wrapped with feelings
>   of bliss . . ."

Masako's love for Yi Eun was deep, genuine, and therefore unquencherable. "I am binding myself in marriage to his warm heart, and not anything else," she assured herself. "The politics of Korea-Japan union is none of my concern. My utmost wish is to love and comfort him in his loneliness as his warm, caring wife and friend. That shall be my duty and my destiny," Princess Masako promised herself.

For 70 years, Masako loved Yi Eun with the same passionate love in good times as well as bad times, in sickness and in health, in life and even after his death.

In the days of her destitution and desperation during the postwar period, Masako could have opted to settle in America, in peace and comfort, with her son who had a promising future as an MIT-trained architectural engineer. Masako, however, decided to go to Korea with her ailing husband and begin a new life as a Korean, knowing fully that Japanese were not welcome in Korea.

Yi Eun's life-long dream was to return to his homeland and live out his life among his people. In Masako's love of Yi Eun there was no other option but to help him realize his dream.

When Masako, as a teenager, felt herself being pulled to Yi Eun, his burden and his heartache and those of his people became her own. "As I came to know His Highness," she reminisced, "his plight became very personal... The more I studied about Korea and its tribulations and sufferings brought upon by Japan, the more pain I felt. They were no longer Korea's or His Highness' but mine."

It was with the same empathy and passion that Masako, now as Yi Bangja, loved Korean children with physical and mental abnormalities, whom even their own people disdained and neglected. In loving them she went out of her way looking for them and bringing them into her heart to share her life with them. Surely it was *dynamic and active compassion* at its best.

One day, upon her return from a short fundraising trip to Japan, Masako entered a dormitory housing the disabled children. As she entered a room, children with twisted arms and disfigured faces struggled out of their bath tub, all wet and with soapy water dripping from their naked bodies.

With joy and excitement, one child clung to Masako' left side and another to her right, the soapy water still dripping from their bodies. Masako hugged them tight, and looking into each child's eyes, she said, "My dear ones, I am here. I am here now. I have just come home."[18]

This story reminded me of an incident in which I was involved personally in 1944, nearly 70 years ago, as an eight year old elementary school pupil. Japan ruled Korea then, and my school principal was a Japanese.

One morning while rushing from the school playground to my classroom I ran smack into the Japanese principal. He loathed being touched by a Korean boy. Shouting curses at me, he kept saying, "Chosenjing! Kitanai, kitanai! (You Korean, filthy, filthy!)"

Koreans, sharing their collective memory of Japanese atrocities and misdeeds committed by Toyotomi Hideyoshi's samurai soldiers in 1592 and 1597 and those of the 20th century, do not hesitate to reveal their anti-Japanese sentiments. They believe that the Japanese have committed heinous sins and crimes against Korea and the Koreans, too many to be forgiven. Those sentiments have been on the rise in recent years as Korea and Japan are at war verbally over a disputed island and other ugly issues from the past.

When a report appeared in the news recently that the next big earthquake would hit the Tokyo area, possibly submerging the entire city in the Pacific Ocean, some Koreans welcomed it on their Twitter and added, "Not just Tokyo, but let the entire land of Japan sink and disappear into the Pacific Ocean forever!"

To this vengeful outburst, a thoughtful Korean responded via social network service, "Please, please. Just calm down, my fellow Koreans! Remember Nashimoto Masako." "The land of Japan" he reminded, "gave birth to Toyotomi Hideyoshi, Ito Hirobumi, Miura Goro, Terauchi Masatake, Minami Jiro, Abe Nobuyuki, and a thousand other cruel samurai, who gave Korea much pain and suffering, but it also gave birth to Nashimoto Masako, who loved Korea more than Koreans!"

Masako is known to Koreans informally as Madame Yi Bangja and formally as the last Crown Princess of Joseon Royal Dynasty, but she is loved, honored, and respected by them as "the mother of Korea's forgotten children" and as "a Japanese who loved Korea more than Koreans."

To an interviewer one day in 1975, Masako said, "As I care for the people in need here, I am convinced that I am becoming more Korean each day . . . His Highness is no longer with us, but I think of him daily in my heart, and I hope that when I see him again I can tell him that I did something worthy after he left us."[19] Masako's love of Yi Eun endured even long after his death, and nothing gave her greater joy and happiness than becoming more Korean each day and doing something he approved.

And for Yi Eun, Korea's last crown prince, it would have been his ultimate personal joy and satisfaction that Masako, his Japanese wife, loved Korea more than Koreans.

Soon after her betrothal to Yi Eun in 1917 Masako was hoping and dreaming for the day when she could reciprocate the cultural and human blessings which ancient Koreans bestowed upon Japan during its formative period. She fulfilled that dream far beyond measure. She not only blessed Korea but loved it and its people with all her heart, soul, mind, and body.

And Masako did so for the land that had taken the life of her Little Jin and broken her young and tender heart to a million pieces.

She was an angel from the land of samurai.

In 1981, the Korean government honored her with the *Moranjang*, the second highest meritorial order of Korea, and on May 2, 1989, she was posthumously honored with the Grand Order of *Mugunghwajang*, the nation's highest order of merit.

Nowhere in her personal writings or in those written by others about her, is there any hint that Masako had ever known about Henry Drummond's *The Greatest Thing in the World*, a treatise on love, but it was through her ability to love and empathize that Masako saw beautiful rainbows in a world beset by cruelties, uncertainties, and contradictions.

Somehow early in her life, she discovered that "love suffers long and is kind . . . does not insist on its own way . . . does not rejoice at wrong, but rejoices in the right . . . bears all things, believes all things, hopes all things, and endures all things."

She also knew that love was the wellspring of life and happiness. When she learned that Princess Deok-hye, after many decades of vegetative existence, regained her consciousness upon her return to her homeland surrounded by her old, loving friends and relatives, she exclaimed, "Ah, such is the power of love and affection. It works miracles!"

With the greatest thing in the world, the empathetic love and active compassion, Masako redeemed her own world of cruelties, uncertainties, and contradictions, for such love sees beauty in the ugly, value in the worthless, and hope in despair.

On May 8, 1989, a public funeral service befitting a crown princess was held for Masako in Seoul under the auspices of the Jeonju Yi Clan Association, in accordance with the mortuary protocols of the royal court of Joseon Kingdom.

It was attended by more than a thousand dignitaries and guests, including Prime Minister Gang Yeong-hoon of Korea and an imperial delegation sent by Japanese Emperor Akihito, represented by Prince Mikasanomiya Takahito, the younger brother of the recently deceased Emperor Hirohito.

An impressive royal bier was borne by 100 high school students in a mile long funeral procession leading to the courtyard of the Grand Jongmyo Ancestral Shrine of Joseon Kingdom.

In front of the bier were 260 multi-colored eulogy flags, sent from all corners of the country, blowing magnificently in the wind.

They were followed by a single long flag on which was written: This is the sacred coffin of Crown Princess Eumin. (Eumin was the name given posthumously to Yi Eun by the Jeonju Yi Clan Association).

Staying close to the bier was Yi Ku, Masako's son, whom she had been longing to be with so dearly.

From the Grand Jongmyo Ancestral Shrine, a royal hearse carried Masako's coffin to Yi Eun's tomb in the Geumgok Royal Cemetery in the eastern outskirts of Seoul City, and it was placed next to Yi Eun's, side by side in the same tomb. Thus, after death they were again together as in life.[20]

At the base of their Tomb stands a simple marble marker identifying the couple buried in it: *Crown Prince Eumin and Crown Princess Eumin of Korea*.

To visitors who know their story, the marble stone stands as an eternal monument celebrating the human spirit which, when imbued with empathetic love and active compassion, transforms misfortunes, adversities, and unwished destiny into patches of paradise as beautiful as the rainbow. © Song Nai Rhee

Tomb of Yi Eun and Yi Bangja, Geumgok Royal Cemetery, Geumgok, Korea

REFERENCES

*T*he author is indebted to the following publications for supplementary information and wishes to express his gratitude to their authors and publishers.

Choi, Bo-shik, "A Saint of our Times: Sophia (Choi Bun-i), the Nun" in *Chosun.com—Society Section*, December 24, 2012. (In Korean)

Chosun Ilbo, a Korean daily published in Seoul by Chosun Ilbo Co, Seoul.

Chung, Henry, *The Case of Korea—A Collection of Evidence on the Japanese Domination of Korea, and on Development of the Korean Independence Movement*, Fleming H. Revell Company, London and New York, 1921.

Dong-A Ilbo, a Korean daily published by Dong-A Media Group, Seoul.

Eckert, Carter J., and Ki-baik Lee, Young Ick Lew, Michael Robinson, and Edward W. Wagner, *Korea: Old and New*. Ilchokak Publishers, Seoul, 1990.

Grayson, James H., "The Shinto shrine cult and Protestant martyrs in Korea 1938-1945" in *Missiology*, 29: 287, 2001.

Honda, Setsuko, *Joseon Ocho Saigono Kotaishihi (The Last Crown Princess of Joseon Royal Dynasty)*, Bungei Shunju, Tokyo, 1988. (In Japanese)

Jansen, Marius B., *The Making of Modern Japan*, Belknap Press of Harvard University, Cambridge, 2000.

Jeong, Beom-jun, *Jegugeu Huyedeul (The Remnants of the Korea's Joseon Kingdom)*, Hwangsojari Press, Seoul, 2006. (In Korean)

Kang, T. and Pyeong-dom Kim, The Great Kanto Earthquake and Koreans (Kantodaishinsai to Chosenjin), Tokyo: Misuzu Shobo, 1963. (In Japanese)

Kim, Eul-han, *Joseon eu Majimak Hwangtaeja Yeongchin Wang (The Last Crown Prince of Joseon Kingdom, King Yeongchin)*, Paperroad, Seoul, 2010. (In Korean)

Kim, Hak-joong, *Yeongchin Wang Byeongsang-gi (Sickbed Diaries of King Yeongchin)*, Weolgan Joong-ang, Seoul, 1970/6. (In Korean)

Kim, Sung Gun, "The Shinto shrine issue in Korean Christianity under Japanese colonialism" in *Journal of Church and State*, vol. 39, no 3, 1997.

Lee, Hyeong-geun, *Gunbeon 1-beon eu Oegil Insaeng (One Way Life of Dog Tag # 1)*, Joong ang Daily, Seoul, 1993. (In Korean)

Lee, Jang-rak, *"Hanguk ddang e mutchirira"* ("I will be buried in Korea") (*Life of Dr. Frank William Schofield*), Jeongeumsa, Seoul, 1980. (In Korean)

Legault, B., and John F. Prescott, "The arch agitator": Dr. Frank W. Schofield and the Korean Independence Movement, *The Canadian Veterinary Journal*, Canadian Veterinary Association, 50(8), 2000 (August), 865-872.

Maeil Gyeongje, a Korean business and economics newspaper published by Maekyung Media Group, Seoul.

McClain, James L., *Japan, a Modern History*, W. W. Norton and Company, New York, 2002.

McKenzie, F.A., *Korea's Fight for Freedom*, Fleming H. Revell Company, New York, 1920.

Myeonghui-weon (Bright Sunshine Foundation), *Gahye Yi Bangja Yeosa Chumo Iship Junyeon Ginyeom Hwabojip (Photo Album of Madame Yi Bangja's 20th Memorial Celebration)*, Myeonghui-weon, Seoul, 2009. (In Korean).

Naff, Robert, *The Great Kanto Earthquake Massacre: In 1923 Americans in Japan witnessed the killing of Koreans* and *Socialists*, OhmyNews (International PODCASTS), 9/29/2006.

Nakamura, Shintaro, *Two Thounsand Years of Japan and Korea*, Tokyo, Toho Shuppan, 1981. (In Japanese)

Otabe, Yuji, *Yi Masako: Kankokujinde Kokainaku (Yi Masako: I have no regrets as a Korean)*, Minerva Shobo, Kyoto, 2007. (In Japanese)

Ryang, Sonya, The Great Kanto Earthquake and the Massacre of Koreans in 1923: Notes on Japan's modern national sovereignty in *Anthropological Quarterly*, vol. 76, no.4 (2003), 731-748.

Rhee, Song-Nai, C. Melvin Aikens, Sung-Rak Choi, and Hyuk-Jin Ro, "Korean contributions to agriculture, technology and state formation in Japan: archaeology and history of an epochal thousand years, 400 B.C.-A.D.600" in *Asian Perspectives*, 46/2 (Fall 2007).

Seomundang, *Dokrip Undong (Korean Independence Movements)*, Vol. I and II, Seomundang, Seoul, 1987. (In Korean)

Storry, Richard, *A History of Modern Japan*, Penguin Press, New York, 1976.

Yi, Pangja, (Translated by Kim Sukkyu and edited by Joan Rutt), *The World is One*, Taewon Publishing Company, Seoul & Los Angeles. 1973.

Yamada, Shoji, *The Korean Massacre during the Great Kanto Earthquake and its Aftermath: The Responsibility of the Japanese Government and People (Kantodaishinsaishi no Chosenjin Gyakusatsu to sono ata—Gyakusatsu no Kokka Sekinin to Minshu Sekinin)*, Tokyo: Soshisha, 2011. (In Japanese)

Yoshida, Seiji, *Chosenjin Ianfu to Nihonjin (Korean Comfort Women and the Japanese)*, Shinjinbutsu Oraisha, Tokyo, 1976. (In Japanese)

GLOSSARY OF NAMES IN THE STORY

Abe Nobuyuki (1875-1953), a Japanese general; prime minister of Japan, 1939-1940; Governor General of Korea, 1944-1945.

Ahn Joong-geun (1879-1910), a Korean patriot and independence activist; was tried by the Japanese court and executed at Lyushun Prison, Manchuria, for killing Ito Hirobumi.

Asaka Yasuhiko (1887-1981), A Japanese prince; the eighth son of Asahiko; married Emperor Meiji's daughter; Masako's uncle.

Bonesteel, Charles H. (1909-1977), an American general from New York; served in World War II and the Korean War; served as the commander of US Forces Korea, 1966-69.

Chiang Kai-shek (1887-1975), a Chinese military and political leader; the head of the Kuomintang, the Nationalist Party of China; fought the Chinese Communists and the Japanese.

Deok-hye (1912-1989), a Korean princess. Daughter of Gojong by Lady Yang; Yi Eun's half sister; taken to Japan as a hostage in 1925; forced to marry a Japanese; became a mental patient.

Doolittle, James H. (Jimmy) (1896-1993): An American general from California; in April 1942 he successfully led 16 B-25 medium bombers and bombed Tokyo and other Japanese targets.

Eom Ju-myeong (1896-1976), a Korean military officer and an educator; a niece of Lady Eom, Yi Eun's mother. He was a childhood friend of Yi Eun and accompanied him to Japan.

Fumi (1891-1933), a Japanese princess. She was the eighth daughter of Emperor Meiji and married Prince Asaka Yasuhiko, Masako's uncle.

Gojong (Yi Hee) (1852-1919), the 126th king of Joseon Kingdom of Korea, 1863-1897; Emperor of Korea, 1897-1907; father of Yi Eun.

Gustav Adolf (1882-1973), the king of Sweden, 1950-1973; had deep interest in archaeology and Asian culture; in 1926, he participated in excavations of an ancient Shilla royal tomb of Korea.

Han Chang-soo (1862-?), an official in Gojong's government; after 1905, became pro-Japanese earning hatred among Koreans; served as the head of the Yi Royal Family Affairs Administration.

Hasegawa Yoshimichi (1850-1924), a field marshal in the Imperial Japanese Army; the Governor General of Korea, 1916-1919.

Hindenburg, Paul von (1847-1934), a Prussian-German field marshal and a statesman; Germany's Chief of General Staff, 1916-1919; the president of the German Reich, 1925-1934.

Hirohito (1901-1989), Emperor of Japan, 1912-1989; Japan's wartime emperor; married Kuni Nagako, Masako's first cousin, in January 26, 1924.

Hirota Koki (1878-1948), a Japanese diplomat and politician; prime minister of Japan, 1936-1937; convicted as a Class A war criminal and executed.

Hodge, John R. (1893-1963), an American general; the commander of US XXIV Corps occupying Korea on September 9, 1945; the military governor of South Korea, 1945-1948.

Hong Beom-do (1868-1943), a Korean independence activist; waged numerous battles against Japanese troops in Northeast Korea and Manchuria with spectacular victories.

Inokuma Genichiro (1902-1993), a Japanese painter; well-known for abstract paintings; lived in France, 1938-40 and in New York, 1955-1975; had a stroke and moved back to Japan in 1975.

Inukai Tsuyoshi (1855-1932), a Japanese politician; prime minister, December 13, 1931-May 15, 1932; tried to reign in the military and for that effort was assassinated by young army officers.

Ito Hirobumi (1841-1909), a Japanese politician; the first (1885-88), fifth (1892-96), seventh (1898), and tenth prime minister (1900-1901) of Japan; resident-general of Korea, 1905-1909.

Ito Hirokuni (1870-1931), a Japanese official; Ito Hirobumi's adopted son; minister of the Imperial Household Ministry in 1920.

Itsuko (1882-1976), a Japanese princess; the second daughter of Marquis Nabeshima Naohiro; married Prince Nashimoto Morimasa in November, 1900; mother of Masako and Noriko

Jang Myeon (1899-1966), a Korean statesman; South Korea's ambassador to the United States, 1949-51; the prime minister, 1951-52; vice president, 1956-60; prime minister, 1960-61.

Jo Myeong-ha (1905-1928), a Korean nationalist; on May 14, 1928, attempted to assassinate Prince Kuni Kuniyoshi, the father-in-law of Emperor Hirohito with a poisoned knife.

Kim Eul-han (1906-1992), a Korean journalist; a reporter for various news organizations in Korea and Japan beginning in 1924; the resident correspondent in Tokyo for the Seoul Daily, 1950-1957.

Kim Hak-joong (1923-2013), a Korean physician; a specialist in cardiology and served as a life-time professor of cardiology at the Catholic University Medical School in Seoul.

Kim Il-sung (1912-1994), a Korean politician; in 1945 became the leader of Communist North Korea, serving as Prime Minister, 1948-1972, and as President, 1972-1994.

Kim Jong-pil (1926-), a Korean military officer and a politician; in May 1961 participated in a military coup with General Park Jung-hee; prime minister of South Korea, 1971-75 and 1998-2000.

Kim Jwa-jin (1889-1930), a Korean independence activist; in October 1920 ambushed and killed more than 3000 Japanese troops in southern Manchuria.

Kim Ku (1876-1949), a Korean independence activist; the leader of Korean Provisional Government in Shanghai; trained guerilla fighters against the Japanese.

Kim Kyu-shik (1881-1950), a Korean independence activist; a leader in the Korean Provisional Government in Shanghai; published *La Coree Libre* in Paris; fought the Japanese in Manchuria.

Ko Hee-kyeong (1873-1934), a Korean official in Gojong's government; fluent in English and Japanese; an officer in the Yi Royal Court administration; became Yi Eun's secretary in Tokyo.

Koiso Kuniaki (1880-1950), a Japanese general and a politician; commander of the Japanese Army in Korea in 1935; Governor General of Korea, 1942-44; Prime Minister of Japan, 1944-45 after Tojo.

Konoe Fumimaro (1891-1945), a Japanese politician; prime minister of Japan, 1937-1939 and 1940-1941; Japan committed the Nanjing massacre during his tenure as Prime Minister.

Kuni Asahiko (1824-1891), A Japanese prince; Emperor Ninko's son by adoption; Nashimoto Morimasa's father; Masako's grandfather.

Kuni Kuniyoshi (1873-1929), a Japanese prince and a full general in the Japanese Imperial Army; Prince Asahiko's third son; his eldest daughter, Nagako, married Crown Prince Hirohito.

Kuni Nagako (1903-2000), a Japanese princess; eldest daughter of Prince Kuni Kuniyoshi; married Crown Prince Hirohito in January 1924; the Empress of Japan, 1926-1989.

Lady Eom (1854-1911), a palace court lady of Joseon kingdom of Korea; after Queen Min's death she became Gojong's favorite and gave birth to Yi Eun; established several schools in Seoul.

Lady Yang (1882-1929), a palace court lady of Joseon kingdom of Korea. After the death of Lady Eom, Yi Eun's mother, she became Gojong's favorite and gave birth to Princess Deok-hye.

Lee Bong-chang (1900-1932), a Korean independence activist; as a protégé of Kim Ku, he attempted to assassinate Emperor Hirohito with grenades.

Lee Hyeong-geun (1920-2002), a Korean general; South Korean representative at Panmunjeom Cease-fire Conference in 1951; South Korean Army Chief of Staff, 1956-57.

Lee Wan-yong (1858-1926), a Korean politician; known among Koreans as one of the notorious "Five Traitors of 1905" who sold out Joseon Kingdom of Korea to Japan in 1905.

Lyuh Wun-hyeong (1886-1947), a Korean independence activist, diplomat, journalist, and sportsman; a leading political figure of Korea seeking to establish a free, independent, unified nation.

Mao Zedong (1893-1976), a Chinese communist revolutionary and a politician; Chairman of the Communist Party of China and founder of the People's Republic of China in 1949.

MacArthur, Douglas (1880-1964), an American general; the Supreme Commander for the Allied Powers following Japan's surrender; commander of the UN forces at the beginning of the Korean War.

Matsumoto Jiichiro (1887-1966), a Japanese statesman and businessman; became the Chairman of the Burakumin Liberation League in 1946; Vice-Chairman of the House of Councilors.

Matsuoka Yosuke (1880-1946), a Japanese diplomat; as Japan's foreign minister (1940-41) helped author the Tripartite Treaty allying Japan with Germany and Italy in 1940.

McKenzie, Frederick Arthur (1869-1931), a Canadian correspondent; one of few Westerners in Korea during its March 1st 1919 independence demonstrations, reporting on Japanese reign of terror.

Meiji (1852-1912), 122nd Emperor of Japan from 1868 to 1912; began Japan's modernization; father of Emperor Taisho; grandfather of Emperor Hirohito; Masako's uncle.

Min Gap-wan (1897-1968), a Korean maiden of the nobility; eldest daughter of Min Yeong-don, Korean ambassador to Great Britain; was engaged to Yi Eun with Gojong's blessing in 1907.

Minami Jiro (1874-1955), a Japanese general; the commander of the Kwantung Army and Japanese ambassador to Manchukuo, 1934-36; Governor General of Korea, 1936-1942.

Miura Goro (1847-1926), a Japanese general; planned and executed the murder of Queen Min on October 8, 1895.

Mullock, Julia (1923-), an American art designer of Ukrainian descent; married Yi Ku in 1959 but was divorced in 1982; in 1995 returned to Hawaii; never lost her affection for Yi Ku.

Nabeshima Naohiro (Chokudai) (1846-1921), a Japanese nobleman; the 11th and final daimyo of the Saga Domain; plenipotentiary minister to Rome in 1880; father of Itsuko.

Nah Seok-ju (1892-1926), a Korean independence activist; a protégé of Kim Ku; attacked Japanese colonial banks in Seoul in December 1926, killing several bank officials.

Nashimoto Morimasa (1874-1951), a Japanese prince and a field marshal in Japan's Imperial Army; chief priest of the Ise Shinto Shrine, 1937-1947; married Itsuko; the father of Masako and Noriko.

Nogi Maresuke (1849-1912), a Japanese general; commander of Japanese Third Army in Russo-Japanese War of 1904-1905; the head of Peers School, 1908-1912; tutored young Hirohito.

Noriko (1907-1992), the second daughter of Nashimoto Morimasa and Itsuko; younger sister of Masako; married Count Hirohashi Tadamitsu in 1926; died three years after Masako.

Park Jung-hee (1917-1979), a Korean general and politician; in May 1961, led a military coup and served as President of South Korea 1963-1979; led South Korea's economic modernization.

Queen Min (1851-1895), the consort wife of Gojong, 26th king of Joseon Kingdom of Korea; murdered by Japanese assassins on October 8, 1895 in Gyeongbok Palace, Seoul, Korea.

Queen Yun (1894-1966), a Korean queen; daughter of Yun Taek-yeong, a government official under Gojong; in 1907 married

Sunjong, the 27th king of Joseon Kingdom and Emperor of Korea.

Rhee Syngman (1875-1965), a Korean independence activist and politician; in 1945, returned to Korea from America as an ardent anti-communist leader; established the Republic of Korea in 1948.

Rusk, Dean (1909-1994), an American lawyer, military officer, and diplomat; Assistant Secretary of State for Far Eastern Affairs in 1950; Secretary of State, 1961-1969.

Saionji Kimmochi (1849-1940), a Japanese statesman; the most liberal politician in prewar Japan; prime minister,1906-1908 and 1911-1912; a member of the *genro* which advised the emperor.

Saito Makoto (1858-1936), an admiral in the Japanese Imperial Navy; Governor General of Korea twice, 1919-1927 and 1929-1931; prime minister of Japan, 1932-1934.

Schofield, Frank William (1889-1970), a Canadian veterinarian and missionary to Korea; reported on Japanese reign of terror in Korea after the March 1st independence movement.

Seo Seok-jo (1921-1999), a Korean neurology specialist and educator; chief of internal medicine at Catholic University in Seoul; established in 1973 Soon Cheon Hyang University Medical School.

Shigemitsu Mamoru (1887-1957), a Japanese diplomat and politician; had diplomatic assignments in the US, Germany, and England; signed Japan's surrender documents on the USS Missouri.

Sohn Byeong-hee (1861-1922), a Korean patriot; one of the 33 signatories who signed the March 1st, 1919 independence declaration.

Song Hak-seon (1897-1927), a Korean nationalist and independence activist from Seoul; in 1919 attempted to assassinate Governor General Saito Makoto to revenge Gojong's death.

Stalin, Joseph (1878-1953), the leader of the Soviet Union from mid-1920s till his death; supported Kim Il-sung and the establishment of Communist North Korea as well as Kim's invasion of the South.

Sunjong (Yi Cheok) (1874-1926), the 27th king of Joseon Kingdom and the Emperor of Korea, 1907-1910; Gojong's son by Queen Min; married Queen Yun in 1907; became a retired Emperor after 1910.

Suzuki Daisetsu (1870-196), a Japanese Zen Buddhist scholar, author, and lecturer; taught a Columbia University in New York.

Taisho (1879-1926), the 123rd Emperor of Japan, 1912-1926; son of Meiji; married Kujo Sadako (Empress Teimei); had four sons: Emperor Hirohito, Prince Chichibu, Prince Takamatsu, and Prince Mikasa.

Teimei (1884-1951), fourth daughter of Prince Michitaka Kujo; married Crown Prince Yoshihito (future Emperor Taisho) in May 1900; the Empress of Japan, 1912-1926.

Terauchi Masatake (1852-1919), a Japanese general and politician; Resident-General of Korea, May-October 1910 and Governor General of Korea, October 1910-October 1916.

Tojo Hideki (1884-1948), a Japanese general and politician; prime minister of Japan, October 17, 1941-July 22, 1944; ordered Japanese attack on Pearl Harbor on December 7, 1941.

Toyotomi Hideyoshi (1537-1598), a Japanese samurai warrior; ended the Warring Period and unified Japan in 1590; became supreme military ruler of Japan; invaded Korea in 1592 and 1597.

Truman, Harry (1884-1972), 33rd president of the United States, 1945-53; approved the use of atomic bombs against Japan; sent US troops to South Korea to defend it against the Communist North.

Yamagata Aritomo (1838-1922), a Japanese general and politician; prime minister of Japan, 1898-1900; a member of the *genro*, which advised the emperor.

Yamamoto Gonnohyoe (1852-1933), a Japanese admiral from Satsuma domain. He served as Japan's prime minister twice in 1913-14 and in 1923-24; the leader of "the earthquake cabinet."

Yamamoto Isoroku (1884-1943), a Japanese marshal admiral; opposed war against the US; served as the commander-in-chief of the Imperial Japanese Combined Fleet during WW II until his death.

Yi Gang (1877-1955), a Korean prince; Gojong's debonair son by Lady Jang; disliked the Japanese and sought to secure Korean independence.

Yi Geon (1909-1991), a Korean prince; Yi Gang's son and Gojong's grandson; married a Japanese woman of nobility but divorced after the war; became a naturalized Japanese citizen.

Yi Jin (August 18 1921-May 11 1922), a Korean Prince; the first son of Yi Eun and Masako and the 29th descendent of the Yi royal linage; died in Korea and buried in Cheongyang-ri, Seoul city.

Yi Ku (1931-2005), a Korean prince; the second son of Yi Eun and Masako and the 29th descendent of the Yi royal linage; graduated from the MIT in 1958 in architectural engineering.

Yi Woo (1912-1945), a Korean prince; Gojong's grandson and Prince Yi Gang's son; a lieutenant colonel in the Japanese Imperial Army; sent to China front during WW II; died in Hiroshima atomic blast.

Yonai Mitsumasa (1880-1948), a Japanese admiral and politician; prime minister of Japan, January 6, 1940-July 21, 1940; strongly opposed the pro-Axis army and the Tripartite Treaty.

Yun Bong-gil (1908-1932), a Korean independence activist; on December 19, 1932 assassinated General Shirakawa Yoshinori and other Japanese officials at Hirohito's birthday celebration in Shanghai.

Zhang Zuolin (1875-1928), a Manchurian warlord, 1916-1928; was killed by a Japanese army officer on June 4, 1928 near Shenyang for his failure to stop the Nationalist forces marching north.

Zhang Xueliang (1901-2001), a Manchurian warlord, 1928-29; the son and successor of Zhang Zuolin; became strongly anti-Japanese and supported the Nationalists.

END NOTES

1 Rhee et al 2007.
2 Rhee et al 2007.
3 Rhee et al 200; Nakamura 1981, pp. 156-157.
4 Chung 1921, pp.235-237.
5 Chung 1921, pp. 237-238.
6 Chung 1921, pp.233-235.
7 Chung 1921, pp. 233-235.
8 Lee, J.R. 1980; Legault and Prescott 2000, pp. 865-872.
9 McKenzie 1920, p. 7.
10 Lee, J.R. 1920.
11 Kang and Kim 1963; Ryang 2003; Naff 2006; Yamada 2011.
12 Kim, S. G. 1997; Grayson 2001.
13 *Dong-A Ilbo* 11/28/1991; Yoshida 1996.
14 Lee, H.G.1993.
15 Kim, H. J. 1970.
16 *The Maeil Gyeongje* 9/21/1968.
17 Honda 1988.
18 Honda 1988.
19 Chosun Ilbo 9/9/1975.
20 *Dong-A Ilbo* 5/4/1989 and 5/8/1989.

11274903R00173

Made in the USA
San Bernardino, CA
11 May 2014